DATE DUE

SEP 0 2 2011		

THE PIRATES' PACT

THE PIRATES' PACT

The Secret Alliances

Between History's Most

Notorious Buccaneers and

Colonial America

DOUGLAS R. BURGESS, JR.

New York   Chicago   San Francisco   Lisbon   London   Madrid   Mexico City
Milan   New Delhi   San Juan   Seoul   Singapore   Sydney   Toronto

Library of Congress Cataloging-in-Publication Data

Burgess, Douglas R.
  The pirates' pact : the secret alliances between history's most notorious buccaneers and colonial America / Douglas R. Burgess Jr.
        p.   cm.
  Includes bibliographical references and index.
  ISBN-13: 978-0-07-147476-4 (alk. paper)
  ISBN-10:   0-07-147476-5 (alk. paper)
  1. Pirates—Atlantic Coast (U.S.)—History.   2. Pirates—Caribbean Area—History.
3. Piracy—Atlantic Coast (U.S.)—History.   4. Piracy—Caribbean Area—History.
5. Governors—United States—History.   6. Governors—West Indies, British—History.
7. Great Britain—Colonies—America—Administration.   8. Great Britain—Colonies—West Indies—Administration.   I. Title.

  F106.B94   2008
  910.4'5—dc22   2008024451

1 2 3 4 5 6 7 8 9 10 11 12 13 14 15 16 17 18 19 20 21   FGR/FGR   0 9 8

ISBN 978-0-07-147476-4
MHID   0-07-147476-5

McGraw-Hill books are available at special quantity discounts to use as premiums and sales promotions or for use in corporate training programs. To contact a representative, please visit the Contact Us pages at www.mhprofessional.com.

This book is printed on acid-free paper.

For Shannon Marie Burgess,
the greatest storyteller I have ever known

Contents

Acknowledgments

WITHOUT THE WILLING AID OF A SCORE OF LIBRARIES AND archives, this book would not have been possible. I am greatly indebted to Ted Widmer and the staff of the John Carter Brown Library in Providence, Rhode Island, not only for providing sources too numerous to list but for harboring this particular reprobate for an entire year of research and writing. Special thanks to the Gilder Lehrman Society in New York and to the helpful staff of the Public Records Office in Kew, England, and of the Bermuda Archives of Hamilton, Bermuda. Thanks also to my family, for all their help and support, and to Albert Bui, for his inexhaustible patience and goodwill. I must also acknowledge my debt to Professors Douglas Cope, Tim Harris, and Seth Rockman.

My warmest thanks go to my editor, Bob Holtzman, for his sage advice and unflagging commitment to this project. It is my dearest hope that the assistance and enthusiasm of all these patient readers is justified by the result.

Preface

I CAME TO THIS TOPIC IN A ROUNDABOUT WAY. IN 2002, AS A law student pursuing a master's in International Criminal Law from the University of British Columbia, I happened upon the old Roman definition of *pirates* as *hostis humani generi*, "enemies of the human race," which I was surprised to discover still holds true today. The purpose of this special definition is to distinguish pirates from all other criminals: as enemies not of the state but of the whole human race, they are entitled to be hunted down across the earth without consideration for borders or extradition treaties. They were, as various jurists from Cicero to Grotius termed them, a challenge to the very concept of statehood. They divorced themselves from the nation-state, formed extraterritorial enclaves, and made war—as Daniel Defoe once wrote—"against the world entire."

Something about this description struck a chord. It was one year since the attacks of September 11, 2001, and the United States was still grappling with the concept of a "war on terror." No one seemed to know quite what this war entailed. How could we fight against an enemy that had no territorial boundaries, no standing army, no recognizable government? Against this shadowy nemesis of organized terrorism, how could we know if we won or lost? The problem seemed to me as much a legal as a political one. We had no legal definition for terrorism per se, only a hodgepodge of acts that we labelled "terrorist": bombings, hijackings, kidnapping—and, as it turned out, some forms of piracy.

Our most critical flaw was in failing to provide a name for the very thing we wished to destroy. Were terrorists ordinary criminals? "Unlawful combatants"? Freedom fighters? In the absence of definition, they could be all of the above. The White House seemed determined to cast them as a military force, to better facilitate capture and confinement, but this proved to be a disastrous mistake. Soon we were reading about abuses in Guantanamo, atrocities in Abu Ghraib, illegal renditions conducted throughout the world. The vacuum of definition was fostering a dangerous new world in which the states and the terrorists pursued one another across a vast chessboard with no rules governing their actions.

Yet the elements of international organized terrorism seemed to bear startling resemblance to those of piracy. First there was the concept of *hostis humani generi*, the idea that certain persons exist, by virtue of their crimes, beyond the ordinary protections of citizenship. Then there were the elements of terrorist crimes themselves: seizure, hijacking, destruction of property, homicide. I began to delve into the history of piracy law. What I discovered was astonishing. Piracy, in contrast to its traditional image as "sea robbery," had, in fact, moved farther and farther away from this parochial definition to embrace all sorts of crimes that had no pecuniary motive at all. Chief among them, I learned, was "maritime terrorism." Perhaps most surprising of all was the term coined under international law for the hijacking of airliners like those of 9/11: *aerial piracy*. This has been the working definition of hijacking since the Tokyo and Hague Conventions of the mid-1970s and was spelled out explicitly in the Montreal Convention of 1979, which extended piracy to include acts committed "by the crew and passengers of a private ship or aircraft against another ship or aircraft."

Working in reverse, I began to formulate a definition of terrorism that borrowed the old customary piracy law of *hostis humani generi*. This appeared first as a master's thesis, then as a law review article in the *University of Miami Journal of International and Comparative Law*, and finally as an article in *Legal Affairs Magazine*. Then, unexpectedly, the idea took off. I found myself quoted in the *New York Times*, answering questions on NPR, and expounding on the idea before the U.S. military leadership at the Army/Navy Club in Washington, D.C.

The idea for this book developed from one crucial aspect of piracy law and its relation to terrorism. In addition to the numerous instances where pirates were cast as enemies of the state, there were countless others where the state itself acted as sponsor. The Elizabethan court was famous for this, sending off corsairs like Francis Drake to harass the Spanish. Often states used piracy as a means of striking at their enemy and hiding the blade: pirates were surrogate navies, sent off to harass enemy fleets and rob their coffers even as the two nations preserved diplomatic relations. This, I thought, was a powerful precedent for the current issue of state-sponsored terrorism.

Many authors have examined the relationship between Elizabeth and her corsairs. What I learned, however, was that instead of being replaced by a new generation of out-and-out pirates, this relationship was transferred from the crown to those men in the colonies charged with enforcing its will: the colonial governors. The evidence of widespread collusion between governors and pirates in the Atlantic world was all over the ground, yet generations of historians had ignored it—choosing instead to focus on romantic depictions of the pirates as proto-revolutionaries waging private war against the English crown. This conception did much for my attempts to link pirates and terrorists as like "enemies" to the nation-state, but it was not entirely accurate. Pirates, I discovered, could be both enemies of the state and, simultaneously, allies of its colonial administrators. This was a new and fascinating wrinkle, opening up a new vista for interpreting the so-called golden age of Atlantic piracy.

The historiography of piracy is varied and fascinating, but rarely have historians attempted to study the interplay between the brigands and the crown on anything beyond the local level. Given the colorful nature of their subject, and the persistent myths surrounding it, most histories confine themselves to the careers of individual pirates. Corrupt governors add anecdotal humor, but little more, to these accounts. Current historians now acknowledge that many governors cosseted pirates within their colonies, yet few inquire as to the reasons for doing so. It is commonly assumed that these men were either merely corrupt or acting on some implicit crown policy. One example is particularly telling. In his seminal survey of American colonial history, Alan Taylor suggests that this policy was not only entrenched but long-standing:

> England's leaders, including Queen Elizabeth I and a long succession of colonial governors, protected and invested in pirate enterprises. New York, South Carolina, and Jamaica were especially notorious for hosting pirates. Needing more naval protection than the official navy could provide, colonial governors gave the pirates official cover as "privateers" licensed to plunder the enemy in wartime. By fencing pirate loot, governors procured the coveted gold and silver so desperately needed by the colonial economies.

This is a tidy but inaccurate summary. First, New York, South Carolina, and Jamaica were no more or less notorious pirate havens than North Carolina, Virginia, Barbados, Bermuda, Pennsylvania, or Rhode Island.

Second, privateering licenses were granted not only in wartime but in the intervening periods of peace as well. Third, as will be seen, the concept of a pirate coast guard was the merest pretense; there are almost no recorded instances of pirates acting in that capacity. Privateering commissions uniformly employed defensive wording to give themselves color of law. It was ignored by both the donor and the recipient. Fourth and most important, Taylor's terminological linkage between "England's leaders"—the crown and the governors—presumes that both were acting under the same policy. This could not be more false. Successive monarchs enacted antipiracy acts almost yearly, expressly forbidding the granting of privateering commissions except during time of war. They were deadly earnest: for the Stuart kings, good relations with Spain became a cornerstone of their foreign policy; for William III, the promulgation of trade with the Muslim lords through the East India Company was crucial for the expansion of England's maritime empire. In both cases, the willingness of governors to grant illegal commissions to pirates posed a grave challenge to crown policy. Consequently, governors frequently found themselves at loggerheads with the supervising Board of Trade at Whitehall. Some, including Benjamin Fletcher of New York, William Markham of Pennsylvania, and Archibald Hamilton of Jamaica, even lost their positions because of over-familiarity with the pirates. Others, including Samuel Cranston of Rhode Island, survived only because the exigencies of communication made it almost impossible to curtail their actions or secure their removal.

Taylor's blithe presumptions are indicative of the general attitudes of most colonial scholars. Yet if one combines the separate incidents of pirate patronage throughout the Atlantic world into a single narrative whole, one finds that nearly all governors practiced a passive-aggressive noncompliance to crown law with regard to the pirates within their colonies; a noncompliance that runs starkly contrary to the perception of servitude, loyalty, and dignity that these crown-appointed gentlemen have long enjoyed. Moreover, the lines of demarcation between pirate and privateer, and even pirate and governor, became increasingly blurred. Henry Morgan, the greatest buccaneer of the mid-seventeenth century, ended his days as lieutenant governor of Jamaica. Similarly, Woodes Rogers, one of the most ferocious pirates in the "golden age," turned respectable, took an appointment as governor of the Bahamas, and became a feared pirate hunter. Such changes of heart reflected the times. The crown, in quick succession, issued proclamations that first commissioned privateers, then outlawed them, then pardoned them, then revoked the pardon and ordered them hanged, then gave privateering commissions anew to those left alive.

While the contradictions between the established and actual history of seventeenth-century piracy are glaring, the task of documenting a "true" account proved daunting. Tracking a coherent account of governors' relationship with the pirates, their respective impulses and motivations, is like nailing jelly to the proverbial wall. Because the governors were understandably reluctant to display their pirate dealings in public, the majority of the surviving sources come only from scandals and trials, when the issue was forcibly thrust into the light of publicity. As such, they tend to involve only the most notorious pirates—Tew, Avery, Kidd, Teach—and only the men at the highest echelons of colonial administration, the governors themselves. This raises a complication for sources. To establish anything beyond a disjointed narrative of corruption in high places, we must infer the rest from what was *not* made public—for example, the correspondence between Governor Cranston and the Board of Trade. We must also include not only the governors but their lesser functionaries—men like lieutenant governors and customs inspectors, such as the duplicitous Tobias Knight—who were as actively complicit as their superiors in aiding the pirates. Taken in sum, these sources paint a vivid and complex picture of colonial commerce and administration that belies the traditional image of loyal crown colonies, merchants, and governing officers on the one hand and bloodthirsty pirates on the other.

To examine the relationship between the governors and their pirate protégés involves more than digging up old scandals and parading them anew. In this cynical century there is nothing astonishing in the revelation that some politicians take bribes or consort with known criminals. What is astonishing, however, is how much this accord between administrator and outlaw some three hundred years before resonates in our own time. As we continue to struggle with the ongoing sponsorship of terrorist organizations, issues of statehood, nationality, loyalty, and even patriotism constantly come into play. While it is always a dangerous endeavor to draw parallels between one historical age and another, the accord between pirates and governors in the Atlantic world seems strikingly prescient. In the seventeenth century, the harboring and sponsoring of alleged criminals by colonial administrators posed a critical challenge to the English state's attempt to enforce its legal prerogative, expand its influence overseas, secure its trade, and maintain its foreign policy intact. One can hardly examine this era without being reminded of the current problems that beset our own nation and its allies in their ongoing attempt to wage and win a war against the nebulous, quicksilver, state-sponsored terrorists.

Yet this is a work of history and should be read as such. Though I first began researching this topic in conjunction with its relationship to contemporary issues, the issue of pirate patronage also has crucial implications for our understanding of law and statecraft in the seventeenth and eighteenth centuries. How can we speak of English "law" in the colonies, if colonial governors are openly and persistently harboring criminals? What made them do so, and what were the repercussions? Most important, does this relationship suggest an independent colonial identity distinct from that of England, perhaps even a precursor to independence? These were the questions that I posed for myself as I began exploring the documents.

The answers, I discovered, have as much to say about who we are as who we were.

THE PIRATES' PACT

-Prologue-

The End of Blackbeard

NOVEMBER 21, 1718

From across Ocracoke Inlet came the sounds of drunken laughter and song. Lieutenant Robert Maynard, in command of a small convoy of His Majesty's sloops, was contemptuous but relieved. Surprise was essential to his plans. And he was far too clever a soldier to be deceived by the apparent jollity of the men he had come to destroy. The legendary ferocity of Edward Teach, alias Tach, alias Thatch, alias Blackbeard, would grow and grow as the centuries passed, but even in his lifetime it was enough to give a prudent man pause. Just a few weeks earlier Blackbeard and his men had been taking their leave of his close friend, a man named Tobias Knight, when the pirate felt the thirst come upon him.

He hove his small river craft alongside a jetty on Pamlico River and called out to a nearby pleasure boat, "Give me a little dram!" It was past midnight, and the men in the boat were wary. "'Tis too dark to see to draw," a local planter named William Bell called back. Blackbeard, enraged, leapt aboard the craft in one jump, several of his men behind him. He was no longer thirsty. "Damnation seize me," he said into Bell's ear, as he held a sword across his throat, "I'll kill you unless you tell us where the money is."

"Who are you and whence come you?" Bell answered, terrified.

"I come from Hell and I will carry you there presently," the old pirate told him.

Now it was evening, and Blackbeard was back on his sloop, the *Adventure Command*. The darkness had come fitfully, heavy clouds pierced by sudden rays of amber light. Maynard ordered the lamps doused, and the two sloops, *Pearl* and *Lyme*, picked their way carefully into the inlet, casting the lead again and again to check the depth as the bottom shallowed out from under them. The lights of the *Adventure Command* winked at them almost welcomingly. A shrill sound—a fife— warbled from her decks. Maynard raised a hand for silence, and the navy ships moved like phantoms across the water. Prudence, Maynard cautioned. As well he might. Though he had fifty-five men under his command, more than double the number on the pirate ship, he had no mounted guns to answer the *Adventure Command*'s eight. Moreover, the seamen and soldiers with him were raw recruits, some taken from their boardinghouses and taverns by the press-gangs just hours before the convoy sailed. Blackbeard's crew were furies from hell, fashioned so by a man whom many believed was the devil himself. More to the point, they had fought dozens of engagements and bore the scars to prove it. With no long-range cannons, Maynard would be forced to overcome the pirates through hand-to-hand combat, a prospect no one relished. It was critical that Blackbeard and his men have no warning of the nemesis that was fast approaching them.

Blackbeard was vulnerable, though, as Maynard knew, and even more than he realized. At the height of his prowess the pirate commanded a convoy consisting of one forty-gunner and several armed sloops, with more than four hundred seamen serving under his colors. Joined with his old compatriots Major Stede Bonnet and Benjamin

Hornigold, the triumvirate boasted a navy that could rival the king's own in these waters. But now Hornigold had turned coat and was working as a pirate hunter for the crown, and Bonnet had gone mad. Blackbeard lost most of his crew to disease and desertion, and two of his ships to storms and poor seamanship. One he had even burned himself, for fear that it contained too much evidence of his piratical practices. Several months ago he presented himself in Bath a reformed man and accepted the governor's pardon. His refuge in Ocracoke Inlet was the desperate act of a worried and nearly broken old pirate. Remaining with him now were only twenty men, including Israel Hands, the first mate whose kneecaps Blackbeard had once blown off in sporting jest, and the sixteen-year-old girl whom the captain had chosen from a Bath brothel to be his fourteenth wife. Worst of all, his last remaining sloop had run aground in the sucking mire of Ocracoke Inlet. Blackbeard and his men were sitting targets until the next high tide floated them free. His retreat to the rum bottle that evening might well have been as much out of despair as good fellowship. Hearing the sounds of sodden revelry, Maynard was confident. He ordered the sloops to drop anchor for the night and settled in for a long watch.

But something was wrong, terribly wrong. Lieutenant Maynard was a Carolina man, as were the soldiers under him, and they were in Carolina waters. Teach was a Carolina man, too, if only by adoption. By rights he was North Carolina's problem, and most especially that of its governor, Charles Eden. He had, in fact, surrendered himself to that august personage several weeks ago. So why was Maynard's commission signed by Alexander Spotswood, governor of Virginia? And why had Spotswood sent him this long way to kill a man who was already—or at least technically—in His Majesty's custody? The answer would come months later from Governor Spotswood himself, in a letter written to Lord Cartwright of the Board of Trade. By this time Blackbeard was dead, and another scandal was swiftly unfolding. Governor Spotswood took the quill in his hand, touched it briefly in the inkwell, and wrote, "My Lord . . . the business required such secrecy that I did not so much as communicate to His Maj'ty's Council here, nor to any other person but those who were necessarily to be employed in the Execution, lest among the many favourers of Pyrates we have in these parts some of them might send Intelligence to Teach."

Now, on the deck of the *Pearl*, Maynard wondered if these precautions had been enough. He had waited through the night, and the first fingers of morning appeared on the horizon. It would be a clear, cool day. The fires were not lit on either the *Pearl* nor the *Lyme*: he would not risk the light or the cooking smells. From the *Adventure Command* came only silence. The pirates were sleeping off their rum. It was time to get moving. A lead boat was dispatched with eight men at the oars, and the two sloops gently weighed anchor. With a favorable wind and no ill currents, they might be within range of the pirate ship in a matter of minutes.

But there was no wind, and the soundings grew ever more shallow. The same Carolina mud that had imprisoned the *Adventure Command* now menaced Maynard and his crew. They were finally reduced to casting oars over the sides of the sloops and scuttling, crablike, toward the enemy. The sun was higher now, glinting on their sails flapping uselessly in the dead calm. Surprise was lost.

Blackbeard, roused from a dead sleep, watched their approach through his glass. The tide was up; he set his men to freeing the sloop, readying her for battle. Finding he could not free his anchor, he cut the anchor cables. The *Adventure Command* drifted free. He ordered her four starboard cannons loaded and the decks cleared for action. The pirates, bleary eyed, hung over, and some still drunk, scurried about purposefully. If their captain had any intimation that this might be the end, he gave no sign of it. When the navy sloops came in range, he let loose the cannons in a thunderous broadside that raked both ships across their bows. The first of Maynard's men fell wounded and dead. They had no cannons to answer but instead kept a steady stream of musket fire, which snapped and whickered around Blackbeard and his crew like angry bees. "Damn ye for villains," Blackbeard roared at the approaching sloops. "Who are you and whence came you?"

Maynard lacked his opponent's oratorical flair. He answered by raising the king's standard and jettisoning all his ballast to keep the sloops from grounding. "You can see by our colors we are no pirates," he shouted back.

"Send your boat on board that I might see who you are," Blackbeard taunted him. The ships were close now; both men could easily make out the features of the other. Not that Blackbeard was hard to miss. Standing well over six feet tall, he towered over his companions. The famous beard was every bit as black and wild as Maynard could have imagined, sprouting like some prehistoric growth from a long, cavernous face with deeply set eyes. Sometimes the pirate wove it into bizarre pigtails tied with pink ribbon; during battle he capped its ends with sulphurous fuse and lit them, wreathing his face in devilish green smoke. Yet even without these histrionics, the most famous pirate of the eighteenth century was still a sight to behold.

"I cannot spare my boat, but I will come aboard you as soon as I can with my sloop," Maynard called back.

This incensed the old brigand almost beyond speech. He was not accustomed to having his taunts thrown back at him. "Damnation seize my soul," he bellowed, "if I give you quarters, or take any from you!"

"I expect no quarter from you nor shall I give you any," said the navy captain coolly.

Blackbeard's answer was a second broadside, all the more terrible for the shorter distance between them. The cannons were loaded not with balls but with partridge shot, small and deadly. In an instant, more than a third of Maynard's men fell dead or injured. The fragile hulls of the sloops were not designed to take such a pounding. The *Lyme,* waterlogged and crippled, fell back. But the *Pearl,* with Maynard at the helm, pressed on. Hurriedly he ordered his surviving crew below both to protect them from the murderous fire and to trick Blackbeard into believing that they had been decimated. There was a scrap of wind, just enough to make headway under sail alone. The *Pearl,* a ghost ship with her decks stark and empty, was now only a few yards from the *Adventure Command.*

As the two sloops came alongside one another, Blackbeard's men appeared at the rails, hurling primitive grenades—"Grenadoes," as Daniel Defoe termed them—onto the decks. These were nothing more than rum bottles filled with shrapnel and gunpowder capped by a short fuse, but they were loud and horrible: perfect complements to a pirate's repertoire. This time, however, they exploded without effect, taking out their vengeance on the scattered corpses that littered the deck. The ruse had worked. Blackbeard turned to his men and cried out merrily, "They are all knocked on the head, except three or four! Let's jump on board and cut the rest to pieces!" He leapt first himself, and the men followed in triumph.

The heavy clomp of the pirates' boots on the main deck was as good a signal as any. Suddenly the hatches flew open and the remainder of Maynard's crew swarmed onto the deck. Blackbeard let out a roar of rage and astonishment. In an instant he knew it was over; the navy men outnumbered his own by well over two to one. But he had sworn to give no quarter, and he would not. Swinging his cutlass, he entered the fray.

Maynard had left the helm and now stood on the main deck, fighting alongside his men. The wind had died again, and the sulphurous smoke of the grenades billowed about them. In the smoke and confusion he could see little of his opponents: a face appearing out of the fog, either friendly or fierce, leaving barely enough time to react. He dispatched the man in front of him and then turned on his heel as a shadow menaced from behind. There he found himself staring face-to-face with Blackbeard. In the same instant, both men raised their pistols and fired. The hammer clicked harmlessly against the flint of Blackbeard's, sending up sparks but nothing more. A misfire. Maynard's shot hit the pirate in the shoulder and he recoiled, injured but not dead. Still acting out the bizarre dance of eighteenth-century combat, both simultaneously discarded their pistols, drew cutlasses, and advanced on one another.

Blackbeard was quicker. He drew back his sword and slashed a brutal arc, aiming for the band of white above the blue brocade that was the lieutenant's throat. Maynard had barely enough time to raise his own sword in defense. But so great was the force behind the pirate's thrust that he broke Maynard's sword clean in half, the blade clattering uselessly to the ground. The lieutenant overbalanced, fell. And now Blackbeard was above him, raising his cutlass for the final strike that would sever his head from his body with a single blow. Maynard fumbled, tried to draw his second pistol. But there was no time, not even for prayer. The blade was scything down toward him.

And missed. Unaccountably. Blackbeard's eyes still stared murderously down, but his arm had fallen short. A quick-thinking seaman, his name forever lost to history, had fallen upon Blackbeard just as he was about to strike and cut the pirate's throat from ear to ear with a long-handled dirk. Blackbeard roared in pain, blood spewing from the open wound. He ignored the seaman and advanced on Maynard again. But by now the lieutenant had regained his feet and drawn a second pistol from its holster. He fired point-blank into the man's body. Still Blackbeard did not fall. By now there was a small band of seamen around him, lunging at his body with their swords like a bull in a corrida. But the cornered pirate would not die. Twenty saber wounds slashed across him, five shots emptied into his body, but still he fought on. The bandolier of pistols strapped across his chest was almost empty. He pulled the last from its leather holster, cocked it, and pointed it at Maynard. But the pirate's eyes were clouded, confused. He swayed slightly, staggered, then fell onto the deck.

For the men of Blackbeard's crew it was as though the devil himself had been smote. They dropped their weapons almost at once; some even jumped overboard. The survivors fell to their knees and begged quarter. Maynard, against his earlier declaration, granted it. "Tho' it was only prolonging their Lives a few Days," Defoe would later write with trenchant candor. They began picking up the bodies of the slain pirates and heaving them over the side. Out of twenty, only eight remained. Maynard left the job of tidying up to a midshipman and crossed over the brief divide onto Blackbeard's sloop, which was now rightfully his own. He made his way to the pirate's cabin. It was small but surprisingly well kept. A journal lay next to the bed, though it would offer little insight into the man who kept it. "Rum all gone," one entry ran. "Knaves a'plotting. Weather clear." Maynard moved on. The desk was as sparse as the rest of the cabin, but on it lay a small strongbox with a lock. A few moments' job with the sharp end of a dirk and it was open. A packet of letters was revealed. One seemed to bear an official seal. Maynard scooped them up and left the cabin.

It was only later, when he had returned to his own cabin aboard the *Pearl* and sat down to write his official report for Governor Spotswood, that Maynard thought to read this strange parcel of correspondence. One can only imagine his eyes widening as he perused it carefully, taking in the words, though scarcely believing them. Here, in a series of written exchanges, was quite a different story from that which had just been played out on the deck of the *Pearl*.

Blackbeard had been warned. That much was immediately clear. From the letters themselves and the testimony of the surviving pirates, an incredible picture emerged. There were letters from prominent New York traders, assuring the pirate of their goodwill. There were letters from Tobias Knight, colony secretary and personal friend and agent of Governor Charles Eden. "My dear friend . . ." Cargo manifests revealed that Blackbeard had been liberal with his prizes, sharing some twenty hogsheads of sugar with Knight and another sixty with Eden. And there were other letters, each bearing the distinctive seal of the Royal Governor of His Majesty's Colony of North Carolina. Maynard must have shaken his head in wonderment. Even as Governor Spotswood was dispatching him south, Governor Eden sent his own emissary, Knight, to warn the pirate of his approach. The first letter from Knight informed Blackbeard that he had "sent him four of his men, which were all he could meet with in or about town, and so bid him be on his guard." The second was even more explicit. In the long, slanting style of the times, Knight had written, "My friend, If this finds you yet in harbour I would have you make your way up as soon as possible . . . I have something more to say to you than at present I can write . . . the bearer will tell you in part what I have to say . . . I expect the Governor this night or tomorrow who I believe would be likewise glad to see you before you go, I have not time to add save my hearty respects to you and am your real friend and servant, T. Knight."

The pirate had heeded his warning but not carefully enough. He had known of Maynard's approach in Ocracoke Inlet but either through carelessness or drunkenness had taken no measures to counteract it. Perhaps he no longer cared. He was still enough of a gentleman, though, to leave one of his crew in charge of the precious letters with the instruction that, should he be killed or captured, they and the entire *Adventure Command* were to be blown to kingdom come. The lad had been engaged in precisely this activity when one of Maynard's men interrupted him.

Now Lieutenant Maynard was in a quandary. The letters lay on his desk, proof enough to bring down a government. But to what purpose? He was a Carolinian, after all. The simple struggle of good versus evil that had played itself out so gloriously earlier in the day now seemed tainted, untrue. He could simply hand over the letters to Eden; they were his correspondence, after all. Or he could deliver them to Spotswood as seized booty, which they also were. The choice was Maynard's.

Maynard's actions over the next few days gave considerable insight into his thoughts. First, he ordered the head of the dead pirate to be severed from its body and mounted triumphantly on the bowsprit. This was done. As the *Pearl* limped into Bath, past the astonished eyes of Governor Eden and his friends, it dangled like a grim figurehead, tongue lolling obscenely between slack jaws. When the *Pearl* came into harbor, Tobias Knight was there, in his role as collector of customs. The head grimaced down at him. What was said between the two men, Knight and Maynard, is not known. But Maynard boldly entered the governor's own storehouse and removed eighty hogsheads of sugar, the exact amount that Blackbeard had presented them. These were loaded onto the *Pearl* and marked for Governor Spotswood as spoils of war. Knight did not object. Daniel Defoe colorfully declared that Knight was so disturbed that he quite literally died of fright several days later, but in fact colonial records show he was well enough to respond to an indictment for corruption in April of the following year. After which, it is true, he succumbed.

Governor Eden was made of sterner stuff. Acting on his own and through channels of friendship and patronage, he denounced Maynard as an adventurer, a pirate, and a thief. The *ex*-pirate Edward Teach had come to Bath and accepted the king's pardon from his own hand, Eden declared, a prerogative that had been granted him by His Majesty himself. What right did Maynard—or Virginia, for that matter—have to interfere? Inflamed with righteous indignation, Eden poured out his aspersions in an acidic letter to the Board of Trade that came dangerously close to accusing Governor Spotswood of pirate brokering.

Meanwhile, the pilfered correspondence was duly delivered to Spotswood, along with the sugar. Maynard had made his choice. But in the weeks that followed the death of Blackbeard, sighs of relief gave way to muttered disparagements against Spotswood and his high-handed actions. Eden, Knight, and perhaps even the New York merchants, not to mention the scores of local gentry that had made considerable money off Blackbeard, had done their work well. Having first been hailed as a hero, Spotswood now found himself forced to defend his actions to the Board of Trade, that gimlet-eyed body with whom the fortunes and destinies of every royal governor rested. His first letter, dated February 14, 1719, was a masterwork of diplomacy. One can imagine the aged

Spotswood seated at his desk, perhaps with the Eden letters at his elbow, struggling to convey the monstrous enormity of the conspiracy in as tactful a way as possible. "As I cannot be unconcerned with any Dangers threatening the King's Subjects," he wrote carefully in a clear, neat hand, "I hope the part I have lately acted in rescuing the trade of North Carolina from the Insults of Pyrates upon the earnest solicitations of the inhabitants there will not be unacceptable to Your Lordships, and it is more necessary I should give Your L'dshps a true relation of that matter . . ." Here he might have paused for a moment, wondering how best to proceed. ". . . because I perceive some of your Officers in that Gov't inclinable to misrepresent it as an Invasion of the Rights of the Proprietors." There, that was the tricky bit. He passed over it and went on to describe at some length the heroism shown by Maynard and his men.

Yet like King Charles's head, the question of his own actions came up again. "Now my Lords," he wrote almost sorrowfully, "it seems to be taken very much amiss that this project of suppressing the pyrates should have been concealed and put on execution without the participation of your Lordships, Gov'r, and, in the next place, that the goods w'ch Tach had piratically taken should be brought into this colony to be condemned." But all was not as it appeared, he assured them. Had North Carolina—or her governor—lifted so much as a finger against the appalling Teach, Virginia would have stayed her hand. As it was, "If the necessity of preventing the growth of so dangerous a nest of pyrates in the very road of the trade of Virginia and Maryland, as well as of your Lord'sps' province, and the secrecy which I was obliged for the effectual carrying on this service, has forced me to pass over some forms with your Government, I hope Success may atone for that omission, and I doubt not that your Lordships will prefer the benefit of so many of the King's subjects . . . to the present Resentments of a few discontented Men." That was that. Spotswood scattered sand on the parchment and shook it vigorously. Then he folded it in half and affixed his official seal. It would take months to reach London, but then again so would Eden's condemnations of him.

It would not be the end of the scandal. Accusation and counteraccusation would fly back and forth between Virginia and North Carolina for months. Both men would find themselves blackened with the tarred brush of pirate brokering. It is quite likely that Spotswood foresaw the futility of it all even as he protested his innocence to the Board of Trade.

This sordid scandal of pirate patronage had been and would be played out again and again like a Renaissance comedy throughout the Atlantic world for more than three decades. Blackbeard's case was neither the last nor the worst. In the long history of piracy in the Atlantic, there were always two stories: the official and the unofficial. The first is one of heroism and valor pitted against rank treachery and treason, of brave governments with valiant navies warring against a band of seagoing miscreants that one historian has dubbed "the lowest form of human scum." The official version is not just a dominant narrative—it is a central theme in the history of the human experience: society versus anarchy, lawful versus lawless, majority versus minority, good versus evil. It has been the subject of countless books, legends, tourist destinations, alcoholic beverages, Halloween costumes, feature films, and theme park rides.

The other story has never been told.

-1-

Enemies of the Human Race

"NOW PIRACY IS ONLY A TERM FOR SEA ROBBERY," DECLARED JUS-tice Sir Charles Hedges in 1696. As one of the foremost jurists of his day, Sir Charles spoke with authority. He went on, "If any man shall be assaulted within that jurisdiction, and his ship or goods violently taken away without legal authority, this is robbery and piracy. If the mariners of any ship shall violently dispossess the master, and afterwards carry away the ship itself of any of the goods, or tackle, apparel or furniture, in any place where the Lord Admiral hath, or pretends to hath juris-diction, this is also robbery and piracy."

Perfectly simple, good, sound law. But his audience was uncon-vinced. The twelve jurymen who sat in judgment that day looked over at the accused, a bedraggled crew of misfits, mariners, and malcontents, and rendered their own decision. Despite Sir Charles's blithe insistence, despite the heavy weight of the admiralty, which hung over the trial like a blue-gray cloud, and despite the unequivocal guilt of the men in the dock, they retreated into the solemn sanctum of their chambers and returned with a verdict: not guilty.

Clearly piracy was not just sea robbery, after all. Ordinary robbers, or highwaymen, received small leniency in English courts. What Sir Charles's words failed to address was that piracy, unlike any other form of robbery, was intricately intertwined with issues of statehood, commerce, colonial relations, and even nationalism. Pirates were not just sea robbers; in an Englishman's eyes they could be seen as defenders of the flag against the dastardly French, Spanish, or Dutch, as agents of the crown, vigilantes, even heroes. They could also be seen as brigands and traitors, reaffirming the spirit if not the content of Sir Charles's words. Yet an important distinction must be made at the very outset. Almost without exception, the only pirates that appeared in England, either in print or in person, were those standing trial for their crimes. This fact cannot be overemphasized, for it makes the aforementioned acquittal all the more remarkable. A trial, by its design, places the accused in an unlovely light; the majesty of the law serves to demonize him and rally public support against him. This is implicit in the very words by which cases are read into the docket: *Regina* versus Smith, or Jones, or Kidd. The king, queen, ministers of state, lords justice, and people of Great Britain all stand on one side of the aisle, the accused on the other. Little wonder then that so few escaped the dock intact.

Yet the eight men on trial before Sir Charles Hedges did just that, at least for the moment. Why? What was so remarkable about piracy that it could lead twelve stolid Londoners to flout a chief justice with aplomb? The answer may be found by extending our perspective. England might only see pirates as figures in a dock or gorily displayed on the cover of a pamphlet, but for its colonies the reality and identity of pirates were quite different. Only a small fraction of the seventeenth- and early eighteenth-century pirates ever reached trial. The vast majority did not, and it is these men that have largely been forgotten by history. Whether England saw them as heroes or criminals, to their own people—the colonists—they were traders, sources of income, town burghers, respected merchantmen, brothers, fathers, husbands, sons, and neighbors. A pirate and his family might occupy the adjacent pew in one's local church (a not-uncommon occurrence, as many pirates were surprisingly pious and occasionally endowed churches from the spoils of a successful voyage), a queue at the local marketplace, or the next chair at an assembly meeting.

In other words, pirates were locals. For the entire period of the so-called golden age of Atlantic piracy, a thirty-year span from the close of the seventeenth century to the second decade of the eighteenth, piracy was intricately intermeshed within the social, economic, and political fabric of the American and Caribbean colonies. The pirates' relation-ships with their fellow colonists, and most important with colonial gov-ernments, offer a new and almost entirely unexplored dimension to the study of Atlantic world history: a radical new perspective that challenges and may even transform much of our perception of the relationships between crown and colony in that era.

Pirates and the Law

Before we can understand the challenge to English law posed by colo-nial sponsorship of piracy, we must first consider the nature of that law itself. English law in the seventeenth century was divided into statutory law, which was brought at the initiative of the English government, and common law, which was derived from the history of individual cases. Statutory law has two principal components: acts of Parliament and Orders in Council. In both instances, a legal policy or criminal offense is articulated directly and the corresponding punishment for disobedi-ence is prescribed. The latter, however, more commonly acts as a response to individual legal or social problems. It is also, along with royal proclamations, the principal source for criminal law in the early mod-ern period.

Throughout the seventeenth century the problem of piracy was addressed primarily by the king in council rather than by Parliament. We find relatively few instances of piracy law articulated by the Com-mons, yet the record of proclamations is replete with examples: between 1603 and 1625, the reign of King James I, there are no fewer than fif-teen separate proclamations dealing solely with the problem of English and foreign piracy. This, as we shall see, reveals much about the relationship between piracy and the crown's state-building agenda throughout the seventeenth century.

The articulation of the "crime" of piracy in English statutory law centers primarily on piratical acts. This returns us to one of the most elemental divisions within criminal law. A crime had three components: the *mens rea*, or mental state of the criminal; the *actus reus*, or acts committed; and the *locus*, where the crime occurred. The king and his ministers were little concerned with the mental state of the accused (though it would come into play repeatedly when considering privateering commissions granted during war), but of the acts themselves and the locale they had much to say. Pirates, one 1606 proclamation declared, "have under colour of friendship and peaceable traffic committed most foul outrages, murders, spoils and depredations within the straits and Mediterranean Seas, as well within the Ports without, to the great offense of all our friends, to the extreme loss and hurt of our Merchants trading in those parts, and to the great displeasure of God and men."

With such a broad range of acts, the definition of piracy under statutory law might best be described as whatever acts of depredation at sea the crown wished to curtail, occurring in whichever locale it was most particularly concerned at that time. While the *actus reus* remained fairly consistent—looting, destruction of property, theft, and murder (though rape and mutiny occasionally appeared)—the *locus* did not. Over the course of the seventeenth century, the English crown would shift its focus to coincide with both political and commercial realities, from the Mediterranean to the Caribbean to the Red Sea, until returning to the Caribbean again as a new century dawned.

Piracy in the common law drew its definition from a very different source. The noted jurist Sir Edward Coke, in his *Articuli Admiralitis*, cites a Roman precept coined by Marcus Tullius Cicero at the height of the Republic. Pirates, Coke writes, are *hostis humani generi*, "enemies of the human race." This was excerpted from Cicero's commentary in *De Legibus* to the effect that "*pirata non est ex perdullium numero definitus, sed communis hostis omnium.*" Piracy was more than the aggregate sum of its separate offenses; Cicero segregated it from other similar crimes—looting, murder, and the like—on the basis of its perceived threat not merely to the property or persons in question but to the state as a whole. The threat of piracy came from its implied challenge to the laws and trade of the state: pirates removed themselves from the state's jurisdiction, formed extraterritorial enclaves, and waged private war for pecuniary ends. Hence one could not speak of them merely as ordinary robbers, for the locus of that theft (beyond the state's borders) transformed it. The concept of *hostis humani generi* is critical for understanding the crime of piracy, not only for its longevity (coined in 44 B.C., it remains to this day in both English domestic law and international customary law) but for the unique status it accorded to pirates under the law. To borrow the expression used by Daniel Defoe when describing the pirates of the seventeenth century, such men "waged war against the world entire." Whatever relationships pirates may have formed within their communities or with local governments, this was the legal attitude of English courts during the entire golden age of piracy of the late seventeenth and early eighteenth centuries.

The best articulation of the English interpretation of pirates as *hostis humani generi* appears in Blackstone's *Commentaries on the Laws of England*. Writing in the mid-eighteenth century, a time when the menace of piracy had waned to little more than nuisance, Blackstone credits Coke for being among the first to rearticulate the Roman precept and goes on to offer a concise definition in the English context:

> As, therefore, he [the pirate] has renounced all the benefits
> of society and government, and has reduced himself afresh
> to the savage state of nature by declaring war against all
> mankind, all mankind must declare war against him: so
> that every community has a right, by the rule of self-
> defense, to inflict that punishment on him, which every
> individual would in a state of nature have been otherwise
> entitled to do.

Other aspects of the common-law definition of piracy devolved from this central premise. Blackstone draws a sharp distinction between the elements of the crime under common and statutory law. The former is defined shortly as "those acts of robbery and depredation on the high seas, which, if committed upon land, would have amounted to felony there," while the latter may include all manner of nonpiratical offenses, subject to the whim of the monarch, including "running away with any ship, boat, ordnance, ammunition or goods; or yielding them up voluntarily to a pirate; or conspiring to do these acts; or any persons assaulting the commander of a vessel to hinder him from fighting in defense of his ship, or confining him, or making . . . a revolt on board." This dichotomy is revealing on several levels. First, we find great latitude given to the king in declaring almost any act at sea piratical. This is partly a function of the difference between statutory and common law: the former is far more elastic, open to revision to meet individual circumstances, while the latter represents the culmination of centuries of case law and is thus largely static. Yet it also suggests that kings may have employed the term *piracy* loosely, applying it ad hoc for political purposes (not unlike our present government's fungible definition of *terrorism*).

The second feature of the common law is more subtle, yet equally startling. On the one hand *pirates* are defined as *hostis humani generi*, accorded status well beyond that of ordinary criminals. Yet the acts constituting piracy are synonymous with those of common robbery and murder ashore. This echoes Sir Charles Hedges's assertion in the Every trial of 1696 that pirates were nothing more than "sea robbers," highwaymen at sea. Which begs the question: are they enemies of the human race or are they ordinary thieves? The English courts never entirely resolved this conundrum, though it is fair to say that *hostis humani generi* was most often employed when the interests of the crown were directly at stake—such as the high-profile trials of Henry Every and Samuel Burgess, among others.

This brings us to the matter of jurisdiction. Here the fissures between statutory and common law were played out in full view of the English public. Prior to the fourteenth century, piracy (as "sea robbery") was a common-law crime. Pirates were thus subject to trial "by God and their peers" under criminal law in the assizes. Assize justices regularly handled piracy cases until the mid-fourteenth century, after which time the issue of jurisdiction became increasingly contentious. The problem was that common-law juries were notoriously reluctant to convict pirates—a result, at least in part, of the fact that juries of their peers, particularly in seaside communities, often identified with the accused, either through social or commercial ties, while those same communities were rarely harmed by the accused. Edward III became so incensed at the rate of acquittal that in 1361 he attempted to wrest jurisdiction of piracy from the common-law courts by declaring piracy a species of treason. An earlier case, decided in 1350, gave some legal credence for this: three English sailors and a Norman captain were tried before the assizes on several counts of piracy. The Norman (who was their captain) was convicted only of robbery, but the Englishmen were found guilty of treason by reason of having taken up arms with a nonsubject against the trade of the crown. Edward turned this decision into an extension of crown legal prerogative by employing its rationale to incorporate piracy within the commission granted to the newly created admiralty courts. The coast of England and Wales was divided into nineteen districts, each granted a vice admiral to oversee all coastal and foreign trade and a judge empowered to decide cases involving the breach or detriment of that trade. His official title was the "Lieutenant, Official Principal and Commissary General and Special of the High Court of Admiralty, and President and Judge of the High Court of Admiralty," and his office remained in use until the late nineteenth century.

A fissure in the law had developed between the crown's attempts to expand its purview and the assize courts' attempts to safeguard their prerogative. Both sides had a valid claim. Piracy, as an international crime, did not merely reflect upon its malefactors, but upon the state from whence they came. Thus when English pirates attacked foreign trade, it posed critical problems for the state's relations with those nations. Conversely, when English pirates attacked English trade, particularly in conjunction with foreigners, it was hard not to claim that some form of treason had been committed. Both were compelling arguments for admiralty jurisdiction.

Yet the inverse was equally true: the elements of piracy were identical to those of ordinary robbery, had been defined thus in the common law for hundreds of years, and so the assize courts rightly regarded piracy as a local matter under their purview. Juries remained reluctant to convict: by 1500 a pirate could only be convicted in the common law if he confessed; possession of seized vessels or goods was deemed inadmissible evidence. The government tried again to circumvent the juries in 1536, establishing special commissions appointed directly by the crown. This attempt at bypass was as unsuccessful as the last; the appointed commissioners were either drawn from or influenced by local merchants whose fortunes were owed to the wages of piracy.

Conflict over jurisdiction was never successfully resolved until long after the threat of piracy had receded. Blackstone, writing of the fifteenth and sixteenth centuries, relates that "formerly [piracy] was only cognizable by the admiralty courts, which proceeded by the rules of civil law. But it being inconsistent with the liberties of the nation that any man's life should be taken away, unless by the judgment of his peers, or the common law of the land, the statute 28 Hen. VIII c.15 established a new jurisdiction for this purpose, which proceeds according to the common law." In fact, the statute merely returned a measure of prerogative to the disenfranchised assizes; the admiralty courts continued to claim "special" jurisdiction over piracy cases where treason could be argued. Sir Matthew Hale in his *Pleas to the Crown* remarks that "the statute alters not the offence, but it removes only an offense by civil law . . . and gives trial per course of common law" for crimes of piracy that were not expressly treasonable. In practical terms this meant that the admiralty courts could assert jurisdiction when the case involved a potential embarrassment for the king, thus assuring a conviction.

As we shall see in the next chapter, the crown was granting privateering commissions as a matter of course in the late sixteenth century, and, as piracy cases dwindled to nil, admiralty jurisdiction lapsed. The issue would not arise until the next century, when the crown's attitude toward piracy was markedly different. In 1663 a jurist named Richard Zouch published an article entitled "The jurisdiction of the Admiralty in England asserted against Sir Edward Coke's *Articuli Admiralitis*," which argued that piracy cases, among others, properly belonged in admiralty court. "The Lord Admiral," wrote Zouch, "may hold connaissance of things done in ports and navigable rivers . . . and other things done beyond the sea relating to Navigation and trade by sea . . . as touching damage done to persons, ships and goods." This right was routinely abrogated by the common law courts, which "do intermeddle with and interrupt the Court of Admiralty in cases properly belonging to that court."

The Crown Behaving Badly

Underlying this legal wrangle were broader divisions over the meaning and context of piracy. Irrespective of its definition as "sea robbery," it bore marked relation to another form of depredation at sea: privateering. Ostensibly the difference between the two is facile. Privateering involves acts of depredation committed under the sanction of the state against ships belonging to an enemy state during time of war, which sanction takes the form of a commission granted by the sovereign. Piracy, conversely, occurs without state sanction, against any shipping friendly or hostile to the state. This distinction loses much of its force, however, when applied to the actual history of piracy and privateering in the medieval and early modern periods. What we find on examination is a confused record wherein the common law definition of *hostis humani generi* often appears simultaneously with active crown sponsorship of privateers, even in times of peace. The trajectory from the fourteenth to the sixteenth centuries is one of condemnation to indifference to active sponsorship, a slow evolution away from the concept of pirates as enemies of the human race toward a new role as sub-rosa agents of the crown.

The first recorded use of privateers in England came during the reign of Edward I, who offered "Commissions of Reprisal" to the owners of merchant ships who had been victimized by pirates. The commission entitled such merchants to seize in turn any merchantman flying the colors of the pirate that had first attacked them. Not surprisingly, there was no necessity to limit one's captures to the amount lost, nor was there any cap on the number of vessels one could legally plunder. A portion of the captured wealth went to the coffers of the crown. The success of these endeavors led many coastal families to take up privateering as a trade, particularly along the densely trafficked English Channel. As the practice became professionalized, it no longer required the imprimatur of the crown, and so the distinction between "legal" privateering and "illegal" piracy diminished. Throughout the thirteenth and fourteenth centuries, in the absence of a standing Royal Navy to curtail it, piracy grew unchecked. Such was the gravity of the situation that the towns of Hastings, Romney, Dover, Hythe, and Sandwich—the so-called Cinque Ports—banded together to form antipiracy patrols and police the channel. Their efforts had limited results.

By the early sixteenth century piracy had become a way of life for many coastal families. The risks were relatively small, the rewards great, and the English crown lacked the ability to constrain it. Monarchs continued to grant commissions of reprisal (Henry VIII granted several during his reign, mostly to harass Spanish trade), and even the construction of a navy in the mid-sixteenth century had little effect; the navy was preoccupied, like its monarch, with external threats. Piracy in England became a profession, passed down (as it would be among the Barbary corsairs and, in some cases, the American colonies) from father to son. Consider the Killigrew family of Cornwall. From their lofty perch at Pendennis Castle, the clan oversaw a vast network of pirates, pirate brokers, and sympathetic merchants—most of whom were either directly or indirectly related to the Killigrews themselves. This unruly aristocratic lot was led by one Sir John Killigrew, vice admiral of the English navy and scion of the Cornwall gentry. Given his position in local affairs it was only natural that the crown would confer upon him the singular honor of leading the commission to catalog and capture pirates along the English coast. Sir John didn't have to look far: his son earned a living from pirate trade, his grandfather had been a notorious old pirate in Suffolk, and his own mother was alleged once to have led a boarding party.

Although most English pirates of this period were not gentry like the Killigrews, many, like them, were drawn from the same community of respectable wage-earning citizens who constituted most assize juries. These included local mariners—both fishermen and traders—who were well known both to their fellow townspeople and to the local authorities. Their piratical activities were rarely directed against local trade (for the simple reason that they would have to face their own neighbors if it were so), and thus the "crime" seemed detached and remote. Small wonder that the vast majority of them were acquitted.

Until the sixteenth century the crown policy on piracy was decidedly negative: it was ordinary juries, not the sovereign, that countenanced acts of piracy. Yet that would soon change. The Killigrews were early forerunners of a transformation in English piracy law, when tacit crown tolerance of piracy gave way to active sponsorship. The catalyst was England's declining relations with Spain. At its source, this conflict was almost exclusively mercantile: English ships were branching farther and farther afield, into North Africa and the Mediterranean, even across the Atlantic to the Caribbean and South America. As they did so, they invariably came into conflict with preexisting trade, which was predominantly Spanish. Worse still, as the sea lanes opened to English merchantmen, the pirates inevitably followed in their wake. Yet it was not a simple matter to distinguish the former from the latter; historians assessing this period almost invariably refer to it as "confused." First, English incursion on Spanish trade was far from peaceable. English ships sacked Spanish ships in the mid-Atlantic, raided Spanish colonies, and captured Spanish forts. The Spanish and their Portuguese allies retaliated in kind. Second, the legal situation was chaotic. The Spanish and English governments, steadfastly maintaining that the pirates acted independently of their will, left a considerable paper trail of proclamations against the pirate menace. In reality, they did almost nothing to deter them. Increasingly, as the century wore on and the rift between the two nations deepened, England grew bolder in its use of the pirates. Thus developed a situation wherein legitimate trade, aggressive mercantilism, and outright piracy commingled and coalesced.

A new generation of mariners was rising through the ranks to answer England's call to arms against the Spanish menace. The first, most famous, and most successful of these was a young Devonshire gentleman named Francis Drake.

-2-

Erring Captains

State-Sponsored Piracy and Its Aftermath

APRIL 4, 1581

The tiny seaport of Deptford, lying several miles from its more august neighbor, Greenwich, was bedecked in flags. As the queen's carriage moved through the narrow cobblestoned streets, the local citizenry cheered and tried to touch the wheels. The progress became a procession, and finally a parade, as Queen Elizabeth and her entourage were trailed by the entire township down to the docks. There waiting for them was the *Golden Hind.*

She was not a prepossessing ship, even by the standards of the day. Just over one hundred tons displacement and a mere seventy feet long, the stubby little vessel looked more like a fat-bottomed Dutch trader than a sleek English privateer. And the captain who stood on her quarterdeck, raising his plumed helmet aloft, was scarcely more impressive. Accounts of his height vary according to the vitriol of the narrator (his detractors claimed he was barely more than a midget), but even his greatest friends had to admit that the *Hind*'s commander was not a large man. He was probably about five feet, one inch in his stockings. Like many small men, the captain tried to disguise his meager stature with sartorial splendor, including very large heels. It was an age of excess in both dress and deportment, but few went quite as far in both as he. From the edge of the wharf Her Majesty could easily make out the glint of sunlight shimmering on his breastplate, the scarlet sash and gaily colored leggings, the ostrich-plumed helmet. The next few hours would become the stuff of legend, an iconic image ranked alongside King John signing the Magna Carta and Nelson holding the spyglass to his blind eye in great moments of English history. Countless painters, woodcutters, and lithographers would reproduce this scene. Yet it is perhaps not surprising that nearly all of them got it wrong.

What actually happened was this. The queen reached the edge of the docks, and the captain came forth to greet her. She turned and introduced a tall, saturnine man with a pointed beard as the Sieur de Marchaumont, special envoy of His Most Christian Majesty the King of France's brother, the Duc d'Alençon. The sea captain eyed the Frenchman with interest. Alençon was the latest in a long series of suitors arranged for the Virgin Queen; rumor had it that this time the marriage was almost a certainty. Bringing his representative to this ship, on this day, was a gesture that could have only one interpretation. The deal was being sealed. Formalities aside, the captain invited his guests below, where a banquet awaited them. Though there is no record of it, it is likely that Marchaumont experienced a moment of trepidation as he descended the narrow, poorly lit stairway. He knew firsthand that English cuisine was execrable; English shipboard fare would be unimaginable.

But here the *Golden Hind* surprised him. A huge table was laid with every delicacy, candles twinkling merrily over roast pheasant and leg of mutton, crisp vegetables wreathed in steam, jellies and candies and puddings. And, of course, wine. Marchaumont might not have recognized the plate, though it was very fine. But his counterpart, Don Bernardino de Mendoza, would have. It bore the Spanish imperial crest.

They dined splendidly. The captain, seated at the right hand of Her Majesty, kept the table entertained with long stories of his adventures. The candlelight lit up a face that was ruddy and round, with light blue eyes and a sandy colored beard. The skin was darkly tanned, against which a livid scar across the left cheek glowed white. The face was mobile and interesting, humorous, perhaps a little cocky at times, but at other moments suddenly very wise. It was not hard to see why he had gained the favor of the ever-susceptible queen.

After dinner they returned to the main deck. A ceremonial sword was produced. Not long ago Her Majesty had promised Senor Mendoza that if the head of the notorious pirate Francis Drake was presented to her she would strike it from its body. Reminding the assembled company of that promise, she playfully handed the sword to M. de Marchaumont, saying that perhaps it would be safer if he did the honors. It was not a spontaneous gesture. Such gestures never were. The queen was commanding an envoy of France to bestow English knighthood upon the man who had brought chaos to the Spanish empire and ruin to its coffers. It was exactly like this particular monarch to cloak a symbol of such potent political ramifications in the guise of a womanly jest. But Marchaumont was not amused. He gravely took the sword and just as gravely ordered the sea captain to kneel. Then, with the power that had suddenly been vested in him by the wigged and gowned lady standing at his right, he dubbed the master of the *Golden Hind* Sir Francis Drake, Knight Commander of England. From the mainmast the royal standard, with its white lilies symbolizing England's long-dormant claim on the French throne, fluttered in the breeze.

The Queen's Privateers

The Elizabethan era was one in which many historians argue the state emerged in its modern form, both at home and abroad. Trade gained supremacy over landed wealth, diminishing the power of the gentry. As the prerogatives of the expanding crown ascended and multiplied, the business of state began to dwarf the small band of aristocrats who had customarily held the reigns of government. A proto-bureaucracy was created. Government became compartmentalized and increasingly professional. England by the end of the century had begun its transformation into the preeminent mercantile marine empire of the next three hundred years.

The irony of this development is that much of it occurred in direct response to feelings of instability and fears of imminent attack. Elizabeth, as a Protestant, inherited a deeply divided nation from her Catholic half-sister, Mary. Having failed to arrange an alliance with the Spanish throne through marriage, Philip II turned instead to exploiting religious tensions within England to unseat the queen and replace her with a Catholic successor, Mary Stuart of Scotland. As diplomatic relations became increasingly hostile, the perceived Spanish threat led to a strengthening of the English military and bureaucratic structures. One of the many consequences was the phenomenal growth of the English Navy and, as a corollary, the equally unprecedented growth of privateering and piracy.

The two forms of sea enterprise, naval and piratical, could not be distinguished from one another in this era. Naval vessels were often sent on pirate voyages; naval captains became privateers. Piracy was never expressly cited as a legitimate means of warfare; it simply became one through usage and circumstance. But its advantages for the English crown were manifest. First, it trained future captains by testing their skills against the Spanish before the navies could meet in force. Second, it bled Spanish resources and frustrated their governance of empire, most particularly in the New World. Third, it vastly enriched the English government, providing for the construction of the new fleet. Fourth, it provided a huge resource of trained and experienced seamen to man the fleet once it was ready.

Most important, however, state-sponsored piracy provoked the Spanish into waging war before they were fully prepared, on the necessity of countering the pirate menace. By 1562 it was estimated that several hundred pirate ships cruised the English Channel alone, and the crown had by this time abandoned even the pretense of curtailing them. The Elizabethans had, unwittingly or not, hit upon a brilliant means of waging war without declaring it. By working through the proxy of privateers rather than the Royal Navy itself, the crown could serenely maintain the fiction that England and Spain were still at peace. With scant means of overseas communication available to them, Elizabeth and her ministers could hardly be blamed for skirmishes among brigands in the periphery.

The Elizabethan era was not the first to produce a relationship between states and pirates. Yet never before had the welfare of the state depended in such great measure on the pirates' activities. It is a testament to the burgeoning importance of colonies and new sources of trade for the nations of Europe that disruption of that trade could alone provide the impetus for war. Even more significantly, the directed use of piracy by the crown set into motion a pattern of English sponsorship that would continue, and evolve, over the next two centuries. In its earliest, sixteenth-century incarnation, this relationship was as simple as it was practical: a commission from the crown to harass Spanish trade and threaten her empire. In most cases the corsairs had multiple backers for their expeditions, ranging from government officials, peers, and statesmen to city merchants and private financiers. Likewise, the acts of piracy committed during these treks ranged from the simple taking of necessary provisions to grand, well-orchestrated raids on Spanish ports. The voyage was deemed a success if the ship returned (they often did not) and if it held sufficient quantities of goods or specie to reimburse its patrons.

The audacity of these voyages required a different sort of mariner to lead them. Pirates of the earlier era had rarely been more than coastal raiders, familiar with the shoals and waters around their home base but utterly unqualified to lead a fleet of ships much farther than the channels. The English corsairs were the first of a new breed: gentlemen privateers whose activities augmented the Royal Navy and increased the fortunes both of themselves and the government. They transformed the profession of piracy by legitimizing it: these were not hired thugs in the paid service of the crown (as their classical and medieval counterparts often were) but highly skilled sailors from respectable, sometimes even aristocratic antecedents. These men—and not the uncouth ruffians of earlier generations—were the direct linear forebears of the seventeenth-century pirates.

Francis Drake was the foremost example of this breed. Acting under commission from Queen Elizabeth, Drake launched numerous raids on

Spanish vessels and Spanish ports, both on the continent and in the Americas. His circumnavigation of the globe, undertaken in 1577, was as much a destructive rampage as a voyage of discovery: the cities of Cartagena, Nombre de Dios, and Callao, among others, fell to him. Like most historical figures (and all pirates), the significance of Francis Drake has gradually been subsumed by the legend. He remains, even to most historians, a larger-than-life Elizabethan cutout. But Drake was much more than that. His colossal success not only made him a hero, it made him a prototype—the standard by which all future pirates would be judged and by which they judged themselves. Even in his own lifetime there were scores of lesser men vying to exceed his record; after his death, and for the next two centuries, there would be legions more. Drake, like Caesar Augustus, became the primus inter pares of the pirate world: the first, the greatest, the inspiration.

While this much is well known, the other side of the coin is far less so. Just as Drake's example would fire generations of mariners, the precedent set by his relations with the crown would likewise gain a momentum of its own. It is true that English royal patronage of piracy would never again reach the zenith of the late sixteenth century, but the mistake most often made is to assume that such patronage withered away in the succeeding decades. It did not. Instead, as the Isles developed their first successful colonies in the New World and installed permanent governments therein, the pattern of sponsorship would be transposed from the epicenter to the outposts, taken from the hands of the monarch and vested in the hands of the royal governors. This was both necessary and practical: pirates no longer sailed, like Drake, from Plymouth or Deptford. Many, and ultimately nearly all, were not even born Englishmen. Their locus of interaction was not in England at all but in the colonies from which they sailed. Hence, their only contact with the crown was through its intermediary, the governor.

The example of Queen Elizabeth and Sir Francis Drake would be repeated, albeit under different circumstances and among very different surroundings, countless times in the seventeenth and eighteenth centuries. Sometimes this relationship would bear the imprimatur of the crown; more often it would not. Yet the paradigm was necessary, for without Drake there could have been no Morgan, Avery, Kidd, or Teach. Like lawyers searching for a case, countless governors would justify their sponsorship of pirates by invoking his example. More than a century later, Drake's exploits against the Spanish in a time of nominal peace would continue to buttress claims for similar depredations in many of the same locales: Hispaniola, Cartagena, Panama.

Disaster Under James I

Captain John Smith—explorer, soldier, colonizer, occasional abductor of Native American princesses—looked upon the sorry situation of the early seventeenth century and summed it up with a short, pithy comment: "After the death of our most gracious Queen Elizabeth . . . King James, who from his infancy had reigned in peace with all nations, had no employment for those men of war; so that the rich rested with what they had; those that were poor had nothing but from hand to mouth turned pirates."

By the time Smith penned these words (1629), the problem of Atlantic piracy had spiraled wildly out of control. It began, as is often the case, with a series of well-intentioned but ultimately disastrous laws. Queen Elizabeth had died in March 1603, and her successor, James VI of Scotland, was invested as James I of England on July 11, 1604.

The first item on James's agenda was to bring to a close the long-standing war with Spain. This was done by the Treaty of London in August 1604. Its terms were flagrantly generous to the Spanish, the first black mark against the new king. Moreover James, unlike Elizabeth, had every intention of honoring them. The principal problem, as he saw it, was the continuance of pirate raids guised as privateering expeditions—an infraction of which both the English and the Spanish (not to mention the Dutch and the French) were equally guilty. True peace could not be achieved until the seas were calm. James resolved to begin the process with an act of good faith. Even before concluding the treaty he issued "A Proclamation concerning Warlike ships at Sea," which summarily recalled all privateers. Three months later, due to the total lack of response, it was followed by "A Proclamation to represse all Piracies and Depredations upon the Sea." This revoked all letters of marque and expressly forbade any officer of the crown from issuing them. The proclamations appeared almost yearly thereafter, an index both of James's resolve and its low currency among the English people: 1604,

"A Proclamation for the search and apprehension of certaine Pirats"; 1605, "A Proclamation for revocation of Mariners from forreine Services" (aimed at Englishmen serving aboard foreign pirate vessels) and "A Proclamation with certaine Ordinances to be observed by his Majesty's subjects toward the King of Spaine"; 1606, "A Proclamation for the search and apprehension of certaine Pirats" (interestingly, the list contains several of the same names as its predecessor two years before); and finally, on January 8, 1609, the circulation of a general "Proclamation against Pirats."

What James intended was to turn back the clock, past the privateering commissions of Elizabeth and even the laissez-faire policies of Henry VIII and his predecessors, all the way to Edward III. Piracy in any form would not be countenanced. Elements of the offense were broadened to include almost any act of depredation at sea, and punishment was swift and ruthless: "Wherein if any manner of person shall be found culpable or willfully negligent, contemptuous, or disobedient, His Majestie declareth hereby that punishment shall be inflicted upon him with such severity as an example thereof shall terrify all others. . . ."

James also took steps to ensure that his pogrom would not fall victim to sympathetic juries. Jurisdiction for all piracy cases, however trivial, was granted exclusively to the admiralty courts. To make this explicit, James's ministers circulated a proclamation devoted solely to the manner by which pirates could be apprehended and detained. Subjects, it declared, were enjoined "that immediately after the sight of this present Proclamation they . . . do make diligent search and inquire in all places for the said persons . . . and to apprehend and commit [them] to the next Gaol, there to be detained, until our high Admiral, or his Lieutenant Judge of the High Court of the Admiralty . . . shall take order in that behalf." A later proclamation said flatly that all such cases "shall be heard by the Judge of the Admiralty without admitting unnecessary delay, and no appeal from him shall be allowed to the defendant." With that, the common law avenue of jurisdiction was effectively closed.

Yet within a few years we find evidence in the proclamations that something had gone seriously awry. In 1604 the crown named only three pirates currently at sea and branded them for capture. By 1606 it listed twenty different ships and their captains, as well as "diverse other complices and associates." Among these, interestingly, were the same three pirates—Henry Radcliffe, William Smith, and John Banister—

that the earlier proclamation cited. Three years later the proclamations have an even more jaded and rancorous tone, a shift in tenor from what the crown will do to what it utterly abhors, without specific remedy:

> The King Majesty [has been] informed . . . of the many depredations and piracies committed by lewd and ill disposed persons, accustomed and habituated to spoile and rapine, insensible and desperate of the peril they draw on themselves, and the imputation they cast upon the honor of their Sovereign so precious to him, as for redresse he is for inforced to reiterate and inculcate his loathing and detestation.

And so on. Having catalogued the list of offenses, the proclamation obliquely identifies the source of the problem. "Most of these great faults," it declares, "are continued by the connivance or corruption in many of the subordinate officers [of the crown], especially such as are resident in and near the ports and maritime counties." The attempt to extend royal prerogative into the localities was being thwarted by the same limitations that had doomed Edward III's campaign to failure: the law, ultimately, is only as viable as the willingness of those charged with implementing it.

Captain Smith was on hand to witness the result. The abrupt cessation of hostilities, the recall of the pirates, and the near abandonment of the Royal Navy created that most dangerous of dividends: a surplus of unemployed malcontents. Historically these have been depicted in proletarian fashion as rough, unlettered seamen, poised on the social scale opposite an effete, homosexual king. Some of them doubtless were as gritty as this image suggests. The majority, however, were skilled and accomplished mariners, ranging from captains of the merchant class to sailors before the mast who had been on dozens of voyages and were experts at their particular craft: cooperage, sailcloth, steering, and the like. England, despite the fact that it was both an island and a primarily mercantile nation, was turning inward. With a few strokes of his pen, James had isolated a significant cross-section of English society—the mariners and those who profited from them—and condemned it to penury.

The results did not take long to manifest themselves, as the record of proclamations attests. Part of the problem was the miserly rewards that even those fortunate enough to find a berth on a merchantman or a navy vessel received. Monthly pay for ordinary service was ten shillings a month, an amount that, already a mere pittance, was frequently garnished to pay for food and sundries while aboard ship. Conditions on board were appalling, and discipline was stringently enforced. "I could wish," Smith mused, "Merchants, Gentlemen, and all settlers forth of ships not to be sparing of a competent pay, nor true payment; for neither soldiers nor seamen can live without means, but necessity will force them to steal; and when they are once entered into that trade, they are hardly reclaimed."

The lure of piracy had other sources as well. The American colonies in the early seventeenth century had not yet tapped into the lucrative slave trade, and consequently much of the manual labor was done by English citizens held under indentured servitude contracts. These could be convicts, vagrants, debtors, or anyone picked up by the press gangs. Shipped across the Atlantic and sold like slaves, this lower strata of English society was released upon the New World vengeful and eager to escape the confining bonds of their contracts. Pirate vessels appearing in harbor were often hailed as rescue craft for such unfortunates. "Once landed in the colonies and having tasted the hardships of forced labor," George Dow writes, "a roving disposition was soon awakened and runaway servants were almost as common as blackbirds. Numbers of these men joined marauding expeditions and eventually became pirates of the usual type."

And yet there was no "usual type" of pirate in the early seventeenth century. Though one Whig historian has quaintly derided them as "runaway apprentices, faithless husbands, fugitive thieves and murderers," the men drawn to piracy in this period ran the full gamut of social backgrounds and experiences. They came from the fishing communities in Newfoundland, the middle-class merchant families of Massachusetts and Rhode Island, New York and Maryland, the plantations of South Carolina, Bermuda, Tortuga, and Barbados. Some came willingly, grateful to be free of the bonds of servitude, others were lured by the prospect of riches, and still others were pressed into service. In the *Calendar of State Papers* we find described the ease with which pirates took both crew and provisions:

> From all the harbors . . . they commanded carpenters,
> mariner's victuals, munitions and all necessaries from the
> fishing fleet after this rate—of every six mariners they take

one, and the one-fifth part of their victuals . . . some of
company of many ships did run away unto them . . . and
so after they had continued taking their pleasure of the
fishing fleet, the 14th of September 1614, they departed,
having with them from the fishing fleet about 400 mariners and fishermen; many volunteers, many compelled.

Nor was piracy confined to English practice. James might have been
ardent in his wish for amity among nations, but he was alone in that
desire. Buried within the Treaty of Vervins between France and Spain,
signed in 1598, was a secret codicil. In the flowery language of the age
it declared that the peace made between them came to an abrupt halt
at the Tropic of Cancer. Beyond that imaginary line (the "ligne de l'enclose des Amities," or, more brutally, "friendship termination line") the
treaty was silent; it was almost as if the ancients had been right, that the
world really did drop off into a void. Within that void it was every man
for himself. The Dutch, meanwhile, sent a staggering eighty ships in the
Caribbean Sea, boasting a combined firepower of 1,500 cannons and
some 9,000 trained soldiers and seamen. Cuba, Puerto Rico, and Bahia
fell, albeit briefly, to Dutch possession.

Worse yet, there were clear indications that the Spanish were not
holding their end of the bargain. In December 1604, just months after
James published his fourth proclamation against English piracy, the
Venetian ambassador to London wrote his doge that the English people were in an uproar once again. Even the crisp, concise language of a
trained civil servant could not conceal the outrage behind his words.
News had come, he wrote, "that the Spanish in the West Indies captured
two English vessels, cut off the hands, feet, noses and ears of the crews
and smeared them with honey and tied them to trees to be tortured by
flies and other insects." Being a diplomat, he was bound to be circumspect. "The Spanish here plead," he allowed, "that they were pirates, not
merchants, and that they did not know of the peace." Then the mask
fell again. "But the barbarity makes people here cry out," he concluded.

Even those charged with implementing James's conciliatory policy
boggled at its implications. Lord Cornwallis, newly appointed ambassador to the Spanish court, observed firsthand the wreckage and financial ruin which a decade of war had wreaked on his hosts. He could not
believe, he wrote secretly, that England should fail to take advantage of
such an opportunity. In a letter dated July 2, 1605, he confided that

Spain and her king "were reduced to such a state as they could not in all likelihood have endured for the space of two years more." Others within James's own council agreed with Cornwallis and quietly began encouraging piratical raids. The decades following the Treaty of London reveal a drastic surge of pirate activity, both in contravention and response to the repeated entreaties from the crown to stop.

Part of the problem was James's flawed policy, but it alone was not entirely to blame. We shall see in the mid-eighteenth century a similar legislative pogrom intended to stamp out the pirate menace, with far more successful results. In the latter example legislative will was joined with actual force: a potent, professional navy committed to hunting down and destroying every pirate in the Atlantic. In the seventeenth century, however, James's yearly proclamations lacked teeth. The Royal Navy, which would have been the only force capable of curtailing the pirate menace, was drastically cut back and left to rot in harbors throughout England. In its absence James relied on the goodwill of nations and that of the pirates themselves. The response of both these parties was much as one might expect and, as Dickens would have said, threw a sad light on human nature. By the later years of his reign James was compelled to attempt a different tack: granting full pardons to pirates who willingly surrendered themselves to the crown. Because the nature of the pardon allowed them to keep whatever they found until that time, pirates cheerfully presented themselves as penitents before the customs officers, received their absolution, and set off on another cruise posthaste.

The second problem was that the potential rewards of a pirate voyage were simply too great to refuse. The flota (consisting of some twenty merchant vessels, among which were two galleons of roughly eight hundred tons each) departed Cadiz every year in June. It beat a leisurely course across the Atlantic, stopping at Puerto Rico and Hispaniola, rounding Cape de Cruz, and putting in at Havana. From Acapulco came some ten or twelve million doubloons of Spanish gold, along with whatever local specie and export might be provided. Then, heavily laden, the fleet turned and began its long trek homeward. The regularity and course of the flota was immutable as the migration of cod; pirates, like fishermen, soon learned to track it with ease. And there were other prizes, almost as lucrative. From Portugal came silks and woolens, bound for Brazil. From the Spanish—in addition to gold and silver—came indigo, logwood, sugar, and spices. While English farmers in North America ground a Spartan existence out of rocky soil and English plantation owners in the Caribbean and the Carolinas looked with chagrin at failing crops of tobacco and rice, the Spanish Americans were mining a king's fortune every year in South America. Pilfered Spanish gold became—and would remain—a staple of English colonial commerce for almost a century thereafter.

A Pirate's Warning

The men who sailed out to intercept the Spanish ships were a new breed, distinct both from the coastal pirates and the gentleman corsairs of the last century, yet containing elements of both. Historians are apt to draw a sharp line between these pirates and their predecessors, similar in nature to that between "pirates" and "privateers." The difference, they maintain, is that Drake and Raleigh acted out the policies of Queen Elizabeth, while their successors acted against the policy of James. Hence legal privateering gives way to illegal piracy, and the myth of the "sorry band of human scum" is born. But this is misleading, for it ignores the actual histories of these men, how they viewed themselves, and how they were regarded by their peers. In fact, their careers reflected both a strong linkage to Drake and the willingness to adapt his legacy to changing circumstances—namely, the absence of war.

The most famous and successful of these was a Shropshire gentleman and lawyer-turned-pirate named Sir Henry Mainwaring. Educated at Brasenose (an Oxford college known for producing clergymen), Mainwaring quickly found life in the city unbearably dull. He left his failing practice in 1608 and purchased a small chaser of some 160 tons, which he named *Resistance*. He also hired the services of a trained and experienced crew (Mainwaring himself had almost no sea experience); in those lean times they were not difficult to find, and one gets the impression that the middle-class lawyer was able to get both ship and crew on the cheap.

Required by law to submit a course plan to the Admiralty before departure, Mainwaring offered a bogus document that purported to be a commission to carry miscellaneous cargo from the West Indies back to London. No sooner than they had left harbor, however, did Mainwaring gather his crew on deck and explain their true purpose. They were not surprised. The nature of Mainwaring's voyage had been an open secret from the beginning. With his crew in accord, Mainwaring changed course and headed through the Straits of Gibraltar, bound for Marmora on the Barbary Coast. Marmora in the early seventeenth century was what Port Royal, Jamaica, would become in the late seventeenth century—a dirty, ramshackle, violent port town that was known throughout the world as a haven for pirates of every race and stamp. Mainwaring was an oddity among them: first in that he was an Englishman, second that he was a gentleman. Perhaps it was for both those reasons that the pirates of Marmora accorded him respect, going so far as to appoint him a provisional governor of sorts.

Mainwaring soon justified their regard with a series of dazzling raids against the Spanish vessels passing through the Mediterranean and Bay of Biscay. Such was the extent of his fame that the Bey of Tunis, who had never laid eyes on an Englishman and never wished to, offered him an equal partnership. The only condition the Bey insisted on was that the pirate renounce his Christianity. Mainwaring, perhaps with some regret, refused. He had no wish to embrace Eastern ways, which he persisted in regarding as vulgar and undignified. He also refrained from attacking English vessels, and such was the force of his reputation that under his command the entire cadre of Marmora pirates did so as well. By 1614 the story of Mainwaring's success in the Mediterranean had spread as far as Ireland and even across the Atlantic to the Americas. When in the fall of that year he arrived in Newfoundland—a favorite place for recruiting pirates—he was welcomed as a hero. Not since Drake had an English mariner so captivated the public imagination.

Beating back to warmer waters, Mainwaring joined forces with another English pirate and embarked on his most ambitious and successful campaign yet. The pirate flotilla tacked back and forth along the Spanish coast, intercepting dozens of vessels and amassing a fortune of some five hundred thousand Spanish crowns. The king of Spain, in a fury, suspended all treaties with England regarding piracy and openly offered privateering commissions to anyone willing to attack English ships. At the same time, he dispatched a fleet of five ships of the line to hunt down the infamous Mainwaring and destroy him.

The five Spanish ships met Mainwaring's three on the approaches to Cadiz in the early hours of the morning. The Spanish vessels were nearly twice as large, with double the number of cannons. Mainwaring scattered his fleet, circling round the enemy and snapping at their heels like terriers. Spanish strategy was markedly different: remain in formation, so as to present as invulnerable a target as possible. Mainwaring was counting on this. His ships—small, fast, nimble—circled around the lumbering Spanish ships and battered at them from every angle. Each time the Spanish would lumber slowly round, bringing their deadly gunports within range of the English, Mainwaring's vessels would dart out of the way. Yet the disparity of size and firepower still weighed heavily on the outcome, and despite near-constant battering, the Spanish fleet remained grouped and undefeated from the first light of morning until well past dark. It was a battle of attrition, the only question being which would hold out longer: the Spanish or Mainwaring's ammunition. By midnight the Spanish fleet was crippled and partially dismasted, two of its ships having lost steering power and forced to maneuver with jury-rigged rudders. They retreated in confusion, with Mainwaring still firing volley after volley at their sterns.

King James was appalled. This was not the first time that a pirate would embarrass the English court, and it certainly would not be the last. But few sovereigns have staked so much on the containment of piracy. Fresh evidence of Mainwaring's exploits was coming in daily from sources as disparate as Ireland, Massachusetts, and the Ottoman Empire. Worse still, it was clear that his successes had struck a chord with the English imagination at a particularly volatile point in the nation's history. Peace with Spain had done little to change its perception as the perpetual enemy, a role that was further exacerbated by its status as the most powerful Catholic nation in Europe. While James labored to patch the rift between Catholic and Protestant nations (as well as the even deeper rift between the two faiths among his own people), plots were almost continually under way to blow up the ground from beneath his feet—at one point literally. In 1605, as James prepared to take the historic step of addressing both houses of Parliament, a small band of Catholic Englishmen led by Robert Catesby plotted to ignite a cache of gunpowder under Parliament and send king and Commons to glory. The impetus, historians suggest, was the realization that the Spanish crown was too heavily in debt (partially as a result of pirate raids) to assist them, and thus they must take matters into their own hands. The plot was uncovered and one of the conspirators, Guy Fawkes, was seized in the caverns of Parliament with a wheelbarrow full of gunpowder, but the threat still rankled. English pamphleteers—the yellow press of their day—did a brisk trade in constant warnings of an impending Catholic uprising. The monarchy seemed in danger from threats within and without. In 1606 a London playwright seeking to curry favor with the Caledonian king captured the anxiety of the age and the fears for James's safety: he titled his latest work *Macbeth*.

Mainwaring's exploits, then, were paradoxically a triumph for the English people and a disaster for their sovereign. Not since Drake had any mariner so thoroughly defeated the Spanish navy at sea nor so successfully depleted their coffers. James was bluntly informed by both the French and Spanish courts that unless Mainwaring was stopped, there would be war. This might have been precisely what many in England wanted, but James knew all too well that the crown could not afford even a minor conflict, much less a full-scale conflagration. Yet still he prevaricated, unable to reach a decision. To brand Mainwaring a pirate and seek his execution would risk both failure (if he were not apprehended) and political suicide for the king and his ministers. Not to do so would have equally dire consequences.

What James arrived at ultimately was a brilliant compromise. Like most compromises it was born out of necessity. He dispatched a swift cutter to find Mainwaring at Marmora and deliver him this message: he could either accept the king's pardon and renounce piracy, or he would face an entire fleet of English ships—augmented by French and Spanish, if necessary—to defeat him. Mainwaring did not hesitate. Though doubtful that any English fleet could catch him, he was still an Englishman first, a pirate second. He sailed for Dover in the spring of 1616 and on June 9 received his full pardon "under the Great Seal of England." The template for the document required that the reasons for the pardon be stated. It read, accordingly, that Captain Mainwaring "had committed no great wrong."

Had the story ended there, Henry Mainwaring would still have earned his place among the great English corsairs, albeit a generation too late. But Mainwaring, having been a liability to James and his policies, became their staunchest defender in later years. With a privateering commission from the king's own hand, he turned his wrath on his former compatriots, the Barbary pirates. In just over a year he had beaten them back severely (at one point the Mohammedans had actually been encamped on the River Thames) and returned to accept a knighthood from his grateful sovereign. In 1623, in recognition of his efforts, Sir Henry Mainwaring was elected to a seat in Parliament, representing Dover.

In 1624, in response to a request from the crown, Sir Henry put pen to paper in an attempt to describe in full the state of piracy under the Stuart monarchy. Like John Smith, but far better informed, Mainwaring attributed its exponential growth to the uneasy peace between England and Spain. But Mainwaring's account was extraordinary, for it described with ease and sometimes gripping candor the reasons for his own piratical career. Part jeremiad, part mea culpa, and a good part travel guide, Sir Henry takes his reader from region to region, exploring the path of the pirates as one who experienced it firsthand. Ireland, he writes, was a veritable "nursery for pirates"; Newfoundland was a rich source both for crews and provisions; Morocco was a fine place for watering and victualling; and the Bey of Tunis was, in spite of being an infidel, "a very just man of his word."

Mainwaring's account is unique, for it allows us—as it allowed James—to see for the first time the phenomenon of piracy not merely as a dry legislative or political matter but as a human experience. One could liken it to Drake's record of his adventures, or even Sir Henry Morgan's of a century later, but in this respect it stands alone: it was written not to glorify the writer but to shed light on the subject. It dealt less with the Sturm und Drang of battle than the myriad problems of finding fresh water, arranging favorable terms with sultanates for the exchange of specie, or securing safe havens to careen the ship and scrape its bottom.

Sir Henry dedicated his work, not surprisingly, "to my most Gracious Sovereign, that represents the King in Heaven, whose mercy is above all his works." From that lofty perch he ventured to make several observations and suggestions. First, the problem of piracy was far greater, he wrote, than anyone at court would acknowledge. "Since Your Highness's reign there have been more pirates by ten to one than were in the whole reign of last Queen," he told James, careful not to make it sound as though His Majesty was at fault. He recommended amnesty and reeducation, putting the pirates to honest employ as swiftly as possible. Most of all, he counseled, the navy must be restored and reequipped, and those itinerant seamen that still haunted the docks of Plymouth and Deptford should be put to sea at once, sailing for the crown rather than against it.

If James was persuaded by the logic of this favored ex-pirate, it still did not change matters greatly. The desuetude of the navy continued unchecked. When James died later that year, pirate vessels were ten- or even twentyfold more numerous than they had been at the close of the last century, and the business of granting peacetime privateering commissions was just as great as it had ever been under Elizabeth. James's antipiracy policies had not been without effect, however. What they accomplished, ultimately, was to transform the practice of pirate sponsorship by relinquishing crown prerogative. The consequences were threefold. First, as we have seen, the cessation of hostilities and near abandonment of the Royal Navy propelled a new generation of unemployed mariners to seek out a living through piracy, a practice that was augmented by the ready supply of crews from the Atlantic colonies.

Second, by declining to grant crown commissions to privateers, James unwittingly fostered the circumstances whereby others would fill the void of sponsorship. Piracy, in other words, was no longer a sport of kings. When James refused to follow the example of Elizabeth, a ready conclave of bankers, lords, admirals, and gentry was ready to take his place. Such sponsorship was, as we have seen, sub rosa at first (hence the necessity for Henry Mainwaring to submit a false course plan), but as the century wore on and relations with Spain and France declined, it became increasingly open and obvious. At James's death this patronage came out into the open and flourished, most particularly in the turbulent later years of Charles I's reign.

Third, James's failure to establish a lasting peace with the Spanish and his unwillingness to work through his council or Parliament toward that end created a vacuum of leadership that allowed other private individuals to pursue their own ends. The history of Jacobean policy is one of lofty ambitions that are undercut, time and again, by the inability of enforcement. Thus by drastically reducing the navy, James nullified the only viable check to English (or Spanish, or French) piracy. Similarly, James's intransigence isolated him, leaving courtiers and ministers to act on their own initiative, counter to the royal will. Even men like Henry Mainwaring felt reasonably assured of their position, comfortable in the knowledge that although they were flouting crown law, no serious penalty awaited them. And they were right.

Patrons, Parliaments, and Pirates

The death of James I and the succession of his son, Charles, in 1625, brought to an abrupt end James's dream of peace between England and Spain. Charles, unlike his father, willingly employed privateers in much the same way Elizabeth I had done. His court followed suit. In 1640 the Spanish ambassador reported in a rage that two belted lords, the Earls of Warwick and Marlborough, had outfitted a small fleet of pirate ships and planned to dispatch them to the West Indies with specific instructions to take whatever Spanish vessels they found. Ambassador de Cardenas lodged his protest with King Charles, along with the oblique threat of open war should the ships depart unchecked. Charles, who had neither Elizabeth's resolve nor James's pusillanimity, handled this latest Spanish tirade in his own fashion: he referred it to a committee. The committee then spent several weeks considering and debating the petition, consulting the Law of the Sea and various ancient statutes on the subject. It heard opinions, held councils, and went through a great deal of parchment. In the meantime the Earl of Marlborough departed from Deptford for the West Indies, bearing the personal commission of Charles I to trade with the Indies and take whatever "hostile" ships he encountered. The meaning of the word was left tactfully obscure. Several weeks later, as Marlborough and his crew were still tacking their way toward Hispaniola, the committee finally rendered its decision. As neither Spain nor Great Britain had ever stringently observed the alleged peace, it concluded, and as the West Indies were well beyond the periphery of state influence so much as to constitute terra incognita from the legal point of view, no reasonable man could object to what went on there or hold any state accountable for it. "Whether the Spaniards will think this reasonable or not," one committee member assured another, "is no great matter."

Pirate patronage was not merely the privilege of lords. The Long Parliament also granted privateering commissions as a matter of course. Thus the Earl of Warwick—newly raised by Parliament to lord admiral—became a sort of pirate-broker in chief. William Bradford, in a contemporary account of the Massachusetts colony, tells of one Captain Thomas Cromwell (a name of some distinction in the coming years but apparently no relation to the lord protector), a Boston man who received a commission from Warwick in 1645 and proceeded to cause havoc among the Spanish traders in the Caribbean. He then returned to Boston in great triumph and presented to an astonished Governor Winthrop the jewel-encrusted sedan chair of the viceroy of Mexico. What the staunchly Puritan governor made of this gaudy papist bauble is not recorded, but he relates in his journal that he offered Cromwell the use of one of the best houses in Boston in gratitude. Cromwell, in the best tradition of his Calvinist roots, refused and lodged instead in a "poor thatched house."

In 1649 King Charles I, having failed in his last gambit to invite a Scottish invasion and thus thwart Parliament once and for all, was put on trial for his life. Nine days later, January 30, 1649, in what was surely one of the speediest legal procedures ever conducted, the king of England was found guilty of treason and executed. The Protectorate, newly formed under Oliver Cromwell, seemed at first to promise a chilling effect on piracy. The Royal Navy, which had been nearly decimated through neglect and lack of funds, was revitalized. Naval colleges were established, producing a corps of professional officers better trained and better funded than any since Elizabeth's time. The fleet was rebuilt almost from scratch, with a new class of frigates and ships of the line introduced. Moreover, in one of his first acts as lord protector, Cromwell sent the newly built fleet to root out Barbary pirates that had been harassing English trade in the Mediterranean for several decades. The results were immediate and gratifying: the pirates, surprised by the sudden descent of English vessels, fled precipitously. It was the first victory the Royal Navy had enjoyed in years.

Yet the promise was short-lived. Cromwell, in fact, would be responsible for a series of acts that did as much to foster piracy in the New World as any of James's disastrous antipiracy laws. These were the Navigation Acts of 1651. The acts provided that almost no goods could be imported into England or the colonies except by English ships manned by English captains. Likewise, the colonies could trade only with the mother country and receive only its trade in return. The acts were enacted to protect British trade from Dutch competition. In England the acts seemed draconian; in the colonies they were ruinous. Merchants watched helplessly as their trade dwindled to nothing, and imports—which were the lifeblood of every colony—slowed to a trickle. Ships sat idle in their ports, and more and more disgruntled seamen were discharged onto the streets. The New England and Caribbean colonies were hardest hit; cities like Newport, Rhode Island, and Port Royal, Jamaica, convulsed. Just as James had created a surplus of unemployed mariners by curtailing the navy, Cromwell had accomplished the same by curtailing the merchant marine. Captains without cargo and seamen without employment turned in increasing numbers to the easy lure of piracy.

At the other side of the equation lay the now-insatiable demand among the colonies for imported goods. Nearly anything that could be brought in—spices, cloth, indigo, foodstuffs, enamelware, and, of course, specie—brought high prices at dockside auctions. Cromwell had miscalculated badly: the acts, intended to bludgeon the Dutch into submission, did enormous harm to English trade and almost none at all to the Netherlands. Piracy became—and would remain—a staple of colonial commerce long after the acts themselves were revoked.

Yet if one aspect of Cromwell's plan failed, another succeeded brilliantly. In a series of stunning victories in the battles of Portland, Gabbard, and Scheveningen, the Royal Navy trounced the Dutch and reestablished itself as the preeminent naval force among the European powers. The Dutch were forced, in the Treaty of Westminster of 1654, to recognize the Navigation Acts (though the acts still did more harm than good), and the Protestant nations pledged to act in concert against a common enemy: Spain.

Piracy was legal once again, and business was bigger than ever.

-3-

"His Majesty's Pleasure"

Henry Morgan and Jamaica

IN 1692 A DEVASTATING EARTHQUAKE STRUCK THE CITY OF PORT Royal, Jamaica. The first tremors occurred at eleven thirty in the morning, shaking the bottles off the racks of grog shops and shattering the bed frames of the brothels. Then it seemed to draw breath and went for the final assault. Half the city—its docks, inns, chandleries, customs houses, and many private homes—simply disappeared. The sea reached out and took them, reshaping the coastline and creating a sort of pirate Atlantis, a sunken city that still lies dormant and largely unlamented beneath the bridges and derricks of modern-day Kingston harbor. There were no seismographs to register the scale of the quake, but its results spoke for themselves. To many it seemed that God himself had reached up from the Caribbean Sea and smote the city with his own hand. One survivor described a scene that had an almost biblical quality: "We continued running up the street whilst on either side of us we saw the houses, some swallowed up, others thrown in heaps; the sand in the streets was rising like the waves of the sea, lifting up all persons that stood upon it and immediately dropping down into pits; and at the same instant a flood of water breaking in and rolling those poor souls over and over."

To many it seemed a just punishment. Port Royal was the first great pirate colony, the so-called Sodom of the New World, entrepôt to the Spanish Caribbean, and, in its day, among the largest trading ports of the fledgling English empire. At its zenith in the late seventeenth century the harbor could hold as many as five hundred vessels, and as early as 1662 there was talk of establishing a royal mint there. A census taken in 1670 revealed some seven thousand residents, but the actual number was probably much higher: like the tourist-driven islands of the twenty-first century, visitors to Port Royal always outnumbered residents. It also boasted the dubious distinction of having more taverns per square mile than any other city on earth. Yet its appearance belied such statistics. Surviving cartography reveals a haphazard cluster of dwellings set along a mishmash of alleyways—"all huddled together," as Michael Pawson writes, "at the end of an otherwise bare peninsula." Its streets were narrow and winding, littered with refuse and excrement thrown from above. Its buildings were wooden and ramshackle; this was a frontier town, from start to finish, and cared little for appearances. In the later period one might find a sprinkling of mansions, inhabited by prosperous merchants, looking incongruous and faintly silly amidst the general squalor of the town. Indeed Port Royal presented itself almost exactly like any other English seaport, whether on the Isles themselves or on the North American continent. English colonial architecture was functional and insular; there was no attempt to suit the buildings to the climate. Thus the arriving sailor could confidently expect to be greeted with the same mullioned windows of his ale shop, the same rigid geometry of planking at his inn, whether he dropped anchor in Bristol, Newport, Charlestown, or Barbados.

Yet what made Port Royal significant, indeed crucial, was its location. That bare spit of land jutted out into one of the busiest trade routes on earth, a thoroughfare for sugar cane, molasses, tobacco, indigo, cotton, rum, slaves, and, of course, Spanish gold. This was of particular interest to the denizens of Port Royal.

By the mid-seventeenth century three European powers had consolidated their holdings on the American continent. The British held dominion over a vast tract of land stretching from the New England colonies in the north to Georgia in the south, as well as inland territory in present-day Quebec and Ontario. The French, with whom the British shared its northernmost possessions (uncomfortably, as history would prove), also had colonies on the southern tip of North America, placing the British colonies in a viselike grip. Most of these, both French and English, were commercial ventures, with the notable exception of the Puritan settlements in Massachusetts, and as commercial ventures none were particularly successful. The New England climate is harsh and forbidding, its soil rocky and hilly. Settlements along the Saint Lawrence produced a brisk trade in beaver fur (useful for gentlemen's hats, among other things) but were hardly worth the effort. The southern colonies were more profitable, if marginally so. Warmer climes produced cotton and tobacco in prodigious quantities, though the perpetual labor shortage and difficulties of transport cut heavily into production and profits.

If the colonies were judged solely on their merit as money makers (which was primarily how their mother countries saw them in this era), the greatest and perhaps only success were the Spanish. Spanish possessions began just south of where the English and French left off, in some cases overlapping with the French in Louisiana and Florida. The Spanish controlled the crucial port of New Orleans, mouth to the Mississippi River, and had virtual monopoly over the entire South American continent. From this they extracted vast quantities of gold, enough to fuel an entire empire. This gold was melted down and recast in large gold coins known—famously—as doubloons, then carefully laid in the holds of deep-hulled cargo ships and sent out into Caribbean Sea, bound for Spain.

That was the geography of the Americas in the mid-seventeenth century. Two distinguishing features are worthy of additional note. First, though the colonies stretched like a great ribbon across the continent, it was a narrow cord. There was almost no attempt to settle or even explore the interior and no need to do so. Cities were formed around ports, and the linkages between them were forged, not on land, but by sea. Many even lacked connecting roads, lending credence to the notion of an Atlantic world in which the New World colonies were more tightly bound by water to each other and to their mother countries in Europe than they were by physical proximity to each other on land. Second, the North and South American colonies remained largely static throughout the next century, even as war raged sporadically between the three powers that controlled them. Aside from border skirmishes, there was little changeover: what was Spanish remained Spanish, English as English, and French as French.

The situation changed markedly, however, once one left the shores of the continents and ventured into the island-dotted seas that stretched from Central America to North Carolina. Here the powers of Europe held a far more tenuous grasp, and consequently possession became a great deal more fluid. Here not only the Spanish, French, and English but also the Dutch and Portuguese claimed territories, some within sight of each other, some even on the same island. Here the wars of the seventeenth century were mirrored, played out by proxy. In the dense cluster of islands with their inadequate defenses and myriad shoals and coves a daring man might take a few hundred men and, within a day, find himself in possession of an entire colony. This was precisely what would happen on the island of Hispaniola, and it would launch one of the greatest piratical careers in history.

Captain Myngs and the Governors of Jamaica

Jamaica's Port Royal lay in the epicenter of the Spanish Caribbean, a strategic windfall for the British in possession. But it was a double-edged sword. The port's location made it ideal to launch raids against the Spanish gold ships that passed to windward almost every day, as well as bedevil nearby Spanish colonies. Yet Port Royal, and Jamaica as a whole, were equally vulnerable to such raids themselves. In the mid-seventeenth century it had no navy to speak of, and its fortifications were laughable. This sorry and precarious situation gave the island's governor, Sir

Thomas D'Oyley, considerable unease. Practically the only formidable power in the colony were the pirates who, for decades now, had preyed on the lucrative Spanish trade. These were a motley collection of English mariners, some lately discharged from naval or merchant vessels, most having drifted onto the island solely by virtue of having nowhere else to go. They lived and bivouacked in hastily constructed camps in Hispaniola and Tortuga but came regularly to Port Royal to spend the proceeds of their captures. This influx of welcome currency naturally brought them to the notice of and in contact with Port Royal's merchant community, who in turn introduced them to the governor himself.

By 1660 the granting of privateering commissions had become one of D'Oyley's chief duties, and he did so with a lavish hand. There was nothing illegal in this; England and Spain were at war, engaged in one of the interminable squabbles that punctuated the century. D'Oyley could scarcely have curbed the pirates' practices, and in acting as he did he managed to accrue a portion of the proceeds for the crown. Little matter that his ad hoc prize courts lacked the approval of the Admiralty; such details could be attended to later. Little matter, too, that the pirates quite frequently extended the terms of the commission far beyond the breaking point, even plundering English ships on occasion. Port Royal was profiting as never before.

Yet scarcely had this unusual alliance begun when it was put to a severe test. In 1661 Governor D'Oyley received news that a treaty had been reached with Spain; the war was over. He hurriedly dispatched a proclamation calling all privateering vessels back to Port Royal "to await further orders." The proclamation was also posted in the marketplace, to the enormous consternation of a populace that had just grown accustomed to the finer things in life. In the last few months of his tenure as governor, D'Oyley looked on with dismay as, in his own words, "the order for cessation sufficiently enraged the populacy, who live solely upon spoil and depredations." He gratefully handed over the whole mess to his successor and departed for England posthaste.

His successor, the seventh baron of Windsor, was given explicit instructions from the Lords of Trade to enforce the peace and establish good relations with Spain. Yet he proved even less scrupulous than D'Oyley. Perfectly aware that political circumstances could alter like the fickle Doctor's Wind that blew through the island at night, Windsor saw little point in extending himself to curb a practice that might well be commenced once again before long. Instead, he commissioned a daring raid on the Cuban cities of Santiago and Campeche, led by Captain Christopher Myngs in the frigate *Centurion*.

Myngs was no ordinary pirate. Dispatched in 1656 by Parliament to take command of a ramshackle and disgraced navy—Oliver Cromwell's plan to retake Spanish colonies in the Caribbean had been a dismal failure, resulting in the near destruction of the English flotilla—Christopher Myngs established himself in the following decade as the de facto admiral of the Caribbean fleet. Tall, florid, with a determined nose and intelligent eyes, Myngs had proven himself to be a competent leader of men from the start; his first act as commander of the fleet was to put down a mutiny on board his own ship, the *Marston Moor*. During the last years of war with Spain, Myngs whipped the tattered English fleet back into shape and led it into several successful forays against the Spanish, first at Santa Marta on the Venezuelan coast in 1657, then at Puerto Caballo one year later.

Yet Myngs also proved himself to be as unscrupulous in pecuniary matters as his governor patrons. Returning from Venezuela in 1659, he refused to remit the captured gold to the crown, claiming instead that plunder taken in an onshore action was not within the prerogative of a navy commission. Myngs, therefore, kept the lot, dispensing some to his shipmates and some—as a courtesy—to Governor D'Oyley. Parliament was incensed, and a warrant was issued for Myngs's arrest. He made the long trek across the Atlantic in the spring of 1660 to face charges of embezzlement at the High Court of Admiralty, only to arrive in London and discover the entire city in confusion and disarray. The Long Parliament was gone, and King Charles II had been restored to the throne. The charges against Captain Myngs were lost in the confusion.

Myngs returned to Jamaica, restored if not rehabilitated. His commission from the recently arrived Governor Windsor in 1662 came as a welcome relief, not only for his finances but for his reputation as well. Myngs planned the Cuban attacks meticulously, just as he had for Venezuela. The invading force was nothing less than a pirate armada. Twelve ships carrying more than 1,500 men fell upon the Spanish fortifications at Santiago in the early hours of the morning. The sight of this fleet on the horizon led many in the garrison to abandon their posts from fear, and the fleet—with *Centurion* at its head—sailed triumphantly into the harbor. Myngs ordered long-range cannon fire against the city's fortress, the Castillo del Morro. The effect of this was stunning: after three hours of steady bombardment, a fissure appeared in the fortress walls. Finally, with a sound like muffled thunder, Castillo del Morro crumbled to the ground. What few soldiers remained scattered hurriedly, and Myngs's men stormed ashore. There was little resistance. In the late afternoon a delegation including Myngs and several others went into the town, and by nightfall longboats were already returning from shore laden with captured gold.

Campeche came next and was harder won. There the Spanish had been warned in advance and made what preparations they could. The fortress guarding the harbor of San Francisco de Campeche was well provisioned, its walls even thicker than those of Santiago. Long-range fire would not suffice this time. Myngs commenced the attack at dawn, as with Santiago, and for the entire day the battle raged. Fifteen hundred English, French, and Dutch buccaneers threw themselves against the city's defenses, wave upon wave. Finally, after more than half of Myngs's men had been cut down, Campeche was exhausted. The city surrendered, and Captain Myngs found himself in possession of some fourteen Spanish ships (which had been at anchor in the harbor during the battle) and 150,000 pieces of eight.

In one week's time Myngs and his sponsor, Governor Windsor, had enriched themselves and Jamaica more than any two men in the colony's brief history. To add the veneer of respectability to the endeavor, a proper prize court was convened on Myngs's return to Port Royal. The gold and plate were portioned out to the masters and crews, with one-tenth of the whole going directly to the Admiralty. Sir Charles Lyttelton, the deputy governor, received £72 from one small brig alone; the crown received £200.

King Charles's Ire

While this was indeed among the most successful raids ever attempted to that time, it was not the first. D'Oyley's tenure had seen literally dozens of such actions. Yet there was one glaring difference. The winds of politics had changed direction radically in the last few years. Attacks on Spanish ports and Spanish ships were perfectly legal when Cromwell was lord protector and England was at war; now both Cromwell and his Protectorate were dead and Charles II, the dissolute and debauched son of the martyred king, was on the throne. The game had changed. Crown coffers were exhausted from the drain of constant war, and the young monarch faced enemies within and without. He did not need, nor could he handle, the distraction of an ongoing conflict. And there were other, more subtle considerations. Charles, though an Englishman by birth and title, had spent all his formative years as an exile in France. He had watched the Puritans that murdered his father consolidate their Calvinist grip on the Isles, while he himself received the instruction of Catholic tutors and was surrounded by exiled Catholic courtiers. His wife was Catholic, as was his brother, the future King James II. Yet with his accession to the throne Charles also became defender of the faith, titular head of the Church of England, a title that had passed from monarch to monarch since the Reformation. Thus he was charged with leading the very men who had engineered his own father's downfall.

Charles's position was made even more precarious by the political climate of the time. England in the seventeenth century was rife with "popish" conspiracies, both real and imagined. The fear of "popery"—that is, a return of Catholicism through regicide or a second civil war—was third only to fear of French invasion and of witchcraft. The three were frequently tied together. Thus Charles had to walk a narrow course, appeasing the remnants of the Puritans within his own government who still held much of the popular opinion, while at the same time accommodating and rewarding those loyal Catholics that had long stood by him and helped arrange his return to the throne. Not to mention maintaining the amicable relations with the Catholic states of Spain and France that had sheltered him for so many years.

The first move was immediate cessation of the Spanish War. It was costly, unpopular, and pointless. Good relations with the former enemy became a cornerstone of crown policy—hence the explicit instructions sent to Governor D'Oyley to that effect. It was of paramount importance not to provoke a second war that would turn his erstwhile allies against him and rally the Puritans once again to the Protestant banner.

Yet almost instantly these good intentions were dashed. Charles received word of the Cuba and Campeche attacks several months after they occurred, owing to the long delay in communication between the colonies and the mother country. That word came from the Spanish ambassador, who flew into an undiplomatic rage when he was informed. Charles, too, was aghast. It suddenly appeared as though his entire government might fall entirely because of the antics of some greedy pirates more than a thousand miles away.

Meanwhile Captain Myngs, blissfully unaware that he had earned the enmity of his monarch, was planning a second assault in the fall of 1662. The Council of Jamaica approved, and Governor Windsor gave the proper commission. Campeche was again the target, a fresh haul of Spanish gold having arrived there the week before. The raid went off splendidly. This time the Spanish were taken entirely by surprise, and after a brief skirmish between the *Centurion*'s guns and those from shore, some 150,000 pieces of eight were captured and brought back to Port Royal. It was a princely haul, one of the richest ever seized. Once again the slow process of complaint began, and in the fullness of time the Spanish ambassador again appeared in the royal bedchamber, shaking with indignation.

This time Charles acted personally. Seething, he drafted a letter to Lyttelton (who had succeeded Windsor as governor) demanding in strident tones that he obey the king's law and suppress these raids at once. Lyttelton's reply, dated several months later, was terse to the point of rudeness and could only have been made by one very sure of his position. There was no purpose, he wrote, in attempting to curtail the pirates' activities; the Royal Navy lacked the ships and the wherewithal to do so. The raids would continue with or without crown consent: the only difference would be whether the crown received a share. The privateers, he reported, were "not to be taken off by the King's instructions, so [he, Lyttelton] has not thought it his duty to call them in."

Lyttelton's logic was unassailable, but his political acumen was disastrous. The difference between illegal piracy and legal privateering might have been semantic to a Jamaican governor, but it was not so for an anxious king desperately trying to avert war with Spain. Lyttelton was replaced as swiftly as practicable by a man named Sir Thomas Modyford, an amiable nonentity who had risen through the ranks of the civil service by a combination of good social contacts and colorless politics. Modyford sailed for Port Royal with a packet of letters, a sheaf of official warrants, a new governor's seal, and the personal instructions of Charles II himself that he must not, under any circumstances, commission any more piratical raids.

If Modyford had arrived with good intentions, he quickly forgot them. Indeed it must have seemed to Charles and the Lords of Trade as though there were some pestilential air in Port Royal, an infectious stench of corruption that tainted men as soon as they encountered it. More likely, however, it was three salient factors that drove D'Oyley, Windsor, Lyttelton, and, finally, Modyford. First, and most obvious, was the money. A royal governor received an annuity of £1,000, which was expected to cover all his expenses, both personal and public. This seemingly generous grant dwindled fast. A successful raid could bring a man like Modyford ten times that amount in one lump sum. Second, and of no less importance, were the difficulties of communication. A fast frigate leaving Jamaica in February might—if it were an exceptionally fine crossing—find its way into the mouth of the Thames somewhere round the end of May. But along the way, the frigate had to contend with storms, icebergs, pirates, and dead calms, which could prevent it from arriving at all. Thus there was no regular channel of communication between crown and colony until the advent of steam travel in the early nineteenth century. Modyford and his confreres had years of grace before their iniquities (if such they were) could catch up with them. By which time, it must be noted, another political volte-face might have occurred, and England might again be at war with Spain. Many a political career was saved by such vicissitudes of fate.

Finally, there remained the enormous difference in perspective between the government at Whitehall and the government in the colonies. In principle they were one and the same: governors ruled at the pleasure of His Majesty and were directly answerable to His Majesty's ministers for all their actions. Their salaries were apportioned from crown coffers, and they were regarded as creatures of the civil service, albeit in far-flung locales, connected by an invisible but tightly bound cord that stretched directly between the colonies and mother England.

This perception was Olympian in scope, for it managed to overlook not merely the myriad demands and differences that each colony presented but also the entire Atlantic Ocean. The truth was that neither the monarch nor any of his advisors had the slightest idea what conditions prevailed in their colonies nor how best to address them. Such matters were left to the men they charged with governance. Thus royal governors were often potentates in their own right, and to meet novel problems each was quickly forced to devise novel solutions—solutions that did not necessarily conform with the rigid instructions of the Lords of Trade. For example, Lyttelton's claims of helplessness in the face of marauding privateers might or might not have been mendacious, but there was a kernel of truth to them all the same. The English colonies were undermanned and undersupplied for most of their formative years. Those on the mainland had to deal with regular incursions from the indigenous peoples they displaced, often with bloody results. Those on the islands, like Jamaica, faced the grim proximity of hostile neighbors who might, at any time and for any provocation, attempt to drive them into the sea. Governors governed in a state of constant anxiety, scanning the horizon for potential threats. This was equally true of the Spanish and French governors, perhaps even to a greater degree, as most of the pirates, from the outset, were English. It is not surprising, then, that wars continued in the New World long after they had been concluded in the Old. This was the frontier, and a very different law held sway.

For all these reasons, Modyford soon found himself acquiescing to circumstance. Still with the king's instructions staring up at him from his desk, the new governor told his assistant, Bennett, that he "thought it more prudent to do by degrees and moderation what he had [formerly] resolved to execute suddenly and severely, hoping to gain them [the pirates] off more safely by fair means and reduce them to planting, to accomplish which he must somewhat dispense with the strictness of his instructions." The key word was *dispense*. Within months Modyford was granting privateering commissions against Spanish trade with clockwork regularity. Prizes appeared in Port Royal in record numbers, and the governor duly collected his share. The precision of his accounts is revealed in another letter to Bennett, dated February 20, 1665, in which he wrote, "The Spanish prizes have been inventoried and sold, but it is suspected that those of Morris and Bernard Nichols have been miserably plundered, and the interested parties will find but a slender account in the Admiralty." At almost the same moment he was sanguinely assuring his lords and masters in London that "upon my gentleness towards them, the privateers come in apace and cheerfully offer life and fortune for His Majesty's service."

Modyford carried the practice of pirate brokering farther than any of his predecessors. In 1666 we find him granting a privateering commission to one Captain Mansfield, who departed in June of that year with a pirate fleet for Curacao. The attempt to take the island failed, and for a short time Modyford's pirates, who now wandered in and out of the governor's house as regularly as office clerks, were forced to settle for smaller captures.

One such prize reached the ears of the ever-disheartened King Charles, resulting in an acerbic personal letter to Modyford ordering him to return the seized vessel to its rightful Spanish owners. Charles's communiqué ran scarcely a paragraph; Modyford's reply was ten pages long and writhing in self-justification. He did not send it to Charles but to his minister and secretary of state, Lord Arlington. Called to account for openly flouting the king's orders, Modyford painted a gripping picture of an island colony bereft of its income by the unwitting harshness of its beloved sovereign. His Majesty had no idea, Modyford told Arlington, of the hardships suffered by Jamaicans due to the cessation of hostilities with Spain. Thus to save the colony from utter ruin and despondency, Modyford granted a few commissions—very reluctantly. "His Lordship cannot imagine what a universal change there was on the faces of men and things," Modyford wrote glowingly of the response, "ships repairing, great resort of workmen and labourers to Port Royal, many returning, many debtors released out of prison, and the ships from the Curacao voyage, not daring to come in for fear of creditors, brought in and fitted out again." No monarch could be so heartless as to deny his loyal subjects a proper living, Modyford concluded. And he was sure that in the divine, bountiful, provident mercy of His Most Gracious Majesty, the continued future of the colony would be assured. Safe in that assurance he was, very humbly, His Majesty's most loyal servant, Thomas Modyford.

The Spanish prize was not returned.

The Rise of Henry Morgan

Even as Charles and Modyford sparred across the Atlantic, the unlikely result of their tussling was already taking shape. Among the hundreds of heterogeneous pirate communities scattered throughout the

Caribbean was a small band of English settlers habiting the Spanish island of Hispaniola. The French called them *boucaniers*, smokers of meat, in reference to both their eating habits and their clothing, which was composed largely of animal skins and gave them a distinctively pungent aroma. Sometime in the late 1650s the Spanish government decided to remove these irksome, smelly foreigners and succeeded in driving them right off the island. The *boucaniers*, or buccaneers, took umbrage. They returned to Hispaniola in a fleet of seized trawlers, brandishing a cache of stolen weapons, and began wreaking havoc on Spanish trade. They were so remarkably successful that they came to Modyford's attention, and he happily issued them privateering commissions. Though hardly one amongst them could so much as sign his own name, they were entered into the records of the Admiralty as adjunct officers, privateers for the crown. Among these marauding bands was a young, unschooled seaman named Henry Morgan.

Morgan was an unlikely candidate to inherit the mantle of great English mariners like Drake and Raleigh. Born to a farming family in Wales in 1635, he drifted into the Caribbean, first to Barbados, then to Hispaniola, in search of a warmer climate and escape. When he assumed his first command, a fishing trawler, he was scarcely twenty-three years old. But Morgan soon displayed a maritime prowess and ruthlessness that exceeded even Drake's. A large, robust, strongly built man with a booming voice, he was a born leader. In Jamaican society he displayed a Falstaffian bonhomie and enormous charm; in battle he was ferocious and inspired. It is not known precisely when Morgan first came to the attention of the governor, but one can easily imagine the encounter: big, bluff, hearty Morgan on the one hand and spare, prim Modyford on the other, each sizing up his man.

Modyford apparently liked what he saw, for in February 1668 he commissioned Morgan for the greatest pirate raid yet, an assault on the seemingly impregnable fortress at Portobello, Panama. Some legal pretense had to be given to justify the raid, and Modyford thought of it at once: Morgan, Modyford instructed him, would "draw together the English privateers and take prisoners of the Spanish nation, whereby he might inform [the government of Jamaica] of the intentions of that enemy to invade Jamaica." The wording of the commission was steeped in the trenchant bellicosity of war necessity; the only complication was that England and Spain were at peace. Taking prisoners and launching preemptive raids went far beyond the usual acts of piracy; Jamaica—and by extension England herself—was declaring open hostilities. It was an unprecedented step, sure to infuriate King Charles and perhaps lead both Morgan and Modyford to the block.

At this juncture Morgan displayed himself a man of surprisingly astute sensibilities. Correctly apprehending the hint conveyed in the idea of "the intentions of that enemy," he reported back from Porto Principe, Cuba, that a massive Spanish fleet was expected to rendezvous at (as luck would have it) Portobello and head on to Havana, where it would join a second fleet and turn again for an all-out assault on Jamaica. It was sheer fantasy. There has never been any evidence to support the existence of this phantom invading fleet, in either colonial or Spanish record. In fact, Morgan had deftly provided his patron with exactly the excuse he needed to justify what was about to occur.

The attack took place in the predawn hours of June 26, 1668. Morgan left his ten ships at anchor and loaded his men—five hundred of them—into canoes. They rowed ashore at approximately 3 A.M., two hours before daylight. Morgan abjured his crew with threats and curses to keep quiet. Surprise was essential to his plans.

Portobello, the "beautiful port," was about as beautiful as a gun turret. Guarding the entranceway to Panama, it had not one but two forts, jutting out like sentries before a small but heavily walled and fortified town. It was considered the most redoubtable fortress in the Caribbean, which was precisely why the Spanish employed it to guard their gold reserves. No pirate nor governor had ever dreamed of taking it. Morgan must have experienced a sense of anxiety, if not dread, as the solid limestone walls loomed above him, growing ever nearer as the boats approached shore. Despite his orders and his ferocious presence, the men were excited and chattering. One of their number, a literate sailor and ship's surgeon by the name of Alexander Esquemeling, later recorded what happened next. "Seeing that they could not refresh themselves in quiet," he wrote, Morgan and his men were compelled to attack the first fortress dead-on. The hail of gunfire whickered and ricocheted around them. Yet once the pirates reached the fort it fell with surprisingly little resistance; it was not as well defended as they had thought. The second, too, fell quickly. By this time the residents of the port had been warned by the gunfire and the frantic tolling of bells and watched as the royal standard of His Most Catholic Majesty fluttered jerkily down. Despite Morgan's grandiose claims that they beat off "three thousand men," the truth was that Portobello was a paper tiger: it looked fierce but was sadly underdefended. Notably absent also was the "invading" armada supposedly poised to strike Jamaica.

Once in the town, Morgan and his band comported themselves with the raucous brutality and wanton cruelty that accompanies every successful sacking. When that was complete, Morgan was ready to accept terms for ransom from the governor of Panama. The final amount was 100,000 pieces of eight, added to another 150,000 taken from the town, as well as a huge hoard of plate, linen, silks, and miscellaneous wares. Morgan brought his pirate fleet to a quiet shoal in Cuba to divide the spoils amongst his men, then tacked back across the Caribbean Sea and entered Port Royal in triumph. There he was met by chief judge of the Court of Admiralty in Jamaica, an august personage by the name of Sir James Modyford, the governor's own brother. Morgan remitted the proper amount to Sir James, who later regretted that he did not attend the fantastic auction that the pirate later held on Port Royal's wharf. "But I was not in cash here," Sir James noted sadly.

The successful raid and the resounding silence from Whitehall in its wake emboldened Governor Modyford still further. He began to quietly prepare the ground for the greatest assault of all: against Panama City itself. Panama was the epicenter of Spanish trade and the seat of Spanish colonial government. It was also the largest city in the Spanish colonies, twice as populous as Port Royal and far more heavily guarded. This was no paper tiger. A Spanish fleet, small but formidable, tacked back and forth ceaselessly on its approaches. As the depot for all the gold and silver mined from Peru, the specie within its walls financed an entire empire. Some historians have likened it to Fort Knox, but that is an understatement. Panama was more like Fort Knox, Wall Street, the Federal Mint, and the Texas oil fields all combined. To sack it could not have any other effect but to bring England and Spain to war, but paradoxically that war might already be won before it started: without Panama, the Spanish would be severely impoverished.

Modyford, though often content to bask in his position and the supposed inviolability that distance from London gave him, was not fool enough to attack the golden heart of the Spanish empire without a single warning note to his masters. He began bombarding the Lords of Trade with letter after letter complaining of supposed depredations against English trade. Some were true, most were not, and the effects were vastly overstated. He entreated them to lift their ban on privateering commissions as a matter of urgent necessity, carefully omitting the fact that he had already acknowledged granting such commissions without pause for several years since the peace. The response from Lord Arlington, however, was chilling: "His Majesty's pleasure is that in what state soever the privateers are at the receipt of this letter you will keep them so till we have a final answer from Spain, with this condition . . . he obliges them to forbear all hostilities on land."

Such words would have dampened any other man, but Modyford was undeterred. It is worth pausing at this point and questioning his motives. Greed was assuredly amongst them, but it seems hardly likely that he would risk not only his position but even his life simply for another haul of Spanish gold. Was it patriotism then? Did Modyford wish to bring war back between England and Spain, for reasons of his own? Again, it is unlikely. This was an age before nationalism, when war was a detached, diplomatic exercise. Modyford may not have liked the Spanish, but neither did he hate them. The most plausible explanation is that Modyford had lived so long as governor in Jamaica, so far removed from his peers and his superiors, that he now believed himself to be outside the English political system. The fragile bonds of patronage that had brought him to power had been severed somewhere in the Atlantic between the two isles, England and Jamaica, and now he was no one's man but his own.

This autonomous streak had deep roots. Roman governors in the Republic era often fell victim to the same pitfall, believing themselves so far from Rome that its long reach could not grasp them. They were not brazen enough to defy it to its face, but they confidently believed that any action taken in the service of their province could be adequately explained and justified. So, gradually, they took on the powers and offices of petty kings. This was one of the contributing factors to the dissolution of the Republic and its replacement by a far more centralized empire.

Sir Thomas Modyford, unaware or indifferent to the hubris of his predecessors, waited for an opportunity. It came in June 1670, when the Spanish launched a small and scattered attack on the north coast of

Jamaica. It was an exercise in sophomoric prankishness: there was little there of value and only a handful of settlers. Yet in his urgent dispatches to Whitehall, Modyford portrayed it as an all-out invasion. The second phantom invasion, in fact. He summoned Morgan—"Admiral Morgan," as he now referred to the pirate—and made him "commander in chief of all the ships fitted or to be fitted for the defense of this island." Morgan was further ordered to "use his best endeavors to surprise, take, sink, disperse or destroy the enemy's vessels, and in case he finds it feasible, to land and attack St. Jago *or any other place.*" Then, setting the commission aside, the two began to make plans to invade Panama.

There was one complication, however. The city of Panama lay on the *Pacific* coast, fifty miles across the isthmus through dense, verdant jungle. For Modyford, this meant that portraying it as a direct threat to Jamaican security was, at best, a challenge. Wisely, he chose not to do so. Instead, Modyford allowed rumors of an impending war with Spain to permeate the colony—rumors that were entirely of his own devising. When the next Spanish raid occurred—a minor skirmish between Spanish pirates and an English coastal trader—it was quickly branded a belligerent act against an outraged English outpost. England and Spain were now at war, at least in this far corner of their empires (or, more precisely, in the mind of the royal governor), and Modyford felt confident he could now justify the taking of Panama as a military necessity. The success of the expedition, he felt, would more than compensate ex post facto.

For Morgan, the location of Panama posed a different problem. Attacking the city meant traversing a huge stretch of terrain, which meant carrying enormous amounts of supplies and artillery through often impenetrable jungle. Only once had Morgan ever attempted an overland assault, against Puerto Principe on Cuba in 1668. At the time they had faced a ragtag band of defenders less than half their own strength and still nearly been repulsed. This time, though 1,800 men were granted him for the campaign, Morgan had far greater worries. Panama would not fall easily, and unlike Cuba, Morgan had little idea of the terrain he would face along the march. It was relatively easy to keep control over a band of a few hundred men; but nearly two thousand was not a band, it was an army, and Morgan had scant experience with the logistics of infantry or artillery.

What followed quickly assumed the mantle of folklore. Thirty ships sailed under Morgan's command on December 18, 1670. Less than a week before, Modyford received a communication from Lord Arlington expressly forbidding any further aggression against the Spanish and reminding the governor that England and Spain were still allies. Modyford was unfazed. The same day Morgan departed, Modyford carefully waited through a cycle of the tides and then posted a response to Lord Arlington, informing him that Morgan had "unwittingly" sailed for Panama, unaware of His Majesty's express instructions to the contrary. But, Modyford assured his lordship, he would send out at once a fast chaser to catch up with Morgan and call him off. Needless to say, the chaser—if indeed there ever was one—never made its rendezvous.

Morgan and his men arrived on the Atlantic coast of Panama on January 2, 1671. Leaving behind two hundred soldiers to secure the fleet, Morgan and the rest left the port of Chagres and traveled west by river, their longboats choking the narrow stream so completely that many of the soldiers crossed from one bank to the other by foot. Poor planning and adversity dogged the expedition thereafter. Unable to carry adequate food, Morgan had blithely assumed that he could take what he needed from the Spanish en route. It had worked in the past. Yet Morgan had not reckoned with the fact that an overland trip of fifty miles with a considerable army takes many days to accomplish, more than enough time for the alarmed Spanish to make their preparations. Every village the pirates encountered was abandoned, most razed to the ground. All the food was gone. On the second day the river bottomed out, and the boats were stranded. Morgan was forced to abandon all his cannons—150 of them—and continue on foot. There were no paths through the jungle, and Morgan sent one hundred men armed with scythes and axes ahead to blaze a trail. The expedition ground down to a snail's pace. The heat was oppressive, and the mosquitoes dense as clouds. Malaria spread through the ranks, killing hundreds. Scorpions, snakes, and even alligators lurked underfoot. Spanish snipers waited in trees, and Indians raided the pirates' camps at night. The men, now delirious and half mad from hunger, thirst, and disease, began to threaten mutiny. After ten days, Morgan's once-proud pirate army was decimated, starving, and belligerent. On the eleventh day they reached a clearing. The steeple of a distant church loomed on the horizon, and beyond that the broad, blue smile of the Pacific.

The pirates, one of their number would later write, "began to show signs of extreme joy, casting up their hats into the air, leaping for mirth and shooting, even just as if they had already obtained the victory and the entire accomplishment of their designs. All their trumpets were sounded and every drum beaten in token of this universal acclamation and huge alacrity of their minds." Better yet, Morgan discovered a large cache of grain and cattle, which the Spanish had unaccountably left intact, and his men feasted for the first time in many days. On the morning of January 19, Morgan assembled his men—a fraction of the original complement—for the final battle.

-4-

Oddsfish!

THE BATTLE BEGAN WITH A TAUNT. IN THE EARLY AFTERNOON THE advance cavalry of Spaniards met Morgan's army and jeered at them, crying, *"Perros! Nos veremos!"* which translates to "Dogs! We will meet you!" Morgan ignored them, and after this schoolboy nonsense had gone on for some time, the Spanish abruptly fled. Then on the evening of the 19th, artillery fire erupted from the fortress at Panama. The account of one of Morgan's men, Alexander Esquemeling, portrays the Spanish as almost childish in their defenses. "The city began to fire," he wrote, "and ceased not to play with their biggest guns all night long against the camp, but with little or no harm to the pirates, whom they could not conveniently reach." Yet after weeks of starvation and illness, Morgan's men were jubilant. "Instead of conceiving any fear of the blockades," said Esquemeling, "they began every one to open their satchels and without any preparation of napkins or plates fell to eating very heartily the remaining pieces of bulls' and horses' flesh which they had served since noon. This being done, they lay themselves down to sleep upon the grass with great repose and satisfaction."

Meanwhile the Spanish governor, Don Juan Perez de Guzman, was making his own preparations. Having taken an oath in the city's cathedral to defend Panama unto the death, he assembled some two thousand foot soldiers in the plaza and gave them their instructions. They were to meet Morgan's men in the plains that lay between their encampment and the city and destroy them before they reached the city walls. Morgan's buccaneers were now outnumbered by more than two to one.

Assault on Panama

The battle that commenced on the morning of January 20, 1671, was among the most mismatched since the Spartans at Thermopylae. Guzman's troops were well fed, well rested, well armored, and covered by heavy artillery. Morgan's men were starving and disease ridden and had abandoned all their artillery in the muck of the Chagres River some forty miles to the east. Even their powder was mostly wet, leaving them to fight with sabers alone. The Spanish troops had two cavalry wings in support; Morgan had none. They held the high ground; he would be forced to charge over an open plain.

Morgan attempted a flanking maneuver, drawing up on the left flank of the Spanish cavalry, which had gathered on a small ridge. It was a tactical success; the Spanish, expecting a frontal assault, fell back before the remainder of their army could reinforce them. Their much-feared artillery was pointed in the wrong direction. Now Morgan had gained a small but tenacious foothold on the Spanish line and pressed his advantage. The pirates, cutlasses drawn, charged against the retreating cavalry. Some of the Spaniards turned and regrouped, crying, *"Viva el Rey!"* but most continued to retreat. "The two hundred buccaneers who went before, every one putting one knee to the ground, gave them a full volley of shot, wherewith the battle was instantly kindled very hot." At one point the terrified Spanish even attempted to startle a herd of bulls into charging at the pirates, to sow confusion in their ranks. But the animals, confused and terrified themselves, stormed through the Spanish ranks instead. After two hours of steady fire the pirates had driven the

Spanish nearly to the city gates. The remainder fled through them to safety; Morgan had the field.

As with most early-modern battles, both sides now paused to regroup on either side of the walls. Besides some six hundred dead, the Spanish had left behind stragglers and wounded in their confusion. Esquemeling, in one of his more contentious passages, describes their treatment: "Some religious men were brought prisoners before Captain Morgan, but he being deaf to their cries and lamentations commanded them all to be immediately pistoled, which was accordingly done."

The final assault on Panama began in the afternoon. It was done in a hail of gunfire: "full and frequent broadsides," as Esquemeling relates. But after three hours of intense fighting, often hand to hand along the perimeter walls, the city surrendered. The governor, who had promised in the cathedral to die before submitting to Morgan, took refuge in its steeple as the battle raged around him. When it was done, Morgan gathered his men in the square "and there commanded them under very great penalties that none should dare to drink or taste any wine . . . because he had received private intelligence that it had been poisoned by the Spaniards." As he had with Modyford and the Lords of Trade, Morgan once again displayed a shrewd understanding of human nature. No such "private intelligence" had reached him; Morgan simply wished to avoid the disorderly and wanton debauchery that his men might otherwise have felt was their due.

The city that the buccaneers claimed as their own was more wondrous than they could have imagined. Even as they looted, Esquemeling and his confreres stared with wide-eyed wonder at the pearl of the Spanish empire. His narration at this juncture is strongly reminiscent of a travelogue:

> All the houses of this city were built with cedar . . . being of very curious and magnificent structure and richly adorned within, especially with hangings and paintings. . . . The churches and monasteries were all richly adorned with altar-pieces and paintings [and] huge quantity of gold and silver. . . . Besides which ornaments here were to be seen two thousand houses of magnificent and prodigious building, being all or the greatest part inhabited by merchants of that country, who are vastly rich. . . . The neigh-

boring fields belonging to the city are all cultivated with fertile plantations and pleasant gardens, which afford delicious prospects to the inhabitants the whole year long.

Just as the first bands of buccaneers had begun to take stock of these wonders, however, a great sheet of flame erupted. From every corner of the city fires broke out and spread rapidly, reducing the cedar frames to blazing infernos in mere seconds. Esquemeling writes that Morgan himself ordered the razing as punishment for the resistance shown earlier by the Spaniards, yet another charge the old pirate vehemently denied. His own report to Modyford states categorically that Guzman himself "ordered the city to be fired, and his chief forts to be blown up, which was done in such haste that they blew up 40 of his soldiers in it." Whatever the cause, the blaze quickly consumed the entire city, and most of the anticipated hoard along with it. Morgan could only stand and watch as one magnificent building after another surrendered to the flames. At this point, Esquemeling would write, the captain's baser instincts prevailed. "They spared in these cruelties no sex nor condition whatsoever," he declared. "For as to religious persons and priests they granted them less quarter than to others. . . . Women themselves were no better used, and Captain Morgan, their leader and commander, gave them no good example in this point."

Morgan and his men remained in the city for nearly a month, sending scavenging parties out into the countryside to round up any valuables that the Spanish had secreted away. In most cases the whereabouts of these treasures were obtained through torture, a practice which, though barbaric, was common to the age. When everything of value had been seized, Morgan gave orders to move the treasure back through the jungle path and down the Chagres River to the waiting boats. He had other worries: the pirates under his command, flushed with victory and the prospect of riches, had become mutinous once again. To remain in Panama longer meant risking dissension in the ranks. Accordingly, Morgan and his men departed for Chagres on February 14. The long trek back across the isthmus had something of a royal procession: 170 mules carried the rich haul from the capture, while several hundred Spanish families marched in chains behind the procession, as slaves. The city of Panama would never be reclaimed, except by the creeping vines of the approaching jungle. Its ruins remain to this day.

The Revenge of the Crown

Admiral Henry Morgan arrived back in Port Royal in April 1671 and submitted at once his own detailed account of the raid. He was hailed as a hero. Modyford, too, had reason to congratulate himself. Though Morgan's account put the actual figure of seized plunder at a very low £30,000, there is strong evidence to suggest that the actual figure was closer to £750,000 or more. The government got its share, and Modyford settled down to the pleasurable task of informing His Majesty's government that the raid that he had done his best to prevent nevertheless netted the crown a considerable sum of money.

But Modyford had finally gone too far. While Jamaicans rejoiced and even Englishmen smiled, King Charles was put in a terrible quandary. The Spanish, whom he had assiduously cultivated for a decade, were outraged and veering dangerously close to war. "It is impossible for me to describe the effect of this news upon Madrid," the English ambassador to Spain informed him. He then went on to do so, at length. Apparently the queen regent had fallen to her knees in prayer, remaining so for hours, as the city went into uncharacteristically bleak mourning. The Conde de Molina, ambassador to England, was more direct. He demanded the immediate capture and trial of the pirate Morgan and the traitorous Governor Modyford as well. That, he said, was the price of peace.

Despite the popular sentiment for both men, it was a price Charles was willing to pay. In a letter written under Charles's direction that same week, Sir Thomas Modyford was to be summarily removed from office and replaced by another Sir Thomas more palatable to the king, Sir Thomas Lynch. Lynch, born a commoner, had achieved the peerage through a £50,000 personal loan to Charles, which was little more or less than a bribe. The two letters, Modyford's and Charles's, crossed in the mid-Atlantic. Of the two, the king's was far more direct. Lynch was not merely to supplant Modyford but "as soon as he [Lynch] has taken possession of that government and the fortress so as not to apprehend any ill consequences thereupon, he [is to] cause the person of Sir Thomas Modyford to be made prisoner and sent home under a strong guard, as he hath contrary to the King's express commands made many depredations and hostilities against the subjects of His Majesty's good brother the Catholic King." There were two points of interest in those instructions. First, that Charles evidently felt Modyford's position to be so entrenched that he deemed it necessary to warn Lynch to take the fortress first; second, that he referred to the Spanish king as "his good brother," a choice of terms that made the new foreign policy abundantly clear and that the Protestant king would live to regret.

So might the process have repeated itself, with Lynch falling into the same pattern of complaisance as Modyford, Lyttelton, and Windsor, were it not for one thing. Governor Lynch proved to be an insufferable prig: a man of little imagination and, as Carlyle would have put it, "sea-green incorruptibility." Yet no one could deny that he was conscientious. His first action on arriving in Port Royal (after a severe attack of gout that incapacitated him for several days) was to summon Modyford and inform him very clearly and very calmly that he was no longer His Majesty's governor but His Majesty's prisoner. To forestall any possible unpleasantness, Lynch next told the governor that his own son, Charles, had been placed in the Tower of London as a security for his father's good conduct. Modyford had no choice. He allowed himself to be carried back to England in chains, in the hold of a trader called the *Jamaica Merchant*. Within a few months he had taken his son's place in the tower.

Next Lynch turned his attention to the pirates, and most especially Morgan himself. Here he was on less certain ground. It is no great matter for one government functionary to act against another, but Henry Morgan was a very rich, very dangerous man. He was also the most popular Englishman in Jamaica, a folk hero for every schoolboy and an inspiration for every out-of-work buccaneer. Even as Lynch mulled over the problem in his mind, the fleet surgeon Dr. John Browne was writing a glowing commendation of Morgan's character to the colonial secretary, Lord Arlington: "I think it fit further to advise your Honor that Admiral Morgan hath been in the Indies eleven or twelve years and from a private gentleman hath raised himself to now what he is, and I assure your Honor that no man whatever knows better . . . the Spanish force, strength or commerce."

To attempt to take a man like Admiral Morgan by force would be to risk civil war within the colony. Instead Lynch acted cannily. He at once issued a blanket pardon to all those who had joined in plundering the Spanish ports and ships, provided they enter the king's service. He also recruited several of Morgan's closest friends and gave them positions of responsibility in the new government. Thus, gradually, the upstart governor removed all the protective walls around his quarry. After almost a year, he felt he was ready. Morgan was far from alone, but his most powerful friends now recognized a new political wind blowing and chose not to stand against it. The old pirate was seized at his home in April and sent to join Modyford in London. It was a dazzling twist of fate for one who had, just a year before, been the most brilliant and celebrated commander in the English-speaking world.

As Morgan was crossing the Atlantic, Lynch and his English allies built the case against him. Particular attention was paid to reports of barbarity among Morgan's troops and by the admiral himself during his stay in Panama. The Spanish ambassador submitted a lengthy report from the Panamanian governor detailing atrocities including gang rape, infanticide, desecration of the Church, and the wanton torture and murder of clergy. Some of it was doubtless true and would be verified by one of Morgan's own men, Esquemeling, in his account of the raid published in 1678. Morgan hotly denied the charges of rape, but he could not deny the devastation. In his own report to Governor Modyford submitted on his return to Jamaica, Morgan had written of the fire in a strangely lyrical hand: "Thus was consumed the famous and ancient city of Panama, the greatest mart for silver and gold in the entire world." Yet it was still an open question whether the atrocities were as bad as was alleged. "The report from England is very high," wrote the ever-optimistic Dr. Browne, *high* being a euphemism for *inflated*, "and a great deal worse than it was; what was done in fight and heat of pursuit of a flying enemy I presume is pardonable; as to their women I know nor heard of anything offered beyond their wills . . . as for the Admiral himself [Morgan] he was noble enough to the vanquished enemy."

Whatever the truth behind the charges of brutality, the acts complained of were no worse than those executed by Drake and many others the century before. Yet there was a crucial difference between Drake and Morgan, one that made Morgan's case a great deal hairier. Drake's actions, however appalling, were done in time of war between England and Spain; Morgan's, however restrained, were committed during peace. For Charles II—and Morgan's enemies in court—that was all the difference in the world. Folk hero or not, Henry Morgan had attacked and decimated a city belonging to His Majesty's ally, the king of Spain. It was high treason.

But the story was far from over. Lynch and his allies had assumed that Morgan's popularity was strictly local; in fact, like Drake, he arrived in London to find himself canonized by the English public. Sympathetic peers dined and feted him, while spontaneous displays of popular support followed after his carriage wherever he went. Yet not all this support was as spontaneous or, indeed, as ingenuous as it seemed. Once again, the rustic pirate had fallen unwittingly into the cogs of English politics. Charles's pro-Spanish policy, while never popular, was now openly despised. The trade war that had erupted between England and Holland soured the public mood still further. The root, once again, was religion. England, a Protestant nation, had allied herself with two Catholic nations, France and Spain, against another Protestant, Holland. Rumors and fears of a popish plot had reached critical mass. Worse still, the war with the Dutch was a military disaster. Thus Henry Morgan's bold destruction of Panama came as an unexpected lift to English spirits, a dazzling victory set against a darkening sky of perpetual defeat. The fact that it was against an ally mattered little; England and Spain might be allies of convenience, but they were enemies of long standing.

None of this should have mattered to Charles. His Spanish policy was dealt a crucial blow by this arrogant, unrepentant pirate and his corrupt governor patron. If anything, the political sentiments that fueled Morgan's triumphant tour through the capital city should have been all the more irksome to the king. But there was another element that neither Lynch nor anyone else could have anticipated. Though a constant source of frustration to the English monarch in his relations with the Spanish, the ebullient, hard-drinking Morgan was a man after Charles's heart. Sent into the king's bedchamber to explain why he had attacked and annihilated a peaceful city several hundred miles from the nearest English settlement, Morgan was unfazed. Repeating almost word for word the carefully fabricated tale of Spanish aggression that Modyford had told the Lords of Trade earlier that year, Morgan stoutly maintained that he believed the governor of Panama was assembling a fleet to invade Jamaica. But surely the governor must have told you that England and Spain were at peace? Charles asked disbelievingly. If anyone had, Morgan answered, it had escaped his memory. He had, he confessed, a poor memory for political matters. The king's eyebrows rose. And anyway, Morgan went on, even if the governor or any of the Spanish officers had told him that, he would never have believed them. The Spanish were nothing but liars; everyone knew that. King and pirate gazed at one another for a long moment. Then, without warning, Charles cried out "Oddsfish!" and burst into laughter. The interrogation was adjourned.

The Pirate Governor

Charles's indulgence might have been motivated by more than sheer panache; Morgan was a popular hero and a potential martyr, which would do the king no great service. Whatever the reasons, by 1675 Morgan found himself rehabilitated and knighted. Admiral Henry Morgan became Sir Henry Morgan and in November 1674 was made lieutenant governor of Jamaica. The irony must have amused the old pirate immensely. He left for his beloved island in March 1675, just ahead of the man chosen to replace Sir Thomas Lynch, a career politician and peer named Lord Vaughan.

The joint rule of Morgan and Vaughan was among the most bizarre in the annals of government. Lord Vaughan was, like his predecessor Lynch, an aristocrat and a gentleman. He took pains on his arrival to ally himself at once with the planter class, landed gentry that held vast estates on the island and had only contempt for the pirate-brokering merchants of Port Royal, not to mention for the pirates themselves. It was these men who had helped Lynch undermine Morgan's influence on the colony; Morgan despised them. Vaughan inherited not only Lynch's government—composed almost entirely of the planter class—but his policies as well, most particularly his staunch antipiracy. To both he was steadfastly loyal. Yet Vaughan also came to realize what the buoyantly optimistic reports of his predecessor had concealed: piracy in the region was not in decline but rather resurgence, and there was little the colonial government could do about it. Lynch had lacked the manpower, the naval force, and the funds. Rather than admit this he instead sent glowing letters depicting a colony freed from a terrible scourge; at one point he confidently assured the Lords of Trade that there were only three pirates left at large in the entire Caribbean Sea. Meanwhile the depredations of the Spanish continued unchecked, and the French were growing more aggressive. Lynch's policies had ironically achieved precisely the reverse of their intent: rather than drive out the pirates, Lynch had simply removed the veneer of legality from their actions and thus divorced them from the restraining influence of the government. As privateers they had some obligation (however tenuous) to hold to the agreement laid out in their commission. As pirates they knew no such boundaries.

Into this volatile climate came Vaughan's lieutenant, Sir Henry Morgan. Morgan understood the confused situation better than anyone else, certainly better than his nominal superior. Even as Vaughan was declaring to the Lords of Trade that "the only enemy to planting is privateering, which I have by all means possible endeavored to restrain and prevent," Morgan was busily reconstituting the surviving pirate bands under his prerogatives as commissioner of the admiralty court. Vaughan could not long remain unaware of his subordinate's activities, and indeed it is likely that Morgan made no secret of them. The gauntlet was thrown down, and one man or another would set the course for Jamaica.

Vaughan began writing acidic letters to the Lords of Trade, urging Morgan's dismissal. In them he used words like *covetousness* and *unfaithfulness*. By May he was driven to even greater candor. "I find Sir Henry, contrary to his duty and trust, endeavors to set up privateering, and has obscured all my designs and purposes for the reducing of those that do use that curse of life." He attempted to paint Morgan as a traitor and a spy, arranging secret deals with the French governors for privateering commissions for his cronies. This was more than unlikely, but it was an era in which accusations and denials flew back and forth with great fluidity and little substance.

In truth, even Morgan himself must have occasionally wondered about his position. His course from piracy to respectability and finally to public service was a parable for the times. In early middle age and still largely illiterate, Morgan suddenly found himself holding court over the very same brigands with whom he had once fraternized—and occasionally still did. Meanwhile Vaughan did all he could to frustrate and embarrass his lieutenant. He remitted all piracy cases to Morgan and watched the ex-buccaneer squirm as he sifted through them. Vaughan also encouraged the governor of Havana to address all his piratical complaints to Morgan personally, resulting in a spate of diplomatic invective breaking all over the lieutenant governor's desk. Morgan delayed and dismissed as much as he could: throwing out cases for lack of witness testimony (the witnesses were either dead or Spanish, and Morgan refused to believe the word of a Spaniard), keeping the Cuban governor at bay. Yet he could not discourage the Royal Navy, which, though sparse in Jamaican waters, still managed occasionally to capture some unfortunate buccaneer that strayed into its path. Then the full majesty of the law took over, and Morgan found himself in the judgment seat. It often seemed to observers as though he looked at the prisoner in the dock with the expression, "There, but for the grace of God. . . ." In a letter written in 1683 to a close friend in London, he was particularly revealing. Referring to a group of pirates that had been brought before him with the sentence of death hanging over their heads, Morgan prevaricated. "I will not proceed against [them]," he wrote, "till his Majesty further commands; and I am heartily glad the opinion of the Court is so favorable, I much abhorring bloodshed and being greatly dissatisfied that in my short government so many necessities have lain upon me of punishing criminals with death." One can almost hear in these words an echo of another of Shakespeare's lovable rogues, Dogsberry, declaring, "Truly, I would not hang a dog by my will, much more a man."

By July 1676, after one year of fractious and hostile coexistence, Vaughan decided the time was ripe to finish Morgan utterly. He sounded out his friends on the council, those loyal planters, and began preparing the evidence for a public trial. Evidence was almost embarrassingly easy to obtain. Morgan cheerfully signed his name to all manner of dubious documents; one sometimes gets the impression he never read them. Vaughan brought a dossier before the Council of Jamaica and named Morgan and his assistant (and brother-in-law) Captain Byndloss as conspirators against the crown. The long list of charges included financing privateering voyages, granting illegal commissions, and engaging in secret deals with the French government on Tortuga.

Morgan appeared in his own defense. Forty-one years old, going slightly to fat, dressed immaculately in the garb of an admiral of the fleet (which, according to the records left by Governor Modyford, he still was), the pirate captain was an impressive sight as he stood before the council. He did not attempt to deny the accusations; he simply dismissed them. It was not the council's concern, he lectured them, on what measures an officer must take to secure the peace in his domain. He did what was necessary and nothing more. When one of the planters repeated the charge of treason, Morgan scoffed. As well he might. Who in Jamaica had done more to bring wealth and prestige to the colony than he?

Morgan and Byndloss were acquitted, to the accompaniment of cheers from the gallery. The public trial was a gamble, and Vaughan had lost. Two years later Vaughan was recalled, still firing parting salvos at Morgan via the Lords of Trade. Morgan would continue as lieutenant governor for two successive administrations, including that, incredibly enough, of the rehabilitated Sir Thomas Lynch. One can only imagine Sir Henry's response to acting as lieutenant governor under the man that had once sent him back to England in chains. Lynch pursued Morgan just as avidly as ever, sending Whitehall report after report of the old pirate's iniquities. "In his debauches which go on every night," one read, "he is much magnified and little criticized by the five or six little sycophants that share them. . . . In his drink Sir Henry reflects on the government, swears, damns and curses most extravagantly."

If Morgan found liberty in his cups to express his "reflections" on the Jamaican government, he had good reason. As Lynch reestablished bonds with the planters—just as hostile and clannish a body as ever—Morgan found himself more and more on the periphery of the council. Not even the presence of his old friend Thomas Modyford among the assemblymen could allay his sense of isolation. Beset with joint pains and liver problems, the curse of a lifelong diet of strong rum, Sir Henry Morgan began to fall back on the rough-and-tumble haunts that were most comfortable to him. "God damn the assembly," one patron heard him mutter, as he staggered out the door of the grog shop into the night.

By May 1682 it was clear that neither Morgan's health nor his political fortunes could withstand another assault. Both he and Byndloss were summarily removed from the council and stripped of their commands. Morgan did little to hinder the process. He was past fifty now and looked much older. A lifetime of prodigious thirsts and appetites was beginning to take its toll. Gout, liver disease, and hardening of the arteries assailed him. A visiting physician left a record of the pirate in

the last year of his life that was starkly at odds with the bluff, hearty figure of old:

> Sir Henry Morgan: aged about 45 [in reality, 53], lean, sal-
> low coloured, his eyes a little yellowish and his belly jut-
> ting out or prominent, complained to me of want of
> appetite for victuals; he had a kicking or reaching to vomit
> every morning and generally a small looseness attending to
> him, and withal was much given to sitting up late, which I
> supposed had been the cause of his present indisposition.

Henry Morgan in his last days seemed almost to welcome the relin-
quishment of power that Lynch and others had brought on him. Now
he could go to the grog shops and the brothels without fear that his rev-
els there would find their way into reports headed for Whitehall. And,
in truth, he had never really enjoyed the trappings of office. "I have been
much more used to the pike than to the book," the reluctant governor
once wrote modestly to his friend Sir Leoline Jenkins. He was still
among the wealthiest men in the colony (though the planters lived in
much greater style) and had few regrets. He could look out the windows
of his large and rambling Port Royal mansion and see the bustling streets
of a city that he, as much as anyone, had helped to create. In July 1688,
perhaps in the knowledge that he was not long for this world, Morgan
was reinstated on the council. He was too ill to attend, however, and in
August of that year fell into his final illness. Not trusting physicians of
his own race (which, considering the era, might have been wise), Morgan turned instead to a Negro doctor, a freeman, who prescribed urine
enemas and plasters of clay and water. Though they did little to help,
they probably did no harm. On August 25, 1688, the same year that
King James II would find himself stripped of his crown and cast into
French exile, Sir Henry Morgan died in his sleep at his estate in the
Cockpit region of the island.

Morgan's death marked a quiet transition, though few would notice
it at the time. The pirates of Morgan's generation—rough, fierce, unlettered men—were becoming marginalized. A new generation of privateers had begun to supplant them. It was a trend that Morgan himself
had approved and encouraged. Piracy was becoming more professional.
Governors Vaughan and Lynch might not have recognized it, but the

men that they continued to pursue and castigate were increasingly more literate, more articulate, more educated, and, most important, more respectable—men drawn from the new middle class, ironically created from the spurious wealth and social trappings that pirate gold had brought to the colony. Similarly, the Caribbean colonies themselves were undergoing radical changes, even by the time of Morgan's death.

Port Royal was perhaps the best example of all. Where once only a few drunken mariners weaved unsteadily on its streets from tavern to brothel and back again, by the last decades of the seventeenth century illegal trade had introduced a cornucopia of finery and haute monde. Ladies from the upper class—that is, merchants' and planters' wives— dressed in the latest fashions popular in London. To read the descriptions of "dry goods" on offer from the shops along Queen Street is to travel back in time. The gentlewomen of the town could choose from a selection of hose, gloves, ribbon, linen, silks, as well as a huge array of fabrics that are as alien to us today as if they were written in Aramaic: dimity, parragon, "French falls," and so on.

Just as piracy was becoming a more professionalized business, colonies like Jamaica were busily extending their trade to cover all the pirates' needs. Ship chandlers, provisioners, shipwrights, and all manner of tradesmen began to spring up along the wharves. There was also a proliferation of enterprise to meet other, more intimate, wants. The number of brothels multiplied exponentially each year: some merely open barns with stall-like enclosures, others bedecked in gilt and swag with the appearance of fine inns. The largest, belonging to a Mr. John Starr, advertised that it offered "twenty-one white women" and, for different tastes, "two black." Less salacious desires also found their satisfaction, as evidenced by the more than one hundred licensed grog shops in the town by 1680. The list of names sparkles with the promise of camaraderie, debauchery, and a whiff of gunpowder patriotism: Black Dog, Cheshire Cheese, Cat and Fiddle, Sign of Bacchus, Sin of the Mermaid, Jamaica Arms, Sugar Loaf, Sign of the George. By 1690 one in four buildings was either a grog shop or a whorehouse.

Port Royal was the first true pirate city, a model for all that would follow. The relationships forged between men like Morgan and Modyford would be replicated again and again for the next two decades, as the colonies consolidated their curious bond with the pirates and, in so doing, distanced themselves from the mother country. The story of pirate patronage begins in the Caribbean, but it would find new and more fertile ground on the American continent. At the same time that Sir Charles Modyford was regretting that he lacked the funds to bid for pirate prizes at auction, he made a rather curious remark on where the spoils were headed. "Some goes now for Old," he said, "but more for New England." Even as early as 1668 the North American colonies were beginning to see the profits of pirate voyages.

As King Charles would have seen it, the contagion was spreading.

-5-

The Pirate Cabal

A ROYAL COMMISSION WAS A GRAND AFFAIR. PENNED ON THICK, creamy parchment in the looped and extravagant cursive of the age, it was the pact that sealed the bond between subject and sovereign. Far more than a contract (for a contract implies equal, or at least comparable, parties), a commission from the hand of King William III was something infinitely precious: it was a badge of trust from God's own anointed representative on earth.

This weighty symbolism was reflected in the wording. One particular commission, dated February 1692, began in the usual form by announcing what the reader already knew: "William and Mary, by the Grace of God, King and Queene of England, Scotland, France and Ireland, defenders of the faith, &c." Then, as the reader's eye passed down through the many titles and honorifics, he finally reached the pertinent part:

> TO OUR TRUSTY and well beloved Benjamin Fletcher, Esquire, Greeting. WEE reposing especiall Trust and Confidence in the Prudence, Courage and Loyalty of you, the said Benjamin Fletcher, out of our especiall Care, Certaine knowledge and mere motion, Have thought fitt to constitute and appoint you . . . to be our Captain Generall and Governor in Chiefe in and over our province of New York, and the Territories depending thereon, in America.

Did Governor Fletcher, one of the greatest pirate patrons of the age, ever reflect back on this sublime expression of royal confidence, the "Certaine knowledge" of his courage, his loyalty . . . his prudence? If not, he certainly had occasion to recall the later paragraphs. Having granted him the power to appoint judges, to hear appeals, to represent the Church of England at all occasions commensurate with his status as the anointed one's representative, and so on, King William abruptly got down to brass tacks:

> AND WEE DOE hereby Give and Grant unto you, the said Benjamin Fletcher, full power and authority . . . to exercise all powers belonging to the place and office of Vice admiral of and in all the seas & coasts about your Government. . . . AND WE DOE Hereby Give and Grant unto you, our Captain Generall and Governor in Chiefe, full power & authority to Constitute and appoint Captains, masters of Shipps, and other Commanders, and to Grant to such Captains . . . commissions to execute the Law martiall.

Therein lay the true source of a governor's power. As the head of state, the chief magistrate, and the military commander of the colony, he had a purview that extended not only into the hinterlands behind but the seas before him. The ability to appoint captains and outfit vessels was the ability to make war. Charged with upholding and implementing the policies of the crown, men like Benjamin Fletcher were also given enormous prerogative to interpret those policies as they pleased and implement them as they chose. As the Atlantic colonies flourished and developed their own individual identities—commercial, social, political—this prerogative and sense of isolation increased. Governors now had to contend with not only external threats unimagined by their Whitehall superiors but the emergence of entrenched and intractable communities that were accustomed to carrying on their affairs sui generis, regardless of crown policy.

Thus the presence of a royal governor translated in legal terms to a conduit for the royal will, a constant reminder of the invisible cord that tied the colonies to the mother country. Yet this conduit had one additional buffer, thanks to the growing bureaucratization of the early empire. Until 1696, when yet another bureaucracy was erected in its stead, colonial matters were handled by an august body known as the Lords of Trade. The Lords of Trade formed the second link in a chain of command that stretched from King William to the lowliest of his colonial subjects. It was they who formulated crown policy for the colonies and communicated it to the governors for implementation. It was they, too, who had the power to censure and replace colonial governors for age, misconduct, or incompetence. In theory, the line from the monarch to the Lords of Trade to the governors and finally to the colonists was one of seamless, undiluted royal prerogative, no less than if the king himself were present at each colonial assembly.

In fact, the chain of command worked quite differently, passing as it did over the imponderable obstacle of the Atlantic Ocean. With no immediate contact from their superiors save the occasional directive, always at least two months old, governors in the Atlantic colonies looked out over the broad band of blue horizon that separated them from their masters and acted accordingly. Governors could suspend legislatures, dispatch the militia, arrest and imprison and even execute with relative impunity. Yet by vesting such authority in a single figure the crown also paradoxically created the circumstances by which its will could be confounded. The implementation of crown policy became a personal decision for the man charged with doing so, and the king and his ministers had scant means of compelling him. Ultimately, then, the matter rested with the individual conscience of each governor.

Given the enormous amount of pressure placed on men like Benjamin Fletcher, the scant resources given them, and their isolation from both oversight and censure, it would not be surprising to find the governors countenancing some illegal activity in their colonies. Smuggling, for example, was widespread and almost impossible to eradicate; consequently, most governors chose to turn a blind eye. They reasoned, correctly, that it did the crown little harm and the colony a great deal of good. But piracy is a special case. It attacked the very foundations of statehood: stable trade, consistent foreign policies, domestic and transnational harmony. Jurists from Cicero to Grotius recognized that by divorcing from the state and establishing themselves as free agents on the high seas, pirates in effect waged war against the entire world. Thus the usual restraints of extradition were removed, and universal jurisdiction was introduced. This concept was not merely a right but an obligation: anyone who found a pirate must capture him and submit him to trial. Governors were not only compelled to capture pirates by virtue of their commissions, they were obliged to do so under international law.

Removed in disgrace in 1699, Benjamin Fletcher has traditionally been derided as the most corrupt and venal of the British colonial governors. Yet much of this reputation was due to the rather spectacular manner of his dismissal, an event that we will consider more fully later on. In fact, Fletcher's activities in New York were no different than those of scores of other governors. Why, then, has history branded him thus? In a word, he made the wrong enemies: men whose own piratical dealings were tactfully concealed as they leveled the charge against Fletcher.

The Glorious Revolution in the Colonies

The story of Benjamin Fletcher and the New York cabal began some years before, as the era of the buccaneers died with Sir Henry Morgan and another came to replace it: the era of the pirate brokers. In January 1688, King James II issued an edict entitled "A Royal Proclamation for the more effectual reducing and suppressing of Pirates and Privateers in America." The title was revealing: England and Spain were at peace, thus *pirate* and *privateer* were synonymous. Yet the proclamation's terms doubtless raised a derisive smile. Such pirates as were willing to confess their crimes were guaranteed pardons, on condition that they not return to their old professions unless called upon to do so. Scores of brigands appeared in colonial offices throughout America and the Caribbean, looking penitent. They then applied for, and received, commissions as "pirate hunters" and were sent off to capture other wayward pirates. These commissions also entitled them to capture "such vessels as may be hostile to His Majesty" and take what little of value they could from them. On return to an English port, they would—by law—make an immediate accounting of their spoils to the local customs agent, who would relinquish an adequate percentage for the crown. The pretense of sending a pirate to capture a pirate was a total legal fiction; these were, with few outward modifications, the same letters of marque that colonial governors had been issuing for decades.

Then in 1688 a cadre of Whig noblemen, disgusted with James's Catholicism and terrified by the possibility of a hereditary Catholic throne, invited the Dutch monarch William of Orange (whose chief qualifications for the monarchy were that he was Protestant and married to James's daughter, Mary) to invade England and take the reigns of office. He did so in November 1688, and after a brief skirmish at Salisbury, James II's army abandoned him—others maintain that James abandoned his army, but either way, a fissure occurred—and the suddenly isolated king of England fled the country, taking refuge in France. The Glorious Revolution was complete.

The overthrow of the Jacobean monarchy and the installment of William and Mary caused a sea change in politics unrivaled since the English Civil War. Historians debate endlessly whether the Glorious Revolution was a "revolution" in the precise meaning of the term—there was no great battle and no purge of the ruling classes, and the business of English government went on almost without pause—but if one judges them solely by their consequences, the events of 1688 were revolutionary indeed. William of Orange, taking a leaf from Charles I's book, inaugurated his reign by resuming an old feud: the succession of the Palatinate. His adversary was the *Roi du Soleil*, Louis XIV of France, defender of the Catholic faith and protector of the deposed James II. William, with the Whig Protestant lords solidly behind him, declared war on France in May 1689. The carefully conciliatory policies of Charles II and the openly amicable overtures of his brother James were dashed at once, the clock turned abruptly backward, and the unfinished business of the Protestant Reformation was given one final and brutal airing.

It did not take long for the repercussions of war to reach the Atlantic colonies. The French pirate De Cussy launched an expedition on the island of Hispaniola in November 1689, which nearly succeeded in driving the Spanish and English (who were now allies against France) off the island. The English retaliated by sacking the French colony of St. Kitts and then turned their wrath on De Cussy himself. At Cap Francois a combined Anglo-Spanish expeditionary force cornered and killed the pirate, but not before De Cussy had dispensed dozens of privateering commissions to French freebooters to plague the enemy's ships. For the first time, English ships were being plundered with almost the same frequency as the French and Spanish. The situation grew intolerable, and not long after, the governor of Jamaica, Lord Inchiquin, requested the prerogative to issue a blanket pardon to all pirates and grant new commissions to attack the French in kind. He died before the Committee of Trade and Plantations could reach its decision, but we find his successor, William Beeston, granting them regularly by 1692—without crown approval. The pirate wars of the Caribbean had begun in earnest.

The Glorious Revolution and its aftermath also had pivotal consequences in the American colonies. Since 1686 the colonies of Massachusetts, Rhode Island, New Hampshire, Connecticut, and New York were combined in a single legislative body, the so-called Dominion of New England. Established by James II, its primary purpose was to enforce the hated Navigation Acts, one of the few examples of Cromwellian legislation left intact after the Restoration. If the Dominion was despised for that reason, it was doubly so for the man placed at its head: the irascible, dictatorial Edmund Andros. Few men in American history have ever been so thoroughly detested, and not until the revolution of 1776 would any one figure so galvanize American outrage. Andros, a Londoner, had nothing but contempt for the colonists under his charge. Legislative meetings were curtailed or abolished outright, town meetings were limited to one per year, and martial law was established. Most galling of all, Andros was a good friend of the papist king, James II.

With the deposition of James, the colonists of Boston seized the opportunity and arrested Andros at his mansion on April 18, 1689. He was sent to England for trial the following year but was released at once (an interesting statement on the divergences between colonial and crown policy) and dispatched again to serve as governor of the much more placid Royal Colony of Virginia.

The sudden departure of Andros from the scene and the subsequent dissolution of the Dominion of New England created a vacuum of power in colonial governance. Consider the case of one William Coward, indicted before the Suffolk Court in Massachusetts on charges of piracy against the ketch *Elinor* in January 1690. By his own admission, Coward was clearly guilty. But when he appeared before the assizes, Coward pleaded no jurisdiction. Apprehended during the Andros regime, he argued that, as the government that arrested and charged him was null and void, so, too, was the complaint:

> And the said Wm. Coward for plea saith that he ought not
> nor by Law is obliged to make any further or other answer
> of plea to the Indictments now preferred against him in
> this Court: for he saith that the Crimes for which he
> stands indicted be . . . committed on the High Seas with-
> out this Jurisdiction and not within the body of any
> County within the same from Whence any Jury can be
> Lawfully brought to have trial thereof. . . . In the case of
> the Commission lately given to Sir Edmund Andros to be
> vice Admirall thereof to be void, it is now remaining in his
> Majesty and cannot be executed or exercised by any person
> or persons without being lawfully commissioned by his
> Majesty for the same.

The fissures in English society that had resulted in James's overthrow also found their counterpart in local society throughout the colonies. A great catharsis ensued, as local elites that had chafed under Andros's dictatorial hand reveled in his downfall and piled imprecations on him. Nathaniel Byfield, a prosperous Rhode Island merchant who himself would figure heavily in the pirate trade in the years to come, wrote joyously:

> Since the illegal subversion of our ancient government,
> this great but poor people have been in the hands of men

> skillful to destroy [us]. . . . For though our foul-mouthed
> enemies treat us as rebellious, because we are a religious
> people, they may be pleased now to understand that if we
> had not been religious, we long since would have been
> what they, if they durst, called rebellious. . . . I have some-
> times challenged any man to mention so much as one
> thing done by our late superiors for the welfare of the
> country, a thousand things we all felt every day doing for
> the ruin of it.

Byfield also provides an interesting account of how the news of the Glorious Revolution reached the colonies. "While these things were going on," he writes, "by way of the West Indies, there arrived unto us several very small intimations that the Prince of Orange had prospered in his noble undertaking to rescue the English nation from Popery and Slavery." Then Sir Edmund Andros intervened. When a messenger arrived from London bearing William's declaration, Andros arrested him at once and charged him with trafficking in seditious materials. Andros and his government roundly denied that the revolution had even occurred, Byfield relates, and "it took all imaginable care to keep us ignorant of the news." Finally, however, not even Andros could stem the tide.

Rebellion in New York

Once the news of William's triumph had been disseminated, expressions of relief and, alternately, consternation appeared throughout the colonies. More important than sheer emoting, however, was the opportunity for these local elites—long disenfranchised under the dominion—to move into key positions of power. Thus, when news of Andros's imprisonment in Boston reached them, a small cadre of fervent Protestants in New York led by German-born Colonel Jacob Leisler responded enthusiastically by seizing Fort James at the southern tip of Manhattan Island (the present site of Battery Park) and renaming it—predictably—Fort William. Leisler announced his intention to hold the fort until the arrival of a governor appointed by King William, most likely with the understanding that, possession being nine-tenths of the law, the appointment would fall to himself. In the meantime Leisler took on the role of acting governor. Among his many assumed duties was the granting of privateering commissions, including one to a local mariner named William Mason, commander of the *Jacob*, in December 1689. Mason took his commission, which limited his prey to French vessels, and immediately set sail for the Red Sea, where the Muslim treasure ships awaited. The *Jacob* would not see New York again until three years later, when a very different government awaited it. Yet Leisler also had grander ambitions. In 1690 he organized the first Intercolonial Congress of America, bringing representatives from all the former dominions to consider how best to counter the French threat. No concrete policy was arrived at, but the significance of the meeting was profound. For the moment, and for the first time, the American colonies were governing themselves.

This brief flurry of independence ended abruptly with the arrival of Major Richard Ingolsby from England in January 1691. Although the replacement governor, Henry Sloughter, had not yet reached New York, Ingolsby demanded that Leisler hand over the fort and relinquish all vestments of office. Leisler refused and called upon the militia to defend Fort William. So began the brief and abortive skirmish known as the Leislerian Rebellion, as Leisler and his followers repelled an attempted invasion by Ingolsby's two companies of infantry. When Governor Sloughter made his belated appearance two days after the attack, Leisler quickly handed over the fort and publicly resigned. It was not enough, however, and in May of that year both Leisler and his son-in-law were convicted of high treason and executed.

The circumstances of the Leislerian Rebellion might seem far removed from the world of the pirates. Yet the events of March 1691 were pivotal, for concealed behind the bare facts of the rebellion were the deep currents of a political, social, and religious schism that would make New York a pirate haven for the next quarter-century. Leisler and his followers have been termed protopopulists, a loose federation of lower middle-class shopkeepers, tradesmen, sailors, and farmers. They identified themselves as ardent Protestants, Whigs, and fervent supporters of William of Orange. The men they chose as their political enemies were those who had profited most under Andros: wealthy merchants like Peter Schuyler, William "Tangier" Smith, Nicholas Bayard, and Frederick Phillipse. Though these men had few political affiliations (some were Tories, others lukewarm Whigs, but nearly all had a massive Dutch indifference to English politics), they had all enjoyed amicable relations with the Jacobean government and its representatives and were often called upon to fill vacant posts in local government. Also, they were rich. When the Glorious Revolution swept the existing structure of colonial administration out of existence, Schuyler, Smith, Bayard, and Phillipse suddenly felt the cold wind of political change. A Whig junta had brought William and Mary to the throne, and what Tories remained in English government either hastened to declare their support for the new regime or, in much smaller numbers, fled to join their exiled king in France.

With a new king and a new Whig government in place, the New York merchants felt increasingly uneasy. The execution of Leisler appeased them somewhat, but it did not settle the issue. Alive, Leisler was a nuisance. Dead, he became a martyr for disenfranchised Whigs who felt betrayed by the failure of the crown to fulfill the promises of the Glorious Revolution. New York politics in the late seventeenth century rapidly devolved into a bitter feud between the Tory merchant class and the Whig middle class: the former desperate to reestablish relations with a hostile crown, the latter equally desperate to unseat them and bring about their own Whig revolution in the colonies. The issue of the governor's seat became a touchstone for all parties.

Major Ingolsby felt reasonably secure of his nomination. He had been instrumental in engineering the downfall of Jacob Leisler and was known to be a friend to the local elites. But when Governor Sloughter suddenly died after less than one year in office, the crown turned instead to another man, a colonel in His Majesty's guards named Benjamin Fletcher. Fletcher, a soldier of fortune and a New York gentleman, had no known political affiliations. As such, he was what might today be termed a compromise candidate. He took the reins of office in August 1692. Governor Fletcher's first year was a contentious one, drawing the lines of many political factions and disputes for the years to come. Desperate to encourage support for the defense of New York from French attack from the north, Fletcher journeyed into the frontier and spent several months with the Mohawk tribe, even learning their language. So successful were his entreaties there that they bestowed upon him the honorific "Great White Arrow."

Yet Indian defense alone would not save New York if it were attacked, and Fletcher turned next to the Connecticut militia. Under the terms of his commission the militia fell under his command, but improperly so. The governor of Connecticut strenuously objected and sent his ally, Governor Phipps of Massachusetts, to England to plead his case. The crown was unsympathetic. A Tory government still held power, and both Robert Treat of Connecticut and William Phipps of Massachusetts were ardent Whigs. In late 1692 the crown granted Fletcher even more power: the governorship of Pennsylvania. It was a move toward consolidation that had been tried before, with Governor Andros in 1686, and would be tried again (although under a Whig regime), with Governor Bellomont in 1699. But for Fletcher the appointment was a political minefield. William Penn, the colony's founder, governor, and, in some circles, patron saint, was summarily dismissed. His colony, which had enjoyed perhaps the most relaxed crown interference among all the Atlantic colonies, was justifiably outraged. Penn quickly circulated instructions to assemblymen to disregard Fletcher's orders and warned Fletcher himself to "tread softly."

Fletcher was not cowed. He summoned the Pennsylvania Assembly in 1693 and demanded that it raise funds to contribute to the defense of Albany. The assembly, acting on Penn's instructions in absentia, refused. Fletcher then solicited, and received, a letter from Queen Mary herself, which buttressed his claim. The assembly relented, under duress, and Fletcher left for New York crowned in glory and trailed by resentment. He appointed a deputy governor to act in his stead, a man whose name would likewise become famous among the pirate brokers in the years to come: William Markham.

Meanwhile the government of Connecticut proved recalcitrant, and Fletcher himself went to New Haven. A series of exchanges survives—published, in fact, by Fletcher in an attempt to draw shame on the colony's shuffling—which reveals the deepening rift between the governor and his unwilling charges. First was Fletcher's letter to Governor Treat on October 14, 1693:

> Sir, in obedience to Their Majesties' commission, directed to me for the command of their militia for the colony of Connecticut . . . I have thought fit to communicate their Majesties' pleasure to you . . . and I have sent this gentleman, Their Majesties' secretary, to you to acquaint you

with what must be further said upon this occasion and to desire your directions how I may best steer myself for the publishing of Their Majesties' commands to render them most effectual for the present service.

A courteous letter with a veiled threat: "Their Majesties' secretary" had in fact been sent for the express purpose of compelling the reluctant Treat to hand over the militia. It was clear that Treat had read past the tone and gotten the message; the record states baldly: "Hereunto His Excellency received no answer." Matters did not improve thereafter. Finally Fletcher summoned the assembly and, much as he had done with the Pennsylvanians, laid down the law:

> Gentlemen, you cannot say you had the power of the militia in the late reign, Sir Edmund Andros having been received and owned your Governor, from whom you received these commissions. . . . Nor can you truly say you had the power of the militia under their present Majesties, Sir William Phipps having a Commission under the great Seal for that Trust, which is superceded and nulled by express words in this commission to me.

By the fall of 1693, through his fervent attempts to secure the Albany frontier, Governor Fletcher had succeeded in alienating the colonies of Massachusetts, Connecticut, and Pennsylvania. Yet one cannot doubt that his diligence—however blunt or politically unwise—reveals a sincere dedication to the problems of his colony and his own responsibility. But Fletcher also had to contend with political factions closer to home: in his own backyard, so to speak. And, as we will see, the internecine disputes of New York society interwove with those of neighboring colonies, with new political alliances forming across borders in the increasingly virulent attempts to unseat Governor Fletcher.

At the crux of the whole matter was the smoldering division between the Leislerians and the Tory merchants. Fletcher had been selected instead of the Tories' own beloved Major Ingolsby, a move that might at first have seemed likely to incur the wrath of men like Phillipse and Bayard. But Fletcher was no friend of the populists, and he knew that he could not hope to maintain the colony without the support of the wealthy merchant class. Bowing to political reality, he actively courted them. The cabal—Stuyvesant, Phillipse, Bayard, Nicholls, and

Smith—were invited to take key posts in the governor's council and hold lucrative positions in trade and customs.

It was a move that could only infuriate the Leislerians and their Whig sympathizers. Governor Phipps of Massachusetts became one of Fletcher's most vocal enemies, pausing in his ongoing stream of invective against him only to encourage the vigorous prosecution of witches in Salem. Meanwhile, genuine friendships developed between Governor Fletcher and his advisors, and by 1694 he had reason to congratulate himself: while Massachusetts languished under the burdens of King William's War (even going as far as to impose a tax on all incoming vessels due to the cumulative effect of "sundry depredations, robberies and damages" done to commercial trade by "piratical sea rovers . . . to the great impoverishing and hurt of the same"), New York was wealthier and busier than ever.

Birth of the Cabal

When Fletcher assumed the governorship, he was in effect taking the reigns of a commercial culture that had been established some time hence and would reach its zenith during his tenure. By aligning with the wealthy merchants and taking them into his counsel, Fletcher not only left himself politically vulnerable, but he also became part of the commercial network of New York, a network that encompassed any kind of trade: slavery, smuggling—and piracy. It is tempting, in fact, to blame much of his subsequent conduct vis-à-vis the pirates on the malign influence of those around him, the infamous "cabal." There are two versions of this story. The first is the classic seduction and corruption tale that the city of New York seems to inspire ad nauseam: honest, industrious Fletcher is lured into the mire of lucre and petty politics of New York, falls in with a shady crowd of Mammonites, and loses his integrity in the process. The second is even more brutal: Fletcher was not lured into anything but rather was venal from the start; the piracy and lawlessness of the colony merely reflected his own blackened greed, and vice versa. This was the dominant narrative circulating after Fletcher's downfall, communicated mostly through the reports of his acerbic successor, Lord Bellomont.

Yet how much of this can we believe? Clearly, both versions rely heavily on the same presumption: that the commercial atmosphere of New York was in some way conducive to piracy, perhaps to the extent that even a governor with more honest ambitions still fell sway to its inexorable force. The first task then, in evaluating the career of Benjamin Fletcher, must be to reckon with the colony that he was chosen to govern.

New York at the end of the seventeenth century was a colony in turmoil, rife with internal disputes between the wealthy merchants and the middle-class shopkeepers, town dwellers and farmers, Whigs and Tories, Dutch and English, Calvinists and Anglicans, and so on. It is always dangerous to generalize over political divisions within a colony, and those historians that have summarily lumped the farmers and the ardent Whigs and anyone who opposed Governor Andros all together and termed them Leislerians surely have oversimplified things. Nevertheless it cannot be denied that when the Leislerians and others complained that the merchant cabal had the colony in a stranglehold, their claim had some merit. Favorable relations between the merchants and several preceding administrations had soured the political climate with the stench of corruption. Consider the journal of Jaspar Danckaerts, a Dutch local who kept a detailed record of the colony in the 1680s. Danckaerts writes that the merchants, desirous to keep tight control over trade in and out of the colony, prevailed on Governor Andros to suspend trade between Boston and New York. This had two consequences: it infuriated locals, who had come to rely on it as an alternative to the West Indian route over which Nicholls, Bayard, and Phillipse had a monopoly, and it created a permanent rift between New York and Massachusetts, which Fletcher, too, would inherit. On a smaller scale, Danckaerts also relates that the merchants, anxious over falling profits from the sale of their imported West Indian rum, convinced Andros to outlaw the distillation of spirits in New York, which he did. In sum, by the time of the Glorious Revolution, the local farmer "remained a child in [the merchants'] debt, and consequently their slave. It is considered at New York a great pleasure and liberty not to be indebted to the merchants, for anyone who is will never be able to pay them."

The effect of the Leislerian Rebellion was to introduce, however briefly, a spirit of Puritan ire and reform into the political mix. As long as Jacob Leisler held Fort William, the long-suffering middle and lower classes were persuaded that they finally had a say in the colony's affairs. It is likely that many, including Leisler himself, believed that the era of the merchant cabal was over. It should not be surprising, then, that with the execution of Leisler and the advent of the pro-merchant Fletcher administration all the preexisting discontent directed against his predecessors would be doubled against him. The farmers and shopkeepers had had a taste of political freedom, only to be subjected, once again, to the crushing tyranny of the merchant cabal.

Thus, when Lord Bellomont arrived in 1699 and began writing scathing letters back to the Board of Trade, he fostered the impression—which remains to this day—that Fletcher and his counselors were so blackened by corruption as to be practically insensible to honest governance. Some of the accusations were true, as we will consider later, but what was misleading about Bellomont's reports was that they presumed that this corruption was in some way singular. In allying himself with the merchant cabal and favoring them, Fletcher was merely walking along a path well trod by his predecessors.

As early as 1668, Governor Lovelace had been accused of granting prominent offices to local merchants in return for a fee, as well as soliciting bribes for sundry services. His successor, Governor Dongan, also fell under attack. A customs collector named Lucas Santen charged that Dongan engaged in illegal trade through his merchant friends, abetted them in avoiding the Navigation Acts, accepted gifts and shares from them in their illegal enterprises, withheld duties to the Royal Purse, and even took bribes for renewing patents. This appalling list should be ameliorated somewhat by the doubtfulness of the source: Santen had been dismissed from his duties by Dongan on account of dishonesty.

True or not, many of these same accusations, particularly the charge of selectively enforcing the Navigation Acts, would surface again during the tenure of the hated Governor Andros. Andros was twice put on trial for the illegal disposal of confiscated goods. Jaspar Danckaerts, who always seemed to have his ear to the ground, repeated in his journal the widespread belief that Andros was in secret partnership with the most notorious of the cabal, Frederick Phillipse.

Phillipse, the proper Dutch burgher, surfaces again and again as the Moriarty, or perhaps the Rasputin, of the story of Fletcher and his relationship with the pirates. Born Fredryck Flypsen in Holland in 1626, he was a carpenter's apprentice who arrived in the bustling Dutch community of New Amsterdam sometime in the early 1650s. There he had the exceeding good fortune to be sent to work for Peter Stuyvesant, one of the colony's earliest entrepreneurs. In his mid-twenties, handsome, and affable and already very ambitious, Flypsen charmed the older man. Stuyvesant became young Fredryck's patron, introducing him into higher social circles than he might otherwise have reached. There he married Margaret Hardenbroeck de Vries, a youthful widow with a sizable fortune. Thereafter events followed a predictable course. When the English annexed the New Netherlands in the 1660s, Flypsen was among the first to present himself to Deputy Governor Richard Nicholls (another charter member of the New York cabal) and swear his undying allegiance to the crown. He also changed his name, and so Fredryck Flypsen the carpenter's assistant became Frederick Phillipse, shipowner and man of substance.

The business of New York (as it was now called) was almost exclusively mercantile, and that was the business which Phillipse entered. By the early 1670s he had a fleet of ships registered in his name, conducting trade up and down the Atlantic coast and across the sea to England, Portugal, and Holland. Phillipse also became a minor figure in the slave trade. In 1675 he was invited to sit on the council of Governor Edmund Andros, a fateful decision which would place him squarely in the center of New York political affairs. By the time of the Glorious Revolution Frederick Phillipse was one of the colony's most respected merchants, a popular and still-handsome man with a very rich wife and a secure place in colonial society.

As a man who derived his income from intercolonial trade, it could not have escaped Phillipse's attention that pirates and the pirate trade were rapidly becoming a fixture in colonial commerce. Even before the Glorious Revolution, complaints filtered back to the Board of Trade that pirates were nesting along the shoals of Long Island Sound, using the many inlets and narrows as beaching grounds for their ships. Nor could Phillipse have been insensible to the growing trade of pirate brokering in the colony, which had its clandestine beginnings in Andros's time and flourished under the sudden legality of privateering during King William's War. But the first evidence of Phillipse's own involvement comes from the deposition taken in 1699 from a notorious pirate-turned-entrepreneur named Adam Baldridge. It was the relationship between these two men, Phillipse and Baldridge, that would bring the New York pirate trade to an entirely new level and enmesh its governor, Benjamin Fletcher, within the coils of piracy.

-6-

King Baldridge
and the
Red Sea Pirates

FROM HIS LOFTY PERCH OVERLOOKING THE PIRATE COLONY OF St. Mary's, "King" Adam Baldridge had reason to be satisfied. Below the ramparts of his castle the harbor glittered, and even with the naked eye he could see the tall spires of masts congregating along the wharves. In the evening the city would be ablaze with the light of torches and the sounds of laughter, song, and the occasional brawl. Just two years ago he had arrived on the island, nearly penniless and hoping to scrape a modest living out of the soil. But he had seen opportunities here. St.

Mary's lay off the north coast of Madagascar, directly in the path of the pirates that sailed up the Mozambique Channel and into the Red Sea, where the Muslim treasure ships awaited them. And so Baldridge abandoned farming (perhaps he had never intended to try it anyway) and began empire building. His contacts with the tribes were helpful in that regard. Now they trusted him—for the moment, anyway—and Baldridge capitalized on that trust. St. Mary's was a pirate paradise, offering everything from cordage to rum to native wenches. But it was still ramshackle and crude. There were still potentialities to explore, and the castle that Baldridge constructed for himself seemed the promise of greater things to come. He was on the cusp of greatness, of trading spurious royalty amongst the natives for real power. He had been in communication with Frederick Phillipse and was now poised to open relations with one of the most powerful merchants in the world. The tiny island that had become his fiefdom would soon be tied, economically and socially, with the colony of New York.

The Pirate King and His Ally

Baldridge was a ruffian. Born and raised in New York, he drifted to Port Royal, Jamaica, around the time that Henry Morgan was serving out his term as lieutenant governor. Baldridge spent his early years shipping out with the coastal pirates that preyed on Spanish trade but met with little success. In 1685, at the age of twenty-eight, he accidentally killed a man in a barroom brawl and was forced to flee the island—to escape not justice but vengeance from the dead man's friends. Baldridge joined a departing ship and made his way across the Atlantic, around the southern tip of Africa, and into Madagascar.

Baldridge's brief piratical career was unremarkable. Sailing in company with other English and French pirates that had made the same journey round the Cape of Good Hope, Baldridge remained some five years on Madagascar. At this time the largest settlements were at Augustin Bay in the southwest, Port Dauphin nearby, Ambonavoula in the north, and the Comorro Islands, which lay in the Mozambique Channel. Another of these islands, smaller than the rest, was known as St. Mary's. The pirates considered it uninhabitable, as the natives were known to enslave any Englishman that encroached on their lands. Baldridge arrived at the island in January 1691.

He would later claim that he settled on St. Mary's hoping to find a quiet spot to farm and perhaps serve as a trading agent with the tribes. This pastoral image notwithstanding, within months of his arrival there, Baldridge was already known as a prominent trader of slaves. Using their labor he constructed a fortress of sorts on the crest of a high hill overlooking the port, bristling with cannons and boasting walls several feet thick. Suddenly the natives began to speak of "King" Baldridge and his castle, and by the end of the year Adam Baldridge was the undisputed "sovereign" of the pirate colony at St. Mary's.

His arrival there coincided with a growing trend that would come to dominate the history of piracy for the next three decades: the Red Sea trade. Gradually, as the Spanish empire in the New World declined, the pirates began seeking new sources of plunder. They found them in a seemingly unlikely and far-flung locale: the waters around the island of Madagascar. Along the route known as the Golden Road, stretching from Mocha in the Red Sea to the west coast of India, the riches of the Indian and Muslim lords were carried mostly by the Muslims themselves or through a charter by the East India Company. James Ovington, a chaplain who visited Mocha in the pivotal year of 1689, records:

> Mocha is the principal port of the Red Sea, to which Ships Traffick from Surat, Cambay, Dieu, Malabar, and other parts of India. Hither also come the Ships from several parts of Europe: England, Holland, France, Denmark, Portugal; as also from Casseen Socatra, Muscatt, and all the Gulf of Persia, which bring hither the Products of their several countries and are met by the Merchants of Barbary, Egypt, Turkey, by the Abasseens and Arabians who buy off their goods for ready money and make little other Returns but Coffee, Sena and some Aloes, Hepetica, and other small things of no great moment.

The "products" to which Ovington refers included a list that would fire the imagination of any freebooter: spices and silk, calicos, leather, made goods, tea, and coffee. But the richest prizes came from the East India Company: great fat-bottomed ships heavily laden with gold, silver, and precious stones. Much as the Spanish had once mined the New World to enrich their coffers, the English government had now concluded favorable terms with the Great Mogul to ensure a constant supply of precious commodities at rock-bottom rates. Few of these, however, would reach the colonies. With the Navigation Acts still very much in force, only English ships could discharge their goods in colonial ports. England had a stranglehold on the Red Sea trade, as well as nearly all others, a fact that the colonists—to a man—resented deeply. Thus piracy in the 1690s became a way to open this barrier, illegally. Pirates were drawn to the Red Sea not only because of the promise of the riches they found there but because of the ready markets for pilfered goods at home. In 1684 Governor Cranfield of New Hampshire wrote to the Board of Trade (then known as the Lords of Trade) of a pirate ship that had dropped anchor in Boston. The merchants of the town had sent out a pilot to bring her safely in, and the pirates—flushed with ready cash amounting to £700 per man—bought out the shops of Boston. The "Red Sea fever," which would culminate after war ended between England and France with the Peace of Ryswick in 1697, would see literally hundreds of mariners (some professional privateers, many more honest merchants on moonlighting sprees) making the long trek across the Southern Atlantic, around the Cape of Good Hope, and into the fray. Perhaps the most concise (if grammatically daunting) statement of this evolution from Spanish Caribbean to Red Sea piracy comes from William Penn, who in 1700 looked back on the succeeding decades and wrote:

> As for Piracy, I must needs say that if Jamaica had not been the Seminary, where pirates have commenced Masters of Art after having practiced upon the Spaniard, and then launched for the Red & Arabian Sea, and at Madagascar have found a yearly supply of flower, bread, ammunition and arms from some of our neighboring colonies, that has perhaps in 10 years time got a million by it, and then have returned these fellows upon us and our Coasts, we had never had a spot upon our Garment.

It did not take long for other pirates to discover the advantages of St. Mary's. On October 13, as Baldridge relates, one George Raynor of New York arrived in the *Bachelor's Delight*, flushed with a successful capture on the Red Sea that netted £1,100 per man. "While they careened

I supplied them with cattle for their present spending and they gave me for my cattle a quantity of beads, five great guns for a fortification, some powder and shot, and six barrels of flour, about seventy bars of iron," Baldridge later testified. Later that month another New Yorker, Edward Coates, arrived, and Baldridge obtained another cache of powder and six more "great guns" in return for his cattle. By this time Baldridge's imperial ambitions were manifest. Clearly he was the man on the spot and intended to remain so, as the eleven "great guns" indicated.

It was in this capacity that he wrote Frederick Phillipse that same month, offering two hundred captured slaves at thirty shillings a head, considerably below market price. If Phillipse found them to his liking there were plenty more, Baldridge assured him. The New York gentleman might also consider supplying this new trading post with other necessities as the need arose. In business terms the offer of the slaves was akin to a free sample, a gesture of trust to inaugurate a long and profitable relationship.

Phillipse responded in kind. Owing to the exigencies of transatlantic communication it was not until mid-1692 that he received Baldridge's note, but he hastened to outfit a vessel to supply the pirate's needs. England and France were at war; piracy, in some fashion, was legal again. Phillipse sent the *Charles*, commanded by John Thurber, with a heavy load of supplies. The list makes interesting reading, for it says much about Baldridge's intentions for his new colony:

> 44 pair of shoes and pumps, 6 dozen of worsted and thread stockings, 3 dozen of speckled shirts and breaches, 12 hats, some carpenters' tools, 5 barrels of rum, four quarter casks of madeira wine, ten cases of spirits, two old stills full of holes, one worme, two grindstones, two cross saws and one whip saw, three jars of oil, two small Iron pots, three barrels of cannon powder, some books, catechisms, primers and horn books, two Bibles, and some garden Seeds and three dozen hoes.

Clearly Baldridge had both farming and construction in mind, but what do we make of the "catechisms, primers and horn books," much less the Bibles? Was he planning to Christianize the local tribes, or were these for the edification and spirituality of the pirates that now constituted nearly the entire populace of the town? In any event, Baldridge sent the *Charles* back with 1,100 pieces of eight and thirty-four slaves—

not the amount contracted for, but as many as he could lay hands on at the moment. Phillipse was not pleased. "It is by negroes that I find my chiefest profit," he reminded Baldridge in a letter. "All other trade I look upon as by the by. . . . Besides, of the 34 negroes that you put aboard there were 15 of them children 3 yrs suckling."

Yet the prospect of a new source of trade intrigued him all the same. "I only expect that a reasonable satisfaction should be made," he went on in a more conciliatory tone, "for I was never known to be sharp or severe with any man, though I had the advantage so to be." As a gesture of good faith (and with an eye on the main chance), Phillipse backed up his words with another shipment, this time in a larger brig called the *Katherine*. Clearly much had been earmarked for Baldridge, but here the pirate is more vague: "She had several sorts of goods in her," he testified, of which "she sold the most to the white men upon Madagascar." In other words, the pirates.

By this time Phillipse believed he had struck gold. Even as the *Katherine* was still making her way back around the Cape of Good Hope, Phillipse was outfitting a third ship, the largest yet, named after his wife, *Margaret*. The man he chose to command her was one who had considerable knowledge of the waters around Madagascar: Samuel Burgess. Burgess was one of those characters that would surface again and again in the history of New York piracy. We first find record of him as serving under Captain William Kidd in the *Blessed William* during a Red Sea pirating expedition in 1690. Then he appears as William Mason's quartermaster on the *Jacob*, the privateer commissioned by Jacob Leisler in 1689. Burgess had also gained some notoriety as a slaver on the Madagascar coast and would return there numerous times throughout the 1690s. It was not surprising that Phillipse knew of him: Burgess was married to one of his cousins. "I have some thought to continue a trade for Madagascar," Phillipse informed him, "and [I] should not be unwilling of a good correspondence that way, provided it was with equal profit and danger on both sides."

A Quiet Conspiracy

For seven crucial years, coinciding with Benjamin Fletcher's tenure as governor of New York, Frederick Phillipse kept the pirate colony of St.

Mary's regularly supplied with rum, clothing, foodstuffs, and gunpowder. When, in 1699, the political winds had shifted once again and a new regime installed in New York, Phillipse's relations with known pirates like Burgess and Baldridge would look very suspicious indeed, no less so than Fletcher's own correspondence with Phillipse. But in fact the relationships that developed in this decade were more revealing of the provincial nature of colonial commerce and governance than any vast criminal conspiracy. Contrary to the popular myth of the pirates as a separate class of proto-revolutionaries, most of the pirates in this era were much like Burgess: local men, respected and well known in their communities, who had engaged in "honest" trade and took to pirating much as one might join a different firm. And, it must be stressed again, privateering was perfectly legal until the Treaty of Ryswick in 1697. English governors had every right to grant privateering commissions, and men like Mason and Burgess were commonly viewed as adjunct naval officers, which in some ways they were. This was buttressed by the passage, in September 1692, of an Act for the Restraining and Punishing of Privateers and Pirates. Despite its title, the act was directed only against those "serving in America in any hostile manner under any Forraigne Prince State or Potentate in Amity with their Majesties without Speciall lycence for soe doing." In other words, only those pirates who had obtained commissions from states other than England would be subject to prosecution. The logical inverse was that those pirates holding English commissions were protected under the law. This left a loophole wide enough to render the act practically meaningless, as Colonel Robert Quarry, former governor of South Carolina and present judge of the Admiralty, wrote to the Lords of Trade in June 1699:

> The Jamaica Act [a common term for the Act of 1692]
> hath made it felony for any of the King's subjects in any
> hostile manner to serve under any forreigne prince against
> any other prince in Amity with his Majesty without
> Lycense, but this Act of theirs hath made noe such provi-
> sion tho' all the roguery that hath been committed by
> those sort of men in the West Indies.

What was most emphatically *not* legal, at any time, was Red Sea piracy. England enjoyed cordial if distant relations with the Great Mogul and through the East India Company received a great deal of trade with enormous profits at both ends. Thus when one speaks of "piracy" and "pirate brokering" during this period, the legal question becomes one of foreknowledge: did men like Frederick Phillipse know that they were in effect subsidizing illegal activity around Madagascar? Did men like Benjamin Fletcher know that the commissions they granted to pursue the French would only serve as a legal imprimatur for Red Sea pirating?

The answer to the first is certainly yes. Phillipse, as the record shows, balanced "danger and profit" and came down heavily on the side of the latter. In the still-small community of New York it was not possible that he did not know the career of Samuel Burgess: in fact, Phillipse not only knew it but relied on it. You do not send a schoolmarm to trade with someone like Adam Baldridge. Particularly because Baldridge, despite his lofty ambitions for St. Mary's, seems a rather shady sort of character. It is likely that Phillipse chose Burgess precisely because he was as tough as the men he would deal with; this is borne out by Phillipse's blunt instruction that if Baldridge had not already "squared his account" with Thomans Mostyn (captain of the *Katherine*), he should be made to do so with Burgess. Phillipse, then, entered the Madagascar trade with his eyes wide open. Should we then pass the judgment of history on him, that he was nothing more than a willing conspirator to piracy?

Not quite. Phillipse might be well aware of what the pirates were doing around St. Mary's, but he himself was not financing piracy expeditions, only selling them garden implements, silk shirts, and rum (and, admittedly, gunpowder). Thus he could honestly maintain, and would later testify, that his only contact with the Red Sea pirates was of entirely legitimate trade. These were fellow New Yorkers, after all. If they chose to make a life for themselves halfway around the world, and perhaps spread England's influence to a new corner, then should not any patriotic merchant do all he could to encourage them? Of course Phillipse himself was moved less by patriotism than by profit, but that itself was no crime. The business of the age was essentially a constant search for new markets, and nowhere was this more the case than among the burgeoning Atlantic colonies.

Yet the securing of funding—though critical—was merely one step of two. The second was the procuring of a commission that could be produced in court in the unlikely (though occasional) event of capture and trial. Here men like Benjamin Fletcher were crucial. From 1692 to 1699, the tenure of his office, he granted some sixteen known privateering commissions, a number which is slightly higher than the average; Governor Richier of Bermuda is recorded as having granted ten, while Governor Cranston of Rhode Island commissioned at least twenty. This evidence comes to us from two sources: accusations made by other governors later in his career (most particularly Governor Phipps and Governor Easton of Massachusetts and, of course, his replacement, Lord Bellomont), and evidence produced by the pirates themselves while on trial in London. This in turn raises the critical question of the sources themselves. When one governor accuses another of pirate brokering, whom do we believe?

One answer would be to look at the sheer volume of accusations. While it is certainly possible that one man may deliberately slander another—and the charge of pirate brokering was a favorite among the governors of that time—this can only be an isolated incident. Pirate brokering is not like witchcraft; it is not a crime without an answer. Governors could, and did, sometimes deny that they had engaged in the act and called upon their accusers to prove their case. This reliance on evidence suggests that an accusation, when made, usually had to have some basis. Granted that basis sometimes took the form of rumor (as in, "it was owned to me by several reports that William Mays had a commission from Rhode Island," etc.), but such was the nature of intelligence gathering in the seventeenth century. Even if we automatically discounted three-quarters of these accusations based on secondhand reports, there would still remain dozens and dozens of pirate-brokering charges. One, five, or even a dozen may be baseless, but to discount them all would strike of absurdity.

Second, there is the crucial evidence of men like Fletcher himself. For in fact he did not deny the charges. He attempted to justify them. Fletcher freely admitted that he granted privateering commissions, as he had every right to do. England and France were at war. Privateering was an essential element of sea warfare. Just as Frederick Phillipse would claim that he had no idea why Adam Baldridge might need four kegs of gunpowder and cannon, Benjamin Fletcher later serenely told the Board of Trade that "it may be my misfortune, but not my crime, if they turn pirates. I have heard of none yet that have done so."

Which brings us back to the question of foreknowledge. Did Governor Fletcher know that the men he sent "on the account"—Coates, Tew, Mays, Glover, Hoar, and others—would promptly abandon the strictures of their commissions and sail directly for the Red Sea? Again, the answer is almost certainly yes. Fletcher, so closely allied with Phillipse and Bayard, could not be unaware of their activities. It is likely, given the political climate of the time, that when a privateer sought out the governor for a commission, one of the cabal may have made the introduction himself. Fletcher might even have taken a share of the voyage for himself, though there is no direct proof of this. The granting of commissions would thus be a routine business matter (Fletcher charged a typical fee of £300), a means of increasing the wealth of the colony should the voyage prove successful, and a favor to his trusted advisors in the council. In this atmosphere of bonhomie and big business it is tempting to consider the activities of Fletcher and Phillipse as conjoined, as indeed (from a business standpoint) they were. But Fletcher's situation is different from Frederick Phillipse's in one crucial respect. For Fletcher was not merely subsidizing piracy, he was sanctioning it. The distinction is a legal one. The members of the council, as private citizens, were guilty of pirate brokering and thus—under a conspiracy charge—piracy itself. This was serious enough, but the charge against Fletcher is graver still. By giving color of law to a flagrantly illegal activity, in full contravention of crown policy, Governor Fletcher was guilty of treason.

One historian has called Fletcher "a man of strong passions and inconsiderable talent: tall, florid, and pompous." Not, at first glance, the craven, Fagan-like character one might expect. And then there remains his conduct regarding the defense of Albany and his alienation of Connecticut, Massachusetts, and Pennsylvania. The Benjamin Fletcher that emerges from the record therein comes across to us as forceful, stubborn, perhaps somewhat arrogant, ardently devoted to his colony, and very likely a patriot. It would be naive to assume that a man with such fervent devotion to duty might still not be tempted to make some profit on the side, but the commissioning of pirate voyages goes beyond mere profit and constitutes a deliberate flouting of crown policy. How, then, do we explain Fletcher's conduct?

The political and social circumstances surrounding Fletcher's appointment are only part of the answer. For the rest, Fletcher's destiny, and his downfall, would be inextricably linked to another man, a proper Rhode Island gentleman and infamous pirate named Thomas Tew.

-7-

Amity, Liberty, and Thomas Tew

YEARS LATER, WHEN THE MEMORY OF THOMAS TEW WOULD PROVE a curse to Benjamin Fletcher, he left an account of his relations with the pirate that generations of historians have derided as almost comically self-serving. Writing in his own defense to the Board of Trade in 1698, three years after Tew's death, Fletcher would stoutly maintain:

> Tew appeared to me not only a man of courage and activity, but of the greatest sense and remembrance of what he had seen of any seaman that I ever met with. He was also what is called a very pleasant man, so that some times after the day's labour was done it was divertissement as well as information to me to hear him talk.

Then came the critical passage that raised many an incredulous eyebrow:

> I wished in my mind to make him a sober man, and in particular to cure him of a vile habit of swearing. I gave him a book for that purpose, and to gain the more upon him I gave him a gun of some value. In return he gave me a present which was a curiosity, though in value not much.

The image was as irresistible as it was incredible: the foppish, bewigged governor gently chiding the rough and profane pirate, perhaps over a bottle of good Madeira wine. Even the Board of Trade was less than impressed. They had heard of Fletcher's relations with the infamous Tew long before. As early as June 1695, the former mayor of New York (and an ardent Whig) Peter Delanoy wrote a scathing attack against Fletcher that included the following charge:

> We have a parcel of pirates in these parts, which people call the Red Sea men, who often get great booties of Arabian gold. His Excellency [Fletcher] gives all due encouragement to these men, because they make all due acknowledgement to him; one Coats, a captain of this honorable order presented His Excellency with his ship, which His Excellency sold for £800 and ever one of the crew made him a suitable present of Arabian gold for his protection; one Captain Tew who is gone to the Red Sea upon some errand, was before his departure highly caressed by His Excellency, in a coach and six horses, and presented with a gold watch to engage him to make New York his port at his return. Tew retaliated the kindness with a present of jewels, but I can't learn how much further the bargain proceeded; time must show that.

The logical inference, which Delanoy's acidic remarks make plain, was that Tew was nothing more or less than a common pirate, and the open "caressing" of him by the governor of New York was flagrant corruption of the worst kind. In this light, Fletcher's touching depiction of their interactions seems farcical and unreal. So unreal, in fact, that Howard Pyle, the nineteenth-century illustrator who provided the most enduring romantic images of the pirates, chose to depict the scene as it "actually" was: Fletcher and Tew sit side by side on a window seat, the governor's face shadowed and turned in profile while Tew's, full of coarse merriment, shines in plain view. The pirate clutches a long-stemmed pipe to his mouth and grins; he is apparently regaling his companion with the tales of his adventures. Thin and spare, there is something almost rodentlike about him. The room is poorly lit and an air of furtive secrecy prevails.

Certainly with the clarity of hindsight we have reason to doubt Fletcher's account, no less than did his interlocutors. By 1697 the Tory governor was under constant attack from a Whig government at Whitehall, from the neighboring colonies that had writhed under his blunt administration, and from the Leislerians in New York—like Delanoy—that were agitating almost daily for his dismissal. He was, so to speak, on the ropes. Yet when the full story of Thomas Tew is told, two salient facts emerge that cast equal doubt over the opposite image. First, Thomas Tew was no rough-hewn mariner raised up, like Milton's Satan, from "that bad eminence" to sit at the governor's table. Second, and even more crucially, Governor Fletcher was hardly the only governor to have amicable relations with the pirate. He was merely the only one to suffer the consequences for so doing. The "ramblings" of Thomas Tew serve, in fact, as a testament to the near ubiquity of pirate sponsorship that emerged at the end of the seventeenth century.

The Luck of Captain Tew

Thomas Tew was a gentleman. His grandfather was Richard Tew, a Northampton man who settled in Newport, Rhode Island, in 1640 and soon became an administrator for the colony. Among the prominent families given special mention in the royal charter of 1663 was "Tew, Esq." Little is known of Tew's early life, but one can make certain inferences from surviving accounts. He appears in Hamilton, Bermuda, in 1691 as a young man, perhaps twenty-five years of age, with ready cash and in possession of a small sailing craft. Clearly he has already spent some time at sea, for he presents himself to the Bermudian gentry as Captain Tew. It is also likely that he had embarked on at least one pirating cruise; during the trial of Governor Fletcher the crown's chief prosecutor, George Weaver, claimed that even in Bermuda "it was a thing notoriously known to everyone that he had before then been a pirate."

Some doubt may arise over the veracity of that source, but this much is certain: whatever his past, Tew was enough of a gentleman (either in manners or means) to gain almost immediate entry into the most rarified circles of Bermudian society. Richard Gilbert, Thomas Hall, John Dickenson, Anthony White, and William Outerbridge all received, entertained, and befriended him. These men were from families that had settled the island with Sir George Somers sixty years before and that still, to some extent, exert commercial and political force over the colony to this day. Not long after his arrival Tew purchased a share of a sloop owned by them, a small vessel with the cheerful name of *Amity*.

Tew then went to Governor Isaac Richier and requested a privateering commission to hunt the French on the west coast of Africa. He and another privateer, a local man named George Drew, were to make their way up the Gambia River and attack the French fortress at Goree. On the surface the voyage seemed credible enough, except for two facts: first, the combined firepower and manpower of the sloops would hardly be enough to mount any kind of credible attack (each had but eight guns and sixty men apiece); second, privateering commissions to Africa, east or west, were notoriously suspect. If, as Weaver indicated, it was already known that Tew had done his share of pirating, Governor Richier could not have been insensible to the true purpose of his voyage.

Still, the exact parameters of Tew's plan remain uncertain. He left with Drew in the late fall of 1691, but there appears to have been some mishap as the two sloops made their way across the Atlantic, and they were separated. Daniel Defoe provides the only account of what happened next. Tew, it appears, had serious doubts about the Gambia project from the start: "He thought it a very injudicious expedition," says Defoe, "which, did they succeed in, would be of no use to the public, and only advantage a private company of men, from whom they could expect no reward of their bravery; that he could see nothing but danger in the undertaking, without the least prospect of booty." Again according to Defoe, Tew put the matter before his crew. Should they press on with the dangerous and fruitless Gambia project or turn instead to the Red Sea trade, where "one bold push might do the business, and they might return home, not only without danger but even reputation"? The crew answered with one voice: "A gold chain, or a wooden leg, we'll stand by you!"

There are many reasons to doubt this narrative, not the least of which being the highly romantic last lines. Given the story thus far, it is far more likely that Tew and his crew set out with Madagascar, not Gambia, in mind. This would also accord with other facts concerning Governor Isaac Richier. Not long after Tew departed, the governor of Bermuda would be embroiled in a scandal over his pirate sponsorship, along with prominent members of his council including White and Outerbridge. In 1694 Richier's successor, John Goddard, began writing to the Lords of Trade, accusing the former governor of pirate broker-ing. Tew was named specifically. Richier responded with a blast of his own. Goddard, he wrote, had packed the council with pirate brokers of his own acquaintance. He had brought several baseless actions against Richier, which were quickly thrown out but nevertheless damaged his reputation. "And all this," Richier concluded, "for no other reason but because [I] refused to give him a certain sum of money that he hath demanded."

The two governors traded insults back and forth, but it was not until 1700 that an officious customs agent named George Larkin was dispatched from London to clear up the matter. By this time both Samuel Day and Benjamin Bennett had succeeded Goddard, and both were accused of pirate brokering. Larkin promptly wrote a report that named every governor back to Sir Richard Robinson of 1690 as a pirate broker, and the Bermudians promptly responded by arresting him. He was taken, he wrote plaintively, "by the Marshall with a file of muske-teers and taken to the castle [probably the present site of the Royal Navy Dockyard], a forlorn place, where there is but one room and the waves of the sea beat over the platform into it in stormy weather." The Bermu-dians, revealing an unexpectedly whimsical side, charged poor Larkin with piracy.

Tew, meanwhile, enjoyed what amounted to a run of fantastic luck. After only a short time cruising the waters around Madagascar he came across a Muslim trader in the Strait of Babelmandeb, nearly twice the size of the *Amity* and carrying more than two hundred seamen. Tew turned to his men and bellowed, "We have found our fortunes!" Then he ordered the decks cleared for action and brought the *Amity* carefully alongside. As they approached, the decks of the Muslim ship suddenly teemed with soldiers, each pointing muskets at the advancing pirate ship. Tew's men were terrified, but he ordered them to hold fast. "Though he was satisfied she was full of men, and was mounted with a great number of guns," Defoe writes, "they [the Muslims] wanted the two things necessary, skill and courage." Tew's gamble paid off. Having fired only a few threatening volleys, the soldiers broke ranks and began laying down their arms and throwing themselves into the sea. Tew led a boarding party, and the Muslim captain struck his colors without firing a shot.

It proved to be a colossal prize. The Muslim ship was bound from the Indies to Arabia, and her hold was packed to the deck beams with gold, silver plate, and jewels. Tew and his men carelessly tossed bale after bale of lesser goods—silks, spices, and the like—into the sea, as they rummaged for more gold. Tew also found that the prize contained so much gunpowder that he ordered the majority of it thrown overboard, lest someone inadvertently touch it off and blow up the ship. Some estimates claim that each of his sixty-man crew was the richer by £3,000 apiece. Adam Baldridge, who recorded Tew's arrival at St. Mary's not long after, put it somewhat lower:

> Arrived the ship *Amity*, Captain Thomas Tew, commander
> . . . having taken a Ship in the Red Seas that did belong to
> the Moors, as the men did report, they took as much
> money in her as made the whole share run £1,200 a man.
> They careened at St. Mary's and had some cattle from me,
> but for their victualling and sea store they bought from the
> Negros. I sold Captain Tew and his Company some of the
> goods brought in the *Charles* from New York. The sloop
> belonged most of her to Bermudas. Captain Tew set sail
> from St. Mary's . . . bound for America.

Yet Tew did not sail direct. Laden down with riches and stores—purchased, as Baldridge notes, from the same ship that Frederick Phillipse had sent the year before—Tew rendezvoused at sea with the French pirate Captain Mission. The story of Mission's Libertatia, a pirate colony on the mainland of Madagascar that rivaled St. Mary's, is heavily clouded by myth and romance. But the bare facts were these: Mission, evidently much taken with his erstwhile English enemy, offered Tew the command of a small flotilla sent to capture slaving ships off Guinea. Ironically, given the wording of Tew's original commission from

Richier, the first slaver he seized was English. Two hundred and forty slaves were taken on board. Several other captures followed, and Tew returned to Madagascar with more than five hundred slaves in total. His vessel, borrowed from Captain Mission, had an equally ironic name: *Liberty*.

Shortly thereafter Tew declared his intention to return home, as he had originally intended. It was well over a year since his departure from Hamilton, and his Bermudian investors would be anxious. Yet Tew was bringing them not only riches but the prospect of a new trade route: having observed Baldridge's relation with Frederick Phillipse, he proposed to be the middleman for a similar arrangement between Mission and the Bermudians. He would, he told Mission, carry the goods himself. Mission responded enthusiastically, and Tew left for Bermuda in the winter of 1692.

Fortune and fate intervened on the return voyage. A wild gale struck the *Amity* somewhere in the South Atlantic, and to save his ship from being dismasted Tew was forced to alter course. Even after the gale had blown itself out the trade winds would not favor him, and the *Amity* abandoned all hope of making Bermuda and sailed instead for Tew's own home, Newport. He arrived in April 1693 and was given a hero's welcome, all the more so after it became known what he brought with him. Tew unloaded a prince's ransom worth of stolen gold, silver, and sundry goods on the dock and promptly commenced an auction. As his exploits in the Red Sea circulated through the usual channels of gossip, Governor Samuel Cranston himself appeared at the piers and presented Tew at society dinners. Thomas Tew was the toast of Newport. The crew of the *Amity* returned as wealthy men and set at once to spending their fortunes in the taverns and brothels of the town.

Tew and the Governors

Tew punctiliously sent on an account of his voyage to his Bermudian investors, along with instructions on how to claim their fortunes (Tew was canny; he did not trust any other captain to carry the gold to Bermuda, but instead buried the larger portion in the Newport sand—shades of Robert Louis Stevenson!—and left £560 with a Boston lawyer with further instructions to remit it to any agent of William Outerbridge). While in Boston, again selling a share of his booty on the docks, Tew solicited a second privateering commission from Governor Easton. Easton had granted them before, and would again, but for some reason this time he refused. Perhaps rumors had reached him of the English slave ship that Tew had captured or of his alliance with the enemy Captain Mission; more likely he was simply not impressed by this arrogant Rhode Island mariner with his newfound wealth. Tew went back to Newport and made the same request to Governor Cranston, who for the fee of £500 promptly granted him license to "harass the French." One wonders why he did not seek out Cranston first.

While his ship was being fitted out in Newport a mad rush to sign onto Tew's next voyage ensued. "Servants from most places in the country running from their masters, sons from their parents and had their children & relations going against their wills," all appeared on the wharves, each proclaiming their skills. News of Thomas Tew's adventures had, thanks to his own perambulations, circulated throughout the Northeastern colonies.

Tew left for the Red Sea again with a fresh crew and a revictualled *Amity* just a few months after he had arrived. Once again his luck held. Off the coast of Arabia the *Amity* encountered a vast treasure ship belonging to the Great Mogul and carrying (according to Tew's own reports, likely exaggerated) one thousand pilgrims and one hundred guns, all headed for Mecca. But the Moorish vessel "made a very poor defense, being encumbered with the goods and number of passengers they carried," and surrendered with nothing more than a token resistance. The pirates found themselves in possession of a heavily laden and almost inoperable craft. One account maintains that they put the Moorish vessel ashore in Aden and released the majority of the prisoners, keeping some one hundred young girls from twelve to eighteen years old for their own enjoyment.

Hereafter the record of Tew's voyage becomes murky. Defoe claims that Tew in this enterprise was accompanied by Captain Mission and proceeds to weave a long tale about their mutual adventures in the pirate colony Libertatia. It is a fascinating story, full of rich narrative detail (including the drafting of a pirate constitution), but the dates do not add up. For Tew was back in the Americas by the spring of 1694 and dead—according to most reports—by late 1695. There just wasn't time for Libertatia, a place that (as most historiography maintains) probably did not even exist.

What is known is that Tew arrived again in Rhode Island in April of 1694, where once again Governor Cranston met him and congratulated him for his successes. Exhausted and vastly rich, Thomas Tew might have had some thought of retiring. Defoe writes that "he had an easy fortune and designed to live quietly at home, but those of his men who lived near him, having squandered their shares, were continually soliciting him to make another trip." So if he had one, his retirement was an exceedingly short one. A traveler who encountered Tew at an inn one night in October 1694 fell into conversation with him, and the pirate was remarkably candid. "He was free in discourse with me," young John Graves would write, "and declared that he was last year in the Red Sea; that he had taken a rich ship belonging to the Mogul and had received for his owner's dividend and his sloop's twelve thousand odd hundred pounds, while his men had received upwards of a thousand pounds each." Graves also records a telling fact: "When I returned to Boston there was another barque of about thirty tons ready to sail and join Tew in the same account."

In that same month Tew left the comforts of his family home in Newport and arrived in New York, where his fame had preceded him. It was not an idle journey; Tew was looking for backers and a fresh commission. Governor Fletcher met him at the pier, as Cranston had done, and "entertained him and drove him about in his coach, though Tew publicly declared that he would make another voyage to the Red Sea and make New York his port of return." It is interesting to note the same circumstance—the fact that Fletcher paraded Tew about in his carriage—appears prominently in two independent sources. What was so significant about these carriage rides? Clearly Fletcher not only entertained the pirate but did so openly, notoriously. Neither man was making any secret of his friendship with the other. For those irate observers who would later call piracy and illegal trade as "the beloved twins of the merchants of New York," such obvious display merely added insult to injury.

Tew remained in New York for several weeks, a guest of the governor. There is some evidence that he might have obtained the backing of Frederick Phillipse for his next cruise, but no actual record survives.

In the matter of the commission, however, Tew was successful. For £300, his voyage received the imprimatur of the crown. Signed at Fort William on November 2, 1694 (the same fort which Leisler had held so doggedly just three years before), Thomas Tew was given a privateering commission to hunt the French along the Gulf of Saint Lawrence. At the bottom appeared the signatures of Governor Benjamin Fletcher and his secretary, Daniel Horan. Beneath them was an almost illegible scrawl: Edward Coates, bondsman. Tew had put up a bond of £3,000 as promise of his good faith, endorsed by Coates. Should he depart from the wording of the commission, not only would he be a criminal, he would forfeit this princely sum.

The farcical nature of the bond—everyone knew perfectly well where Tew was headed, and it certainly wasn't the Saint Lawrence—was demonstrated by the bondsman himself. Edward Coates was a pirate. He had served with Mason on board the *Jacob*, the same ship that Leisler had commissioned in 1691, and taken his own sloop, the *Nassau*, on a Red Sea excursion in 1692. Though not as successful as Tew, Coates had enriched his New York backers by £500 on the first voyage and 2,800 pieces of eight on the second. On both occasions he acted under the commission of his good friend Governor Fletcher. In 1695, not long after Tew departed on his last cruise, Coates would present the governor with the *Jacob*, valued at £2,000, as a present. The whole issue of bonds was a common ruse, as evidenced by how they were handled ex post facto. Later investigation revealed that pirates regularly gave bonds declaring their "honest" intentions, which the governor's secretary—having entered them dutifully into the records—promptly destroyed as redundant scraps of paper.

Tew left America for the last time in November, joined by the interestingly named Captain Want and Captain Wake, two pirates from the Carolinas who had also been in Governor Fletcher's favor. In June 1695 he arrived at the mouth of the Red Sea, where he met up with another famous pirate, of whom much will be said later: Henry Every. In those first summer weeks Tew's third voyage seemed to have all the promise of his last two. A Moorish vessel that surrendered without firing a shot (which seems a common theme among the Red Sea traders) proved to contain more than £60,000. Shortly thereafter another vessel hove to, which included among its stores several caskets full of jewels and a ruby-encrusted saddle for the Great Mogul. Then, suddenly, all mention of the pirate Thomas Tew disappears from the record, almost as though the sea itself had swallowed him. As with Every, Baldridge, and other pirates of the golden age, accounts of his end vary widely. One thing was certain: Tew never returned to Rhode Island. Given that, the most likely story of his demise comes from Defoe, who relates that not long after his successes in the summer of 1695, during yet another engagement with a Moorish ship, "a shot carried away the rim of Tew's belly, who held his bowels with his hands some small space. When he dropped, it struck such terror in his men that they suffered themselves to be taken without making resistance."

Tew might have been dead, but he was still much anticipated by his investors, his sponsors, and the merchants of New England. As late as 1697 Jeremiah Basse, governor of New Jersey, was writing to the Board of Trade:

> In all I am told that there are [pirates] gone from Boston, New York, Pennsylvania and Carolina, from each one ship and from Rhode Island two. . . . The persons expected to return are Tew's company, and all those that sailed from New York and Rhode Island. It is expected that they will try to conceal themselves in the Jerseys or Pennsylvania, being little inhabited about the harbor, they reckon themselves safe there. I am told that some persons have already been preparing for their reception there.

Another man eagerly awaiting Tew's return, but for very different reasons, was the governor of New York, Richard Coote, First Lord Bellomont. After Benjamin Fletcher's fall from grace in 1699, Bellomont was eagerly amassing any evidence of his predecessor's relations with the pirates. When Tew came back, he would be the showpiece of Bellomont's charges against the late governor. Almost immediately after taking office, Bellomont wrote to the Board of Trade to prepare the ground. "Captain Tew has a commission from the Governor of New York to cruise against the French," he informed them:

> He came out on pretence of loading negroes at Madagascar, but his design was always to go into the seas, having about seventy men on his sloop of sixty tons. He made a voyage three years ago in which his share was £8,000. . . . Colonel Fletcher told Tew he should not come there [New

York] again unless he brought store of money, and it is said
that Tew gave him £300 for his commission. He is gone to
make a voyage in the Red Sea, and if he makes his voyage
will be back about this time. This is the third time that
Tew has gone out, breaking up [disbanding his crew] for
the first time in New England and the second time in New
York.

Bellomont also took the opportunity to note in passing that one
Captain Gough, who kept a ship chandler's shop in Boston, had made
a tidy fortune out of victualling Tew and his compatriots.

Pirates and Patrons

The case of Thomas Tew survives because of the fantastic sums that Tew
accrued during the course of his brief, violent career. But it is the
penumbra around the story that is most interesting, as it reveals much
about the workings of pirate patronage and the Red Sea trade. Nearly
all accounts of the period make a great deal of Tew's purchase of a commission from Fletcher for the infamous sum of £300. Few, however,
note that it was actually the third such commission: the first was purchased from Governor Richier of Bermuda and the second from Governor Cranston of Rhode Island. Similarly, the amount involved was
not exceptional; Governor Cranston charged £200 more. Tew's example thus negates the supposition that Fletcher was in some way anom-
alous in his favoring of pirates—a crucial point, as we turn to look at
the careers of other governors and the political climate of the age.
Indeed, Tew's perambulations from one colony to the next; his collection of a diverse crew (including the Carolina men Want and Wake);
his dealings with other pirates like Coates, Mission, and Avery; and his
commerce in New York with Frederick Phillipse and in Madagascar with
Adam Baldridge—all come together to create a vivid picture of the inter-
connectedness of piracy in this period. Within this panorama the role
of the governors takes on its proper significance: one part among many,
all working in apparently seamless harmony, but crucial nonetheless in
itself. Consider the words of Lord Bellomont in 1697:

> The place that receives them [the pirates] is chiefly Mada-
> gascar, where they must touch both coming and going. All
> the ships that are now out are from New England, except

Tew from New York and Want from Carolina. They build
their ships in New England, but come out under pretense
of trading from island to island. . . . On first coming they
generally go first to the Isle of May for salt, then to Fernando for water, then round the Cape of Good Hope to
Madagascar to victual and water and so for Batsky where
they wait for the traders between Surat and Mecca and
Tuda, who must come at a certain time because of the
trade wind. When they come back they have no place to
go to but Providence [i.e., New Providence, Bahamas],
Carolina, New York, New England and Rhode Island,
where they have all along been kindly received.

Benjamin Fletcher is remembered most as Tew's patron (thanks to
the recorded disparagements of Lord Bellomont), but just as other governors sponsored Tew, other pirates solicited—and received—Fletcher's
patronage. First was the aforementioned Edward Coates, inheritor of
the *Jacob* and close friend of the governor. Another was William Mason,
the *Jacob*'s first commander and the same pirate who had first received
his commission from Jacob Leisler. When Mason returned from Madagascar in 1692 he found a very different government awaiting him. But
being both canny and careful, he was quick to ingratiate himself with
Fletcher and was rewarded with a second commission, this for the *Pearl*,
a sizable vessel of two hundred men and sixteen guns. Arriving in Rhode
Island in 1694, much like Thomas Tew, he sought out Governor
Cranston. Also like Tew, Mason was a gentleman; his grandfather was
none other than Cranston's predecessor, Governor Samuel Gorton.
Cranston granted a new commission with alacrity, and Mason was off
to the Red Sea again. Retiring to New York in 1699, he was reputed to
have amassed a fortune in excess of £30,000.

Another example of Fletcher's sponsorship was Richard Glover, a
well-known and respected slaver who received his commission from
Fletcher to carry slaves from the Madagascar coast in 1694. He had previously completed several of these voyages. Yet, as James Lydon notes,
slavers do not usually require twenty guns and more than one hundred
men. Nor do they sail with piratical escorts: in this case, John Hoar.
Hoar, captain of the *John and Rebecca* (named, touchingly, after himself
and his wife), purchased a privateering commission from Fletcher for
Canadian waters, the same boilerplate that Tew received just a few

months later. Glover and Hoar embarked on a long, if unspectacular, pirate voyage. When Hoar at last arrived in St. Mary's, his only booty was a cache of chintzes and calicoes taken off a Persian trading vessel.

Fletcher's council, no less than himself, profited from the pirate trade. Frederick Phillipse was perhaps the most obvious case, albeit not the only one. Nicholas Bayard and William Nicholls (the former deputy governor) were accused by Lord Bellomont of acting as "agents" in piratical deals; Stephen Brooke, William French, Thomas Willet, Thomas Clark, and William Smith were all alleged to have met frequently at night in the old Whitehead Inn, where financing deals with notorious pirates were thrashed out. Again, one must take all this evidence with a grain of salt, coming as it does from one who had a particular interest in blacking the names of Fletcher and his cohorts. Harder to deny, however, was the case of another council member, James Emott, who admitted to acting as Fletcher's personal representative with many notorious pirates. He had acted for the other councilors as well.

Pirate trade had become so entrenched by the late seventeenth century, thanks to the active sponsorship of men like Benjamin Fletcher, that it had assumed the mantle of legitimate business. One historian described New York during this period as "abound[ing] with well-dressed beaus and their brocade-bedecked wives or sweethearts, and with pirates who swaggered about the streets with rolling gait, and sometimes staggered, as they squandered their booty." Surely there is some romanticism at work in this depiction, but it is indicative all the same. There can be no doubt that piracy infused a welcome stream of ready cash into a marketplace that still reeled under the effects of the Navigation Acts. And the profits were enormous. It is estimated that in 1695 alone, five years before the Red Sea trade reached its zenith, there were some sixty pirate captains sailing in and out of New York, each with crews numbering between seventy and one hundred men, and that each man's share averaged between £1,000 and £1,500 per voyage. This was an era during which the average laborer in England earned less than £100 per year. One brave and impecunious customs agent reported to the Board of Trade in 1698 that he estimated the annual dividend of pirate trade for the colony of New York to be somewhere in the region of £100,000. The question for governors was whether the benefit of turning a blind eye to such trade outweighed the political risks. In most cases they determined it did.

Addressing the Pennsylvania Assembly on the eve of his appointment as governor, Fletcher lectured them that "there is an act against pyrates and privateers, with limitation of time for their coming into the province & entering into bonds for their future good behavior, which was drawn in England and sent with me to be enacted in New York." This, he said, meant that "pirates and privateers may become good men at last, and the design of that Law is to draw them from their evil courses, and that they may become good subjects & inhabitants amongst us, to help our government. . . . I hope it will meet with no opposition." It didn't.

Tew, Glover, Hoar, Want—these were men from respected families, whose mercantile careers had made them, if not wealthy, at least solidly middle class. They were not highway robbers perched on lonely roads, waiting to spring on local coaches. Their depredations occurred far away, against men and nations whom a solid, insular New Yorker like Benjamin Fletcher could only feel contempt. " 'Tis no sin for a Christian to kill a heathen," Richard Glover would later claim, and most in the Atlantic colonies would have agreed with him. When Fletcher spoke of pirates becoming "good subjects and inhabitants amongst us," his only obfuscation was the tense; as far as he was concerned, they already were. Time and again, his writings and protestations made this clear. Even when he was knowingly lying, his respect for the pirates—his innate sense that they were *"de notre monde"*—crept through:

> Captain Tew brought no ship into this port. He came as a stranger and came to my table like other strangers who visit this province. He told me he had a sloop well manned and gave bond to fight the French at the mouth of Canada river, whereupon I gave him a commission and instructions accordingly. . . . It may be my misfortune, but not my crime, if they turn pirates. I have heard of none yet that have done so.

Whitehall didn't seem to know quite how to handle such flagrant disregard of its orders. As far as the Lords of Trade were concerned, there was no difference between a pirate and a highway robber. That the governors might see things differently was tacitly acknowledged in an antipiracy proclamation of September 10, 1692:

> And for the better and more speedy execution of justice
> upon such who have committed piracies . . . be it further
> enacted that all felonies, piracies, robberies, murders or
> confederacies that hereafter shall be committed upon the
> sea . . . shall be enquired, tried, heard, determined and
> judged in such form as if such offense had been committed
> on the land.

Even though the 1692 act, and acts that followed, explicitly extended culpability to those "that shall in any way knowingly entertain, harbor, conceal, trade, or hold correspondence by letters" with pirates, the sum effect was negligible. Colonists continued to trade with pirates as though the acts had never been promulgated, and governors routinely ignored them. In 1696 the Commissioners of the Customs gloomily reported that "in the case of the encouragement of privateers by Governors," the king could certainly order the governors to "give no privileges to privateers, unless they first give security in £1,000 for good behavior." But there was no means of enforcing this order, beyond the governor's own good faith. And, worse yet, "we understand from Mr. Randolph that what are here called privateers are in reality freebooters, who ought to be wholly suppressed."

They ought indeed, but how? That was a question which the Lords of Trade never fully answered. As long as the men charged with pursuing the pirates neglected to do so, what force could compel them? Nevertheless, Fletcher's bland denials and coy concealments are revealing. They demonstrate that, even though piracy was swiftly becoming a respected staple of colonial commerce, governors still hesitated to act in open and obvious contravention to the royal will. A pattern of subterfuge was developing. Governors could no more discourage piratical trade by their own colonists than they could halt piratical depredations by their erstwhile enemies, France and Spain. In plain terms, they lacked the manpower. The Royal Navy gave sparse protection to their colonies, and only a coherent and zealous military response could have even begun to check the pirate hegemony on the Atlantic coast. Hence, governors like Fletcher erected the plausible ruse of privateer/pirate hunter, which gave color of law to the pirate's activities, facilitated trade, and kept the dignity of the crown intact.

It was a ruse that worked well, so long as none came along to challenge it. Cranston, Richier, Markham, and many others enjoyed long and profitable careers, even though the Lords of Trade knew perfectly well from numerous complaints that they countenanced and subsidized piracy. But when the political winds shifted in Whitehall, and a new government came to power, Benjamin Fletcher would find himself isolated and disgraced. The first thunderclap came as early as February 1696. Disturbed by reports from Peter Delanoy and others, the Lords of Trade wrote Fletcher that "further complaints have been made to His Majesty from other colonies and especially from Jamaica, that the great temptation to Piracy by the entertainment given to pirates in several places had been other means of seducing their inhabitants from them." This was standard boilerplate; His Majesty had bewailed the favor given to pirates since the days of James I. The next sentence was more worrisome, however: "And His Majesty, being highly sensible how such practices tend to dishonor the English name and nation, has therefore ordered us strictly to require the respective Governors of all this Plantations to take due care for the future that no Pirates or Sea Robbers be anywhere sheltered or entertained under the severest penalties."

Still nothing altogether out of the ordinary. It looked like the usual protestation. But then Fletcher read the next lines with mounting horror:

> We are obliged in giving you to recommend it so much particularly to your care, by reason that in the information lately given on Tryal of several of Every's crew, your government is named as a place of protection for such villains and your favor in particular to Captain Tew is given as an instance of it.

Accusations from men like Peter Delanoy were of no great matter, but this was something else again. An accusation could be denied, explained, even ignored. The long ocean passage made certain of that. But, as Benjamin Fletcher now realized, a trial at the Old Bailey was poised to blow the lid off the entire business of pirate patronage and lay the culpability of the governors before an avid—and outraged—British public.

Blackbeard, alias Edward Teach, takes aim at Lieutenant Maynard in this contemporary wood-cut. The image is surprisingly accurate: at the base Maynard's men swarm up onto the deck of the *Pearl*, and behind Blackbeard is the shadowy figure of the seaman who cut his throat. THE GRANGER COLLECTION, NEW YORK

QUEEN ELIZABETH KNIGHTING DRAKE ON BOARD THE "GOLDEN HIND" AT DEPTFORD, APRIL 4, 1581
From a drawing by Sir John Gilbert, R.A.

A scene that never happened. Queen Elizabeth I knights Francis Drake on the deck of the *Golden Hind*, April 4, 1581. In reality, the honor of granting the knighthood was given to M. Marchaumont, envoy of the King of France. Drake was among the most notorious of the sixteenth-century privateers, providing the precedent and model for legions of pirates for more than a hundred years. PRINT COLLECTION, MIRIAM AND IRA D. WALLACH DIVISION OF ART, PRINTS, AND PHOTOGRAPHS, THE NEW YORK PUBLIC LIBRARY, ASTOR, LENOX, AND TILDEN FOUNDATIONS

Sir Henry Morgan, famed buccaneer and later lieutenant governor of Jamaica, from the frontispiece to the Dutch edition of Alexander Esquemeling's account. COURTESY OF THE JOHN CARTER BROWN LIBRARY AT BROWN UNIVERSITY

JOHAN MORGAN,
geboren in de Provincie van Walles in Engelandt
Generaal van de Roovers op Jamaica.

Henry Morgan and his men sack Portobello on June 26, 1688. Morgan's exploits against the Spanish and his close relation with Governor Thomas Modyford of Jamaica bridged the gap between the state-sponsored privateering of the sixteenth century and outright piracy of the seventeenth. THE GRANGER COLLECTION, NEW YORK

Die Anlandung der Englischen Trouppen zu Neu York   Debarquement des Trouppes angloises a nouvelle York

A view of New York during the tenure of Governor Benjamin Fletcher. Through an alliance between governor, merchants, and pirates, New York became a preeminent trading port in the Fletcher era. COURTESY OF THE JOHN CARTER BROWN LIBRARY AT BROWN UNIVERSITY

Nineteenth-century lithographer Howard Pyle's depiction of the meeting between Thomas Tew and Governor Benjamin Fletcher. The pirate regales his governor with adventuresome yarns, while Fletcher's face is obscured in shadow. Fletcher would be remembered as among the most brazen of pirate patrons, a reputation he only partly deserved.

Richard Coote, First Earl of Bellomont. Sent to the colonies in 1699 to eradicate the scourge of pirates, Bellomont quickly became embroiled in a controversy of his own.

Captain Kidd arrives in New York in this fanciful nineteenth century rendition. Kidd greets the ladies, while at right the governor and one of his adjutants anxiously confer. In fact, Kidd approached the American coast warily, dropping anchor in Long Island and sending an emissary to sound out Governor Bellomont. This scene would have had greater validity several years earlier, when Thomas Tew arrived in the colonies to a tumultuous welcome.

Captain Kidd is arrested in the home of Lord Bellomont, governor of New York, July 6, 1699. Kidd had counted on Bellomont, his former patron, to protect him from charges of piracy. But the political climate had shifted after the Every trials, and the Whig Lords' attitude toward the pirates had hardened. THE GRANGER COLLECTION, NEW YORK

A letter from Captain William Kidd to the Whig Lords, dated December 30, 1700. Kidd was writing from Newgate prison, begging the lords to release him from the close confinement he had suffered there for nine months. Kidd's capture and return to London proved a serious embarrassment for many of his erstwhile backers, including the then governor of New York, Lord Bellomont. THE NATIONAL ARCHIVES, UNITED KINGDOM

Woodes Rogers, governor of the Bahamas, shown here with his family late in life. A former privateer, Rogers became governor of the Bahamas in 1718 and quickly set about transforming the islands from a pirates' nest to a viable colony. Rogers was among the first generation of colonial governors to actively address the pirate menace. NATIONAL MARITIME MUSEUM, GREENWICH, LONDON

- 8 -

Henry Every, "As Yet an Englishman's Friend"

MAY 30, 1694

Captain Gibson had a terrible hangover. He awoke early in the master's cabin of the English-registered sloop *Charles II* to the sound of blocks shrieking and feet pattering overhead. The little room pitched and heaved—heavy swell for riding at anchor, he thought. The *Charles II* had put in at the Spanish port of La Coruna for supplies and passengers and to accept a commission from the Spanish government to hunt French smugglers. But thus far the captain had spent little time arranging either: he was "much addicted to his Punch," according to later chroniclers, and had found ready supply of it ashore. Most of the work had been done by his industrious, ever-cheerful first mate. This was all right with Gibson, though the mate's manner toward him—a curious combination of deference and half-concealed amusement—was somewhat disquieting. Even more disquieting was the sight that now met his groggy, bloodshot eyes. The objects on his nightstand swayed ominously, and the light through the aft windows was strange: the sun, for some reason, had apparently risen in the west. It was this last incongruity that made the desperately ill captain turn fretfully in his bunk and reach for the summoning bell. He rang it several times.

The first mate appeared promptly, as was his custom. He was beaming. That was customary too: accounts described him as "middle-sized, inclinable to fat and of a jolly complexion." Two men stood behind him. They were less jolly: one was holding a pistol casually pointed to the floor. "What is the matter?" Gibson asked the first mate.

Nothing at all, the mate replied, still smiling.

"Something's the matter with the ship," Gibson insisted. He might not have been much of a mariner, but the movement under him was stronger than anything delirium tremens could conjure up. "What is the weather?" he pressed. "Does she drive?"

"No, no," the other man assured him. "We are at sea with a fair wind and good weather."

Gibson sat bolt upright on his bunk. "At sea!" he cried. "How can that be?"

The first mate was grinning now. "Come, come," he said, "don't be in a fright. Put your clothes on and I'll let you into the secret."

As Gibson struggled into his trousers, the first mate told him the whole story. The crew had elected to abandon the fruitless task of hunting French smugglers; many, in fact, had signed on the *Charles II* with the express purpose of seizing the ship and sailing her "to make our fortunes" in the seas around Madagascar. Among these was the cheerful first mate, Henry Every.

Every and his crew had laid their plans quietly and well. More than half the crew of the *Charles II* had been with him from the start, including all the officers save the second mate, David Creagh. Every, whose talents for persuasion would soon become legendary, then went over to the escorting ship, the *James*, and picked up an additional sixteen conspirators. Every gave them a code phrase to signal the mutiny, and on the morning of May 30 the plan went into action. A longboat from the *James* pulled up alongside the *Charles II*. The phrase—"Is the drunken boatswain on board?"—was duly bellowed from the boat. "Aye," Every called back. The longboat came alongside, and the *James* men swarmed on deck. Those few among the crew that had either refused to join or were unaware of Every's plans were quickly co-opted. Creagh, the second mate, heard the commotion above and hurried onto the deck, only to find a pistol aimed at his face. He was escorted meekly below again. The crew gently raised the *Charles II*'s anchor, while others went aloft and loosed the sails. Captain Humphreys, captain of the *James*, cried out to Every that some of his, Humphreys's, men were deserting. Every replied calmly that he knew that perfectly well. The *Charles II* hoisted topsails and began to make its way carefully out of the harbor. Humphreys tried, with his reduced crew, to give chase. Failing in that, he signaled the commander of the local *guarda costa*, a Dutch frigate patrolling the harbor, that the *Charles II*'s crew had mutinied and were escaping. The Dutch captain looked through his glass at the cool way in which Every and his crew conducted themselves on deck and made his own decision. The *Charles II* passed by unmolested.

When the greenish shoal seas gave way to big blue Atlantic rollers, Every took a couple of hands with him and went to respond to the captain's summons.

"You must know," Every concluded, "that I am captain of this ship now. And this is my cabin, therefore you must walk out. I am bound for Madagascar, with the design of making my own fortune, and that of all the brave fellows joined with me."

Every then offered the unfortunate Gibson a choice: he could come with him as his second mate (an extraordinarily generous gesture, considering Gibson's ineptitude), or he could be put ashore in La Coruna. Gibson, summoning what was left of his dignity, chose the latter. He and a few other crew, including second-mate Creagh, were put off in a longboat and given a compass to guide them back to shore. Then the *Charles II*, soon to be renamed the *Fancy*, turned to starboard and made course for the Cape Verde Islands, en route to the Red Sea.

Rake's Progress

Henry Every, alias Long Ben Avery, alias Henry Bridgeman, was a study in contradictions. His piratical career would be more profitable than any before or since, his name second only to that of Blackbeard in the pantheon of seagoing rogues, yet he was neither a particularly good mariner nor an inspired leader of men. He could be witty and generous, or sullen and cruel, depending on his mood. He professed himself to be patriotic yet was one of relatively few pirates in the seventeenth century to sail without a privateering commission—at a time when such commissions were readily available to anyone who wanted one. This in turn would give rise to another irony: Every's depredations, which occurred in the Red Sea and without any color of law whatsoever, would nevertheless reveal more about the quiet accord between Atlantic governors and pirates than any other.

Every's only consistent characteristic was a quicksilver opacity. Despite his fearsome reputation, he was less a great pirate than an exceptionally gifted confidence man. Nothing about him was ever as it seemed: the true man concealed, as many of his closest friends admitted, behind the basilisk, inscrutable smile. Even his early life is shrouded in mystery. He appears to have been born in Devon, perhaps even in the same village as Henry Morgan, around 1653. One account claims that his father was once a captain in Cromwell's navy. Yet it is likely that a different role model inspired him. As a young man he must have been well aware of Henry Morgan's reputation and would likely have idolized him. It might have been Morgan's example that led Every to a seafaring career, but the exact nature of that career is not known. Some accounts place him, like his father, in the Royal Navy, but there is nothing to substantiate this. The first record of Every comes in 1693 from an agent of the Royal Africa Company, who identified him as a slave trader serving under a commission from Isaac Richier, the much-maligned governor of Bermuda. Something of Every's jolly duplicity surfaces in the description left by the agent: "I have nowhere met the negroes so shy as here," he wrote, "which makes me fancy they have had tricks played on them by such blades as Long Ben, alias Every, who have seized them and carried them away."

Even his compatriots didn't quite know what to make of him. At trial in 1697, one of his crew offered a depiction that was almost comically contradictory:

> [Every was] daring and good tempered, but insolent and
> uneasy at times, and always unforgiving if at any time
> imposed upon. His manner of living was imprinted in his
> face, and his profession might easily be told from it. . . .
> He still had many principles of morality which many sub-
> jects of the King have experienced.

If indeed Every still possessed an English morality, it did not much affect his choice of prey. Reaching the Cape Verde Islands, the *Fancy* hoisted the flag of Saint George and swiftly took three small English vessels, seizing victuals and trinkets from them. Every then sent a raiding party ashore, where they found and captured the Portuguese governor and brought him back on board as a hostage. They released him in exchange for ransom and then left for the Guinea coast. There Every played his "tricks" again, soliciting a local chieftain to exchange gold dust for a share of the *Fancy*'s plundered cargo. When the Negroes arrived on board with the gold, Every promptly took it and shackled them in the hold. He would later offer several of them as slaves to the Portuguese government as an act of good faith.

Every and the *Fancy* then headed south along the African coast, stopping at Fernando Po and Cape Lopez and finally at Anamabu. In December 1694 the *Fancy* rounded the Cape of Good Hope, arriving in Madagascar the following month. He stayed only long enough to take on fresh provisions from Adam Baldridge (who duly noted Every's presence on the island, along with Tew, Glover, Hoar, and Wake), then he made at once for the island of Johanna. There, in the protection of a sheltered bay, Every careened his ship and began stripping off much of the upper works, making her nimbler and faster. As he did so, Every composed a curious testament that he left with the local chief, along with instructions to pass it along to the first English nonpiratical vessel that arrived. The chief did as requested, and by May 1695 the English governor at Bombay, Sir James Gayer, held it in his hands. Half apologia, half bravado, its patriotism counterbalanced by a distinctly cunning streak, it was a document much like Every himself:

> February 28, 1695,
>   To all English Commanders, let this satisfie, That I was riding here at this instant in the Ship *Fancy*, Man of War, formerly the *Charles* of the Spanish Expedition, who departed from Croniae [Coruna] the 7th of May 1694, Being (and am now) in a Ship of 46 Guns, 150 Men, and bound to Seek our Fortunes. I have never as yet wronged any English or Dutch, nor ever intend whilst I am Commander. Wherefore as I commonly speak with all Ships, I desire whoever comes to the perusal of this to take this Signall, that if you, or any whom you may inform, are desirous to know what wee are at a distance, Then make your Ancient [i.e., ensign, flag] up in a Ball or Bundle and hoist him at the Mizenpeek, the Mizen being furled. I shall answer with the same and never molest you, for my Men are hungry, Stout, and resolute, and should they exceed my Desire I cannot help myself. As yet an Englishman's friend,
>
>   HENRY AVERY

What Every's motives were in crafting this letter we can only guess. Clearly he had a healthy fear of capture and wanted to do all he could to discourage the English from "molesting" him. Hence his outright lie that he had "never as yet wronged" any English ship, conveniently overlooking the three trading vessels he plundered off Cape Verde and his own mutiny on the *Charles II*. One can only surmise that, in the absence of a privateering commission (unlike Tew, Want, and the others, Every had never had the opportunity to solicit one from a sympathetic colonial governor), Every was essentially writing one for himself. Whatever his intentions, neither Sir James nor anyone east of the Atlantic seaboard was likely to condone his actions. The letter from colonial agent Robert Blackborne that contained Every's document had a codicil that put the matter very plain:

> That the said pirate had in pursuance of his said declaration pillaged several Ships belonging to the Subjects of the Mogul . . . is known, Whereby the said Governor and Company [that is, the East India Company] have reason

to fear many great inconveniences may attend them not
only from reprisals which may be made upon them at Sur-
rat . . . but also from the interruption which may be given
to their trade from port to port in India, as well as to their
trade to and from thence to England.

For Englishmen in America, the Red Sea pirates were a source of
trade; for those in the Red Sea itself, as well as in England, they were a
detriment to it. Such was the crucial difference in attitude toward piracy
in the colonial period and a source of deepening divisions between
England and the Atlantic colonies. Thus Every's "commission," which
might have been welcomed in the Caribbean, fell on unsympathetic
readers. Even before he had left Johanna, an East Indiaman had begun
to pursue him, catching the *Fancy* by surprise on the afternoon of March
15. Fortunately for Every, his ship was ready. "He was too nimble for
them by much," the colonial agent for the Great Mogul reported grimly,
"having taken down a great deal of his upper work. . . . This ship will
undoubtably [sail] into the Red Seas and we fear disappoint us of our
above expected goods."

The colonial agent was more right than he knew. Until his departure from Johanna, the piratical career of Henry Every was mediocre at
best. His prizes were small, gained more through trickery than seamanship. His crew was probably as hungry as he said, and a substantial portion of them were abandoned on Johanna during Every's hasty escape.

But then Every had a tremendous stroke of luck. Tacking swiftly
back to Madagascar, still in search of plunder, the *Fancy* came upon a
fleet of ships moving in convoy off the coast. When they put into the
shoals, Every set out in a jolly boat to reconnoiter with them in a small
trading post known, if contemporary accounts can be trusted, as Meat.
Every greeted them cordially and learned their identities. He must have
been astonished. Captains Want, Wake, Farrell, Mays, and Tew had
banded together and now sailed in armada fashion, fanning out like a
fishing net to capture any Muslim ship unfortunate enough to
encounter them. Each of them bore a commission from a colonial governor, which they flashed at him. Contrary to popular conceptions of
New York or Jamaica as the sole source of pirate patronage, during testimony at trial one of Every's crew provided a list of names and commissions that implicated nearly the entire Eastern Seaboard:

The *Dolphin*, Captain Want, commander, was a Spanish bottom, had sixty men on board and was fitted out at the Orkells [Whorekills] near Philadelphia. . . . The *Portsmouth Adventure* was fitted out at Rhode Island about the same time, Captain Joseph Faro [Farrell] Commander. . . . Then three sail more came to them, one commanded by Thomas Wake, fitted out from Boston in New England, another the *Pearl* Brigantine, William Mues [Mays] Commander, fitted out in Rhode Island, the third was the *Amity* Sloop, Thomas Tew Commander, fitted out at New York.

Henry Every, out of sheer chance, had fallen upon one of the greatest pirate fleets that ever sailed.

The armada left Madagascar and positioned itself strategically in the sea lane, waiting for the Muslim fleet that Thomas Tew had heard—from Adam Baldridge, naturally—was due to pass through at any moment. Every sent his men aloft and settled in for a long watch. On the morning of August 15 vigilance seemed to bear fruit. A Mocha sloop hove into view, and Every seized upon it avidly as the vanguard of the treasure fleet. Interrogating the captain of the captured vessel, he learned the truth: it was not the vanguard but the rear guard. The Muslim fleet had passed right through in the night.

Every summoned the other captains and told them the bad news. Some were in favor of abandoning the attempt; others wanted to chase after the fleet. A vote was held, and they elected to make chase. By the next day this decision proved to be the right one: a slow-moving trader named the *Fateh Mohamed* came into sight, which upon seizure was found to be carrying some £40,000 of silver. This capture, which would have made Every a very wealthy man, was diminished somewhat when parceled out to the crews of all six ships. Every began to regret his decision to join the convoy.

Then, some ten leagues off the coast of Surat, another ship appeared on the horizon. From a distance it looked like a Dutch East Indiaman, and Every hesitated to pursue. Indiamen were ferociously well armed and could—with a few well-placed shots—blow the *Fancy* right out of the water. When Every prevaricated, his crew became mutinous. "Every only cannonaded at a distance," Defoe later wrote, "and some of his men began to suspect that he was not the hero they took him for." Seeing the other pirate ships turn their bows to join in the fight, Every was emboldened. He closed the distance between the *Fancy* and the unknown ship and watched as she hoisted her colors: they were those of the Great Mogul. The Indiaman appeared to be making some kind of defense: men scurried along her decks, cannons rumbled out on their trucks. Every loaded his own with shot and prepared for a broadside.

The Muslim ship's volley came first, but it was Pyrrhic. One of the starboard cannons exploded, killing all the men around it and spreading mass confusion among the crew. In the ensuing melee Every and his men pulled alongside and boarded her, and after only a few moments of fierce fighting the terrified Muslims struck their colors.

She was the *Ganj-i-Sawai*, soon inevitably anglicized to *Gunsway*. The Arab name was more appropriate: it meant "Great Treasures." Goggling at the sight that met his eyes, Every could scarcely believe his good fortune. The ship was carrying several members of the Great Mogul's court, including the mogul's own daughter and an elderly concubine who served as her guardian. They were returning from a pilgrimage to Mecca. "It is known that Eastern people travel with the utmost magnificence," writes Defoe, "so they had with them all their slaves and attendants, their rich habits and jewels, with vessels of gold and silver, and great sums of money to defray the charges of their journey by land." While Every began to take stock of the riches on board, his men turned their attentions to the women. An English colonial agent for the Great Mogul gave a chilling report to the Lords of Trade of what happened then:

> It is certain that the Pyrates, which these People affirm were all English, did so very barbarously by the People of the *Gunsway* and Abdul Gofor's ship, to make them confess where their Money was, and there happened to be a great Umbraws Wife (as Wee hear) related to the King, returning from her Pilgrimage to Mecca, in her old age. She they abused very much, and forced several other Women, which caused one person of quality, his Wife and Nurse, to kill themselves to prevent the Husbands seeing them (and their being) ravished.

The agent concluded ominously, and lyrically, "All this will raise a black cloud at Court, which we wish may not produce a severe storm."

The storm was coming, but for the moment it still seemed far away. The carnage caused by Every's men was even worse than the agent had reported. Several of his crew would later testify that they had participated in gang rapes, many resulting in mutilation and some even in murder. The men were tortured and then thrown over the side. Though Every may not have participated in these outrages, he certainly did nothing to stop them.

He had other things on his mind. The treasure of the *Ganj-i-Sawai* amounted to some 500,000 gold and silver pieces, plus numerous jeweled baubles and miscellaneous silver cups, trinkets, and so on. It was the richest pirate haul ever taken, exceeding the record held by Thomas Tew by a good margin. The East India Company would later file an insurance claim for £600,000, though that was almost certainly an exaggeration. Plus there was the *Ganj-i-Sawai* herself. With sixty-two guns, five hundred crew members, and the capability of carrying six hundred passengers, she was claimed by Khafi Khan, the Indian historian, to be the most formidable ship in the Muslim fleet. This, added to Every's share from the *Fateh Mohamed*, made him the wealthiest pirate in the world.

At least until the other pirates showed up.

Every did some quick calculating. Farrell in the *Portsmouth* had not come into the fighting; Mays and Tew had gone off in search of treasure elsewhere and thus had no idea of this incredible windfall. Only Captains Want and Wake had joined him in the battle, yet all would sooner or later expect their share when they rendezvoused. Every, that consummate trickster, saw no reason to be a gentleman among thieves. He summoned Want, Wake, and Farrell to his cabin on board the *Fancy* and offered them a proposition. Their ships were feeble and weak, he said, none mounting more than six guns apiece. His own had forty-six. "He bade them consider," Defoe wrote, "that the treasure they were possessed of would be sufficient for them all if they could secure it in some place on shore; therefore, all they had to fear was some misfortune in the voyage." Best to leave it to him, said Every, and sail in close convoy so that they could be assured of his fidelity. The credulous pirates agreed, and "the thing was done as agreed to, the treasure put on board of Avery, and the chests sealed."

Every waited until nightfall. Then, just as he had in La Coruna, he carefully slipped his anchor cables and picked his way silently out of the convoy. When the first morning light illuminated the scene, Every and the *Fancy* and the greatest pirate booty in recorded history were all gone.

The *Fancy* moved swiftly round the point of Bengal, pausing to take on provisions and sack a small Indian trader, which produced the surprising haul of 1,700,000 rupees. When they had put to sea again, Every and his crew were faced with a momentous decision. They were, at that moment, the wealthiest pirates that ever lived. The treasure in the *Fancy*'s hold would ensure a life of comfort and ease for every man on board. But like most great criminals, once the initial flush of success drained away, they were unsure of what to do next. The *Ganj-i-Sawai* had made their fortunes, but it had also made them marked men. Surely no place where English law could reach them would be safe. The logical choice, which appears to have been considered, was Madagascar. They could lose themselves forever there, with no fear of reprisal. But others balked. Despite Adam Baldridge's attempts at settlement, Madagascar offered few luxuries for a wealthy man. It was a fine place to revictual and satisfy one's lusts but little more. What was needed, they said, was a place where they could reestablish themselves as respectable men and still enjoy the fruits of their capture. They pressed for America.

Henry Every had his doubts. Though he could not know of the incredible outrage his actions would soon provoke throughout the known world, he certainly suspected that he would not be a welcome figure anywhere English law could touch. While some argued for New England (which was home to a good portion of the crew) and others for New York (where Governor Fletcher still kept amiable court), Every suggested the Bahamas. New Providence was known to be a congenial place for "gentlemen of fortune," and the governor there—a man named Cadwallader Jones—was known to be persuadable.

An argument ensued, though the exact nature would never be known. It was finally resolved to sail for New Providence, as Every had advised, but a substantial portion of the crew refused to follow. A number of French, Danes, and Englishmen were put ashore in the Mauritius, where they took their shares and disappeared from history. Every then made a brief return to his old habits, putting in at the Portuguese island São Tomé for yet another revictualling and offering as tender an outrageously false bill of exchange. The bill, presented no doubt with great solemnity to the dark-eyed Portuguese traders, was drawn on the Bank of Aldgate Pump and signed by the dubious personages Timothy Tugmutton and Simon Whifflepin. Even as a colossally wealthy man, the trickster Every couldn't resist engaging in a little flimflam.

Halfway across the Atlantic things grew more serious, as Every's crew mutinied outright, demanding that the captain make instead for Cayenne, in French Guiana. Though only twenty pirates stood with him, somehow Every managed to quell the uprising. The *Fancy* arrived in New Providence in late March 1696. Every at once sent a boat ashore with a courteous letter to Governor Jones, introducing himself and his crew and requesting safe harbor.

Every in New Providence

But unbeknownst to Every, he had walked into a political scandal of epic proportions. Governor Jones, whom Every had rightly suspected of being a friend to the pirates, was facing charges in his own council. One Thomas Bulkley, deputy secretary of the Bahamas, openly accused his governor of "arbitrary and tyrannical exercise of power, of neglect to fortify the place, of malversation of the public funds, and of inviting a notorious company of pirates to make war upon [English] subjects." The council promptly imprisoned Jones and appointed Bulkley to prosecute him. Then, just as the zealous Bulkley began assembling his evidence, the worst happened. "Jones," he later wrote, "continued to get a party of pirates and seditious persons to rescue him and his papers from the Government's hands, seized me and took my books from me and imprisoned me in heavy irons on board a ship infected with pestilence." There the unfortunate Bulkley was held for more than a year, as his wife died and his lands were seized and destroyed.

But the council had not been idle. Even with Jones assuming de facto control, they had written in secret to the Board of Trade and laid their troubles before it. The board answered by sending another man, Nicholas Trott, to supplant the egregious Jones. What followed bore marked similarity to the continuance of government in Jamaica a generation earlier. Trott assumed command in early 1696 and at once pardoned his predecessor, appointing Jones "to high places of trust." Trott also allowed Bulkley to languish in prison, proffering an additional charge of high treason against him on behalf of Jones and his cadre. Bulkley, who was scarcely in a position to appreciate irony, appeared in the dock with Jones as his prosecutor. The council, however, remained steadfast, and he was acquitted soon thereafter. Released and vindicated but practically penniless, Bulkley launched his own attack on Jones. He petitioned Trott to charge the disgraced governor, knowing full well that Trott would refuse and thus be revealed as the creature he was. But Nicholas Trott was canny. He did not refuse to prosecute Jones but rather agreed and then delayed the trial, citing one excuse after another. In the meantime he secretly arranged for transport and allowed Jones to escape the colony and Bulkley's wrath. The deputy secretary was obliged to abandon his shattered home, spend the remainder of his fortune on a passage to England, and present his case directly to the Board of Trade. "I have been obliged to leave everything," he wrote them from a rooming house in Kensington, "and come three thousand miles to obtain justice. I beg that the Proprietors may be compelled to compensate me for the damage done to me by their agents Jones and Trott."

Henry Every reached New Providence at the apex of the scandal, just at the time when Trott had assumed command. Thus his petition to Cadwallader Jones was answered, graciously and at length, by Nicholas Trott. Philip Middleton, one of Every's crew, would later recall the exchange in an examination before the London magistrates:

> A letter was writ to Mr. Nicholas Trott, Governor of Providence [sic], which letter this Deponent saw and heard it read, and declareth that the contents were that, provided he would give them liberty to come on shore and depart as they pleased (or words to this purpose), they promised to give the said Governor twenty pieces of eight and two pieces of gold a man and the said ship, and all that was in her.

This was confirmed by another deposition, by crewmate John Dann, who told the magistrates that the letter proposed "bringing their ship thither if they might be assured of protection and liberty to go away, which he promised them." In fact, he promised them a great deal more. Trott, according to Middleton, wrote back to Every "in very civil terms, assuring Captain Every that he and his company should be welcome (or words to this purpose) which said assurance was made good to them by Governor Trott after their arrival in Providence as effectually as they could desire."

If Every was surprised at receiving an answer from Trott, a man he had never heard of, he was comforted by its reassuring tone. He set at once to raising the bribe from his crew. It was, by several accounts, a princely sum: "Captain Every contributed 40 pieces of eight and four pieces of gold and every sailor (being one hundred men besides boys) twenty pieces of eight and two pieces of gold a man, which sum being collected were sent to Governor Trott."

As if to seal the deal, Every also made a present of the *Fancy*, a ship he had no real further use for and which already was attracting a great deal of uncomfortable attention abroad. The ship was of little value to Trott, but her guns—some forty-six twelve pounders—were invaluable. Every, the salesman par excellence, even threw in some casks of Madeira wine and a collection of African elephant tusks.

But New Providence did not prove to be the Illyria that Every had hoped. Despite the open amity of Trott and Jones, the Bahamas were sparse and even less populated than Madagascar (Trott would later claim that the city of New Providence had only sixty inhabitants at the time of Every's arrival, meaning that the pirate crew would have outnumbered the settlers two to one). Unable to spend their gains ashore, and frightened of setting out to more populated (and correspondingly more dangerous) locales, Every's men remained on board the *Fancy* and drank themselves into a perpetual stupor. Both the *Fancy* and her crew dwindled into desuetude until finally a violent storm rent the ship from its moorings and cast it on nearby rocks. The pirates were unharmed, but the *Fancy*—which according to Middleton had been improperly ballasted—was a total loss. It was time to leave New Providence.

The Board's Revenge

Meanwhile, the storm of international protest over the capture of the *Ganj-i-Sawai* was drawing inexorably closer. Much as the English had feared, the Great Mogul responded to this latest and greatest atrocity with vengeance. He ordered his army to Bombay, the key port for English trade, and closed four others: Surat, Broach, Agra, and Ahmedabad.

Sixty-four East India Company representatives were summarily jailed; one was even stoned to death. In October 1695 the Bombay representative wrote his superiors grimly:

> The 13th in the morning the *Gunsway*, one of the King's ships, arrived from Judda and Mocha, the Nocqueda [captain] and merchants with one voice proclaiming that they were robbed by four English ships near Bombay of a very great sum, and that the robbers had carried their plundered treasure on shore there, on which there was far greater noise than before. Upon this the Governor [Itiman Khan] sent a very strong guard to the factory and clapt all our people in irons, shut them up in a room, planked up all their windows, kept strict watches about them, that no one should have pen, ink or paper to write, stopped all the passages, that no letters might pass to us.

The Great Mogul's ire placed the East India Company in a touchy position. On the one hand, outrages such as this against the English people could not be tolerated. On the other, the mogul had a point. Indian trade was the crowning jewel of England's burgeoning mercantile empire, and anything that jeopardized it jeopardized England as well. Yet the central tenet of the mogul's claims was that it was England herself that was deliberately sabotaging this trade, for ends beyond his imagination. It was a hard accusation to refute. If England lacked the sufficient naval forces to police her own citizens, the mogul complained, what guarantees could she offer that any trade could be securely maintained?

Sir John Gayer, the company's representative in Bombay, rather weakly replied that not all pirates in the Red Seas were English. As proof, he handed over a scruffy sextet of Frenchmen captured at Mohilla. The Great Mogul executed them at once but was not convinced. The East India Company had filed an insurance claim for £350,000 for the loss of the *Ganj-i-Sawai*; the mogul instructed his representative, Itiman Khan, to double the claim. The message was clear: either the English were to find a way to curb their errant subjects, or the India trade would grind to a halt.

The Board of Trade reacted with unprecedented fervor. Because it was beyond its powers to stop all acts of piracy, the best the board could do would be to make an example of one in the hopes of deterring the others—an example that, moreover, they could use to placate the Great Mogul. That example was Henry Every. Even as the *Fancy* entered Caribbean waters, Whitehall was hurriedly dispatching messages to governors throughout the Atlantic world. Henry Every was to be taken: alive if possible, dead if necessary. Each and every pirate hunter in reach would be commandeered and commissioned to track him down. The proclamation appearing in print on August 10, 1696, had the force of a clarion call:

> Whereas we formerly received information from the Governor and Company of Merchants in London Trading with the West Indies that one Henry Every . . . had under English colours committed several acts of piracy upon the seas of Persia. . . . We do hereby command all His Majesty's Admirals, Captains, and other Officers at Sea, and all His Majesty's Governor Commanders of any forts, castles, or other places in His Majesties plantations, and all other officers and persons whatsoever, to seize and apprehend the said Henry Every.

The proclamation also contained an interesting provision, almost unique in Admiralty records to that time, and a tangible yardstick of the Board of Trade's desperate resolve. In bold strokes, it turned the pirates against themselves:

> And we do hereby further declare that in case any of the persons abovenamed (except Henry Every, alias Bridgeman) or any other persons who were in the said ship with Henry Every . . . so as they may be seized and taken, in order to be brought to Justice, he and they making such [disclosure of Every's whereabouts] shall have His Majesty's gracious pardon for their offenses. And we do hereby further declare that such person or persons . . . shall have the reward of five hundred pounds promised in the said former Proclamation for the discovery and seizure of the said Henry Every.

The response to this extraordinary document—part indictment, part bribe—was the first worldwide manhunt in recorded history. Governors hurriedly dispatched cutters to hunt him down, and a brisk trade was done for information on his whereabouts.

If New Providence had been uncomfortable before, it was now intolerable. Nicholas Trott had received his proclamation along with the other governors and promptly disregarded it. Pressure came from other quarters, however. Several of the pirates, desperate to reach a new safe haven, had written to Governor William Beeston of Jamaica. They had reason to trust his discretion: he was, like Trott, a known pirate broker. Beeston was not prepared to countenance the most hunted men on earth. He promptly and primly wrote in turn to the Board of Trade: "They [Every and his men] are arrived in Providence and have sent privately to me, to try if they could prevail with me to pardon them and let them come hither; and in order that I was told that it should be worth to me a great gun, but that could not tempt me from my duty." Beeston took the additional step of writing directly to Trott, guilelessly inquiring whether his esteemed colleague was aware that he was playing host to the most notorious band of criminals in the Atlantic.

Trott knew he must act, and quickly. If Beeston knew Every was in New Providence, soon others would as well. Pretending to have just received the proclamation from the lord justices (in fact it had arrived a month earlier, and Every had been a resident for more than seven months), Trott issued a warrant for the arrest of Every and his men. Then he quietly tipped them off and allowed all but a handful to escape.

What followed is unclear, as the pirates disbanded and made their hurried attempts at escape. Though much evidence would later surface at trial, the majority of Every's 113-man crew simply disappeared. In the end, only a dozen were captured, and six of those executed. For years the survivors would surface in odd places: Virginia, Pennsylvania, Jamaica, Connecticut, the Carolinas, even England.

But one man would never be found, and that was Every himself. The romantic story followed from the initial legend of the *Ganj-i-Sawai*: Every married his Indian princess and set down in some uncharted Caribbean isle to live out his days a contented and wealthy man. Daniel Defoe, writing two decades after the incident, had a darker end for the great pirate. He claims that Every made first for Boston "and seemed to have a desire for settling in those parts." This would have been extraordinary indeed, as Massachusetts was one of the least favorable colonies for pirates, and the town of Boston (unlike the more congenial New

York) was quite unknown to Every. Defoe maintains that Every afterward went to Ireland and from thence to Devonshire, his birthplace. Having successfully landed in the very heart of the nation sworn to destroy him, Every now faced the problem of living incognito. He had long since changed his name to Benjamin Bridgeman (a ruse that, as the lords justices' proclamation makes clear, was quickly discovered) and, in an age before Interpol, had little difficulty reestablishing himself in Bideford under an alias. The problem came, Defoe claims, when the pirate tried to capitalize on his earnings:

> They [Every and his friends] agreed that the safest method would be to put them in the hands of some merchants, who being men of great wealth and credit in the world, no enquiry would be made how they came by them. . . . In some time his little money was spent, yet he heard nothing from his merchants. He wrote to them often and after much importunity they sent him a small supply but scarce sufficient to pay his debts.

In the end, according to the tale, Every went in person to the Bristol merchants and demanded restitution. Perhaps he believed his reputation could frighten them. If so, he was disappointed: the merchants promptly "silenced him by threatening to discover him," leading Every to the weary conclusion that "our merchants were as good pirates at land as he was by sea." Thus the old pirate died a penniless beggar in Bideford, "not being worth as much as would buy him a coffin."

It is a fitting end: ironic, moralistic, and satisfying in the best tradition of Restoration literature. The cheating pirate, who gained more from trickery than bravery, is cheated in turn. As such, Defoe's account has long been viewed with deep suspicion. Yet some of the facts seem, at first glance, to bear out his story. Shipmate John Dann claimed at trial that he had crossed the Atlantic with Every and a number of other men, putting in at Donley on the north coast of Ireland. From there Dann said he had heard that Every traveled to Dunaghadee, and later someone informed him that the captain was at Dublin the same time as himself. At one point Dann "heard him say he would go to Exeter when he came into England, being a Plymouth man." After that the trail went cold, though Dann added—as an afterthought—that "most of the men which came with Captain Every to Ireland are now in Dublin."

Yet ultimately the end of Captain Every—quicksilver and duplicitous to the last—was less important than the fate of his crew and the story of their adventures. Through the zealous prosecution of the Board of Trade a handful had been caught in various locales throughout the colonies and in England itself—though, in truth, many of the captures owed more to the foolishness of the pirates than the perspicacity of their pursuers. Several were caught in County Mayo, Ireland, having made conspicuous arrival in the port with a small sloop loaded to the gunwales with silver plate. Others were turned over by sharp-eyed goldsmiths when they attempted to pawn their loot. John Dann (who would soon be the chief witness in the prosecution of his shipmates) was uncovered in a rooming house near London when a nosy chambermaid found the lining of his coat gave off a strangely metallic rattle and discovered it contained some £1,045 of gold sewn into the lining.

Not all were so unfortunate, and even among those captured a significant number were acquitted. Such was the case of John Devin, one of those whom Trott had scooped up in his staged "raid." To make it look more convincing, Trott at once convened a petit jury to try the case. We will never know what transpired then, but the outcome could scarcely have been left to chance: Devin was acquitted on all counts and even presented by the court with a certificate "as a Testimony of his, the said John Devin's, innocency relating to the supposed charge of piracy." It was just as well they did so, for no sooner had Devin arrived in his home port of Boston than an overeager citizenry arrested him for the same charge. Devin instantly produced the certificate "under the hand of Ellis Lightwood, Esq., chief judge of the Island of Providence," and was cleared once again.

In the end, only six of Every's crew would appear at the Old Bailey in the fall of 1696. By that time the story of the *Fancy* had become a cause célèbre throughout the Isles. The six men—Joseph Dawson, Edward Forsythe, William Bishop, James Lewis, John Sparks, and William Mays—would be the most famous criminals in English history to that time. And the trial, lasting more than several months and for two attempts, would bring the quiet accord of pirates and governors squarely into the harsh light of public scrutiny.

-9-

Trials and
Tribulations

THE TRIAL OF THE *FANCY*'S CREW, CONDUCTED OVER TWO SEPA-
rate sessions in the fall of 1696, remains one of the most fascinating
examples of English jurisprudence. It introduced a new phrase into the
lexicon of piracy—*sea robbery*—and enshrined Lord Justice Charles
Hedges as the foremost expert in maritime criminal law for a century
to come. More concretely, it was one of the first great media trials, conducted entirely within the glare of public scrutiny, its details regularly
published in pamphlet form for an eager, bloodthirsty English public.
The mechanism of a trial as an instrument of public discourse and dis-
semination, a form that would reach its apex only in the twentieth century, was still largely unknown in the late seventeenth. Great trials were

heretofore conducted largely behind closed doors; the Star Chamber had been abolished less than a century before.

Executions, on the other hand, were very much a public affair. Dying speeches of condemned men, pleas for God's mercy, or spontaneous confessions were duly recorded (or embroidered) and circulated in pamphlets among the literate public. Pamphlets were written to be read aloud, often in public gathering places such as taverns. As such, they became increasingly lurid, tailored to titillate their audience.

Perhaps it was inevitable, then, that the public's curiosity would eventually extend beyond the execution (which is, after all, only the coda to the story) and ultimately to the details of the trial itself. While no exact date can be placed on this transformation, we do find in the late seventeenth century a marked change in the manner that trials were reported. Previously, chroniclers were content to provide a brief summary of the charges, the evidence brought against the accused, and the verdict. Yet by the early eighteenth century entire trials were being reported, complete with dialogue. The trial becomes in printed form more like a play, with accused and accuser engaged as actors.

The Every trials provide a telling example of this watershed. The first trial, conducted at the Old Bailey in October 1696, has all but disappeared from record. It exists now only in echoes from the second trial, held just days after. From it we can glean a few salient facts. First, the six pirates were charged with offenses stemming from the capture of the *Ganj-i-Sawai* and the corresponding losses for the East India Company. This was hardly a surprise. The *Sawai* affair was a serious embarrassment to the company and a grave threat to future trade. Every and his cohorts had disturbed the most delicate machine of all, the cogs and wheels of mercantilism. By doing so they had endangered not only England's commercial stature but her political stature as well. The chief prosecutor put the case in precisely those terms to the twelve earnest subjects in the jury box.

But they didn't listen. Perhaps it was because the *Ganj-i-Sawai* was a Moorish ship (even with her Anglicized name *Gunsway*) or perhaps because the events seemed very far away, against a people whom they neither knew nor cared about. The lacunae of trade alliances likely meant little to them. Neither did the outrages alleged against the Muslim men and women aboard the captured ship—who were, after all, "merely heathens." What they *did* understand was that an English ship with an English captain had given the Moors a bloody nose and taken a king's ransom from the greedy Indian potentate. Accordingly, having listened to both prosecutor and lord justice lecture them on the evils of piracy and outrages against the East India Company, they acquitted the six men on all counts.

Trial of the Century

The crisis this verdict posed for the king and his ministers can well be imagined. They had promised the Great Mogul swift and brutal justice for Every and his men; already they had had to ameliorate that claim. Every was still at large and likely to remain so. The booty captured from the *Ganj-i-Sawai* had spread to the seven winds. The men in the dock—six out of almost two hundred—were nothing more than deck hands (with the exception of William Mays, who was a pirate captain in his own right); the big fish had all escaped. Worse still, Every's colossal success had emboldened scores of other mariners to try their hand at the Red Sea trade.

The great legal minds of the age went into an anxious huddle, and new charges were swiftly brought. The pirates, who must still have been amazed at their good fortune, suddenly found themselves thrust into the dock once again. The record states, not without some irony:

> The Witnesses for the King were then called and sworn, and in the opinion of the Court gave a full evidence against the prisoners, which was very clearly summed up by the Lord Chief Justice . . . but the Jury, contrary to the expectation of the Court, brought in all prisoners Not Guilty, whereupon the session was adjourned to Saturday the 31st of October, and the prisoners were committed upon a *new* warrant for several *other* piracies.

This time the trial report survives, as a pamphlet published by John Everingham of Ludgate Street. Several things are of special note. First, not only has this pamphlet survived, but it is available in several libraries, indicating it must have enjoyed a healthy circulation. Second, it pro-

vides one of the earliest examples of a complete court record disseminated for public reading: the opening speeches, the witness testimony,
even the words of the pirates themselves. For almost the first time the
English public could hear the voices of the men in the dock—not as
dying speeches but in active and vigorous defense of themselves and
their actions. Such was the furor surrounding the trials that any record
of their goings-on would be eagerly read and circulated, and we may
assume that word of the pirates' testimony reached colonial shores as
well. This would be all the more critical, for the trial revealed something
else that neither the government nor Sir Charles Hedges could have
anticipated: the active patronage of colonial governors.

Because the matter of the *Ganj-i-Sawai* had already been decided,
for good or ill, in the first trial, the charges in the second trial were
mutiny and piracy surrounding a much earlier event: the taking of the
Charles II all those months ago in Coruna. Though far less sensational,
the indictment stood on firmer ground. There was no question the
accused were guilty. Moreover, they were not likely to inspire the unpredictable patriotism of the Albion juror. Here was no tale of romantic
derring-do against the Moor but rather a sordid one of theft and deceit.
The defendants could not plead any other excuse than that they were
compelled by the devious Every: to a man, they all did so.

But this time Sir Charles Hedges was leaving nothing to chance.
Addressing the newly sworn-in jurors, he began by apologizing to them
for the inconvenience. It would not have been necessary to summon
them at all, he said, were it not for the waywardness of their predecessors:

> I wish that all others who were concerned in the dispatch
> of that day's business had the like presence [as yourselves]
> to do the same, the Public Justice of the Nation would not
> then have had any manner of reproach, neither would you
> have had this further trouble. But finding that it hath hap-
> pened, it is become absolutely necessary for a further and a
> strict inquiry should be made after these Crimes which
> Threaten and tend to the Destruction of our Navigation
> and Trade.

Thus setting a somber tone, Hedges went on to offer a brief oratory
on the nature of piracy and its threat to the common good. Noticeably
absent in his potted definition was any mention of the Great Mogul or

the East India Company. Such highfalutin matters had boggled the last jury; this time Hedges confined himself to bare facts and local homilies. Piracy was nothing more than simple robbery, he told them, and a pirate at sea was no different than a highwayman ashore. Hedges had knowingly employed a resonating comparison. Highwaymen were the bane of England, in numbers so great as to sometimes bring internal travel to a virtual standstill. And nowhere were there more than on the roads to and from London, just outside the Old Bailey's walls.

Having recast the defendants as far less palatable criminals, Hedges concluded by offering the jury a unique set of instructions. The presumption of innocence was not needed here, he told them. "You are not obliged in all cases to require a clear and full evidence, but only to exercise till you find, and are satisfied in your consciences, that there is sufficient and just cause to put the party accused upon his trial." Then, when the jury could be in no doubt as to what was expected of them, Hedges closed piously: "I hope that what has been said on this unexpected occasion will not be looked upon as intended to influence the Jury; I am sure it is far from being so designed. Religion, Conscience, Honour, common Honesty, Humanity and all Laws forbid such methods." With that in mind, the indictment was read aloud.

Then, almost immediately afterward, things began to go awry. As a piece of theater, the trial had been planned down to the smallest detail—perhaps too much so. The first witness appeared and duly swore that he had served on board the *James*, companion ship to the *Charles II*, and observed firsthand Every's machinations at Coruna. One of the pirates rose at once and demanded if the witness had seen him in Every's company. No, came the response. One by one the pirates rose and asked the same. It soon transpired that the witness had seen none of them: "It was so dark that we could not see them."

Moving briskly on, the court called one David Creagh, the second mate of the *Charles II/Fancy*, who had resisted Every's attempts at mutiny and later departed with the sodden Captain Gibson. He was quite prepared to swear that he had seen each of the six men in Every's company, as indeed he must have. Unfortunately Creagh's career after leaving the *Charles II* had not been so illustrious. "This man is a prisoner for piracy, my Lord," one of the pirates piped up. It was true: Creagh had enjoyed a brief and unsuccessful piratical career, ending in the Old Bailey. His testimony was the price of his survival, a fact that cast little positive light on its quality.

But Justice Holt was not impressed. "What if he be?" he asked. This seemed to have a quashing effect on the prisoner, who answered, "I do not understand Law, I hope your lordship will advise us."

"I will do you all right," the judge told him. "If he be so, that is no objection against him; he may be a good witness for all that."

Still, a shadow had passed over Creagh and over the trial as well. If the justices had hoped to dispel it with their next witness, John Dann, they were quickly disillusioned—not by Dann but by a chance question that opened a new and dreadful series of speculation. In the midst of inquiring after Every's activities in the Red Sea, Dann had freely used the word *privateer* to describe his compatriots Tew, Want, and Wake. Seeking clarification, Justice Holt asked him, "You call them privateers, but were they such privateers as you were?"

And the answer came back: "Yes, my Lord. I suppose they had commissions at first, but I suppose they did not run so far as that."

This was unsettling news, and one could almost feel a palpable sense of urgency as Justice Holt hurriedly changed the subject. Philip Middleton, called to the stand after Dann, readily confirmed that he had served with each of the accused aboard the *Fancy*, and none had been coerced by Every. Having been briefly derailed, the trial was now jerked firmly back on course. Middleton seemed at first to be a splendid crown witness: informative, eager, helpful, and possessed of an extraordinary memory. So detailed and comprehensive was his testimony that the prosecution allowed itself to digress, and the whole picture of life on board the *Fancy* began to emerge. It was riveting stuff. Middleton told of the attack on the *Ganj-i-Sawai* and the joyous divvying up of the spoils. "What might the shares be?" one of the justices asked.

"Some a hundred pound," Middleton answered, "some six hundred, some five hundred, and some left according to what the company thought he discovered."

"How much was it that you had?"

"About a hundred pound."

Then the judge, perhaps caught up in the moment, asked, "What became of it?"

"John Sparks robbed me of it," Middleton answered grimly.

Sparks was one of the defendants. "The King's counsel have done with the Evidence," another justice interjected anxiously, before the witness's credibility could sink any further.

Later testimony produced other surprises. Defendant William Mays, still desperate to save his skin, inadvertently dropped a bombshell. When he claimed in his defense that he had merely been compelled by Every, Justice Hedges, springing the trap, leaned over the bench and asked him sweetly whether in that case Mays had ever bothered to "discover" himself to a king's official after leaving Every's employ.

"Yes, at Virginia," Mays answered at once. The import of this must have taken a moment to sink in: Virginia had never reported any crew of Every's arriving at its shores. Perhaps the man was lying. Hedges resolved to test him:

> Q: Where did you first arrive in England?
> A: At Bristol.
> Q: When you came to Bristol, did you discover it to any Magistrate?
> A: When I came to Bristol I had a design to discover it to the Lords of the Admiralty.
> Q: Did you go to a Magistrate?
> A: I was several days in the King's Collectors house, and did discover the whole to him, and at Providence.
> Q: You speak of Providence, but in England who did you discover it to?
> A: I was sick, and could not go abroad.

New Providence, where Nicholas Trott had been appointed on the promise of cleaning out the Augean stables of Jones's administration. Virginia, the crown colony where Edmund Andros—the same Andros who had been forcibly deposed from New York a decade before—now improbably held sway. Could either be knowingly complicit in Every's piracy? There were two possibilities. Either Mays's testimony was fabrication entirely (would that it were so!), or Mays had craftily sought to surrender himself before governments that he expected would be far more indulgent. And if that were the case, something very untoward was going on in the colonies.

If the course of the trial had been unpredictable, its conclusion was not. The jury retired and duly came back with a guilty verdict for all six accused. The lord justices breathed a sigh of relief. Earlier in the trial Justice Holt had asked the clerk of the court if any of the former jurors had been returned. "If you have returned any of the former Jury," Holt said bitingly, "you have not done well, for that verdict was a dishonour to the justice of the nation." But this time it was a new jury, and whether convinced by the charges or cowed by the justices, they did as instructed. Joseph Dawson, Edward Forsyth, William Mays, William Bishop, James Lewis, and John Sparks were each sentenced to death by hanging. The record of the trial ends thus: "According to the sentence, Edward Forsyth and the rest were executed on Wednesday, November the 15th, 1696, at Execution Dock, that being the Place for the Execution of Pirates. FINIS."

Birth of a Scandal

Yet even after the tongue is stilled, the printed word survives. The testimony of the accused pirates appeared in print just days after their bodies had been cut down from Execution Dock, and the whole of England could now read of alleged pirate commissions and safe harbors in the colonies. The trial, far from reaffirming English law over its wayward subjects, had in fact exposed the crown's vulnerability for all to see. The situation was further complicated by separate affidavits signed by the pirates Dann and Middleton, which proceeded in great and damning detail to implicate Governor Trott. In exchange for their lives, the two pirates surpassed their performances on the stand, offering exhaustive testimony on nearly every aspect of the *Fancy*'s voyage. This included the exact amounts paid to Trott, as well as hints that other pirates from Every's crew had found succor throughout the American colonies.

Not long after came the response of Governor Cranston to the charge, raised at trial, that he had knowingly commissioned the pirate Mays. In response Cranston sent a letter to the Board of Trade, which came too late to save Mays but reaffirmed all that he had said, and then some. Cranston denied utterly all the "vicious" charges leveled against him and his colony. "The government of Rhode Island was never concerned in nor countenanced any such things," he said roundly. But in answer to questions about Mays's commission, he responded that he had granted the commission in good faith and that Mays had been unwillingly seized by Every and his crew and forced into piracy. Mays had now been dead for more than six months.

The diaspora of Every's crew and the notoriety that followed them had other, more lasting consequences. As the manhunt continued, reports of sightings filtered back to the Board of Trade with alarming regularity. Almost as disturbing as the pirates' unmolested liberty was the treatment most received, even after news of the trial and executions had reached American ears. Like radioactive particles moving through the human body, everywhere the men of the *Fancy* went, they illuminated the corruption around them.

One such place was Pennsylvania. Removed from William Penn's proprietorship and placed in the hands of Governor Fletcher's chosen deputy, William Markham, the colony had become a pirate haven. A colonial surveyor would later, rather incredibly, blame the Quakers: their particularly individualistic strain of Christianity had fostered in them a stubborn independent streak, he said, and their traditional taciturn mien concealed all manner of illegal activities. Colonial administrator and local justice Robert Snead, however, put the blame on a more specific source: Governor Markham. "On the 10th of August, 1696," he wrote Sir John Houblon at the Board of Trade, "a proclamation came to my hands and another to William Penn's deputy, William Markham, who took no notice of it." It was the proclamation quoted earlier, commanding all colonial governors to extend their utmost efforts to capture Every and his men. Mr. Snead "went at once to the Governor and told him that several of Every's men were here, well known to him and all persons. He [Markham] said he knew it not. I told him here was enough to prove it, and that if he did not apprehend them I did not know how he could answer it." Markham blandly replied that if seamen brought good solid income to Philadelphia it wasn't his affair to ask how they got it. "He refused to hear the proclamation when I offered to read it to him, but seemed very angry, so I left him."

No sooner had the egregious Snead left than Markham at once summoned the pirates he had mentioned and warned them to lay low. But Snead had anticipated this and took action. Prevailing on a pair of "fellow justices"—even threatening them with deportment to England when they protested fear of the governor—Snead secured arrest warrants and apprehended three of Every's men not far from Markham's mansion. Stephen Claus, Robert Clinton, and Edmund Lassells were duly taken with great ceremony to the local jail, and Snead sat down to write a self-congratulatory report.

But Markham had not been idle either, and his network was far more intricate than Snead's. One of Snead's own deputies hurried across town to inform the governor of what had transpired, and Markham at once sent the money to secure the pirates' bail. Thereupon a strange and almost comical tug-of-war ensued between the governor and the judge, with Claus, Clinton, and Lassells caught in the center. Having returned home in triumph, Snead learned to his horror that the men were released. Hurriedly he dispatched a guard and arrested them again. Back they went to the local jail, but this time Snead remained and interrogated them himself. "The Governor was much displeased with me," Snead reported piously, and "called me before his Council and asked what I had against those pirates to hinder their discharge. I told him there was proof enough that they were Every's men, and had the proclamation read." But Markham was not to be deterred, and the pirates were released once more.

This apparently sent Snead into a frenzy. In his letter to Houblon he justifies it by pointing to the pirates' alleged atrocities and open contempt for the law: "They ran away from Jamaica with a ship, went to the Persian Seas, and took and murdered many. A princess, who was given in marriage to a great man, was on her way to him by sea when they took the ship; they killed most of the men and threw her overboard. They brag of it publicly in their cups." Perhaps it was no more than righteous ire that moved this particular administrator, or perhaps it was his sense of being an outsider. Snead was not a member of the local gentry, nor of the Quaker cabal that controlled so much of Pennsylvania's business. He had few contacts in the city and fewer friends; Markham had seen to that. "I am but a stranger here," Snead told Houblon wretchedly, "having moved my estate and my family from Jamaica two years before." Whatever the cause, Snead's anger led him down a dangerous path. He wrote at once to the Board of Trade, accusing Markham of accepting £1,000 of bribes from the pirates, and then ordered them arrested once again.

Markham's response was swift and brutal. "He sent for me," Snead wrote, "threatened to send me to jail and dared me to do it [apprehend the pirates], telling me I should not frighten people with my warrant, I had done too much already. He abused me very much and caused my arms [pistols] (which I wear for defense against these rogues) to be taken from me."

Snead does not record his answer to Markham, but his actions were stunning: he arrested the pirates and committed them back to jail for the third time. Unbeknownst to Markham, Snead thought he had an ace up his sleeve: a London packet was due in any day, carrying with her an agent from the Board of Trade with express instructions to round up Every's men throughout the colonies. Snead had only to hold out and play his dangerous game. Finally, in September 1697 the packet arrived. But it was not all that Snead had hoped. The "gentleman from England" promised to set guards over the captured pirates and assured Snead that they would be dispatched to London on the first available frigate. No guard was posted, however, and two escaped. After Markham blandly refused to spare a frigate for the purpose of transporting the remaining prisoners, the matter was effectively closed. "The gentleman's name was Robeson," Snead reported grimly, "a man of pusillanimous spirit, who was frightened by the Governor."

Disgraced and betrayed, with no recourse left to him, Snead poured all his troubles out in a long report to Houblon and the Board of Trade. He closed rather ironically by requesting the board grant him a commission to hunt out the pirates himself, since no one in America would apparently do so. "Please take care that the commission be so firm that the Governor cannot upset it," he advised, "and I will do my part faithfully."

The board did not grant Snead his commission, but his report was circulated widely. Many dismissed it as sour grapes: how could Governor Markham, a man of much esteem, knowingly protect men whom the crown had ordered him to destroy? More important, *why* would he? Unable to furnish an answer, Houblon and his confreres must have concluded that Snead was simply angling for a grant; in any event, they did not reply. They would not get the answer to their question until much later, when the truth finally emerged: Markham had married his own daughter to one of Every's men.

Yet there were other charges in Snead's report that were harder to dismiss. Besides protecting Every's crew, Markham had apparently done a brisk business in granting privateering commissions to known pirates.

"He has lately given commissions to other such rogues," Snead told Houblon:

> One [Captain] Day came with a large ship full of sugar and indigo to Carolina, sold the cargo, laid the ship up, bought a vessel for piratical purposes and came here. The Governor granted him a commission, and they are gone on their errand, as they themselves own. On the 16th inst. I received from his Excellency a copy of a letter from the Council of Trade ordering the apprehension of all these pirates. I understand that the Governor had one directed to him and also the proclamation, to be published forthwith. But he did not do so until he had warned the pirates, who made their escape. . . . Next day the proclamation was published.

Snead was quick to ascribe a single cause for Governor Markham's conduct: "All people see how Arabian gold works with some consciences," he wrote sourly. But as other reports of piratical commissions reached the board, doubts began to emerge. The complicating factor was that these commissions were, technically, still legal. Unlike smuggling or other forms of illegal trade, privateering had been an essential and legitimate source of income since King William had declared war on France in the second year of his reign. The problem was distinguishing false commissions from true. How could a governor know what use a captain might make of this document? Would he stay within its bounds, or sail at once for the Red Sea? More important, *did* the governors know? Surely some had used this ambiguity to their advantage— notably Fletcher, Richier, Cranston, and now, apparently, Markham.

The Board of Trade began sending out feelers, asking governors to report on the status of piracy within their colonies and of the colonies around them. The ongoing manhunt for the crew of the *Fancy* was employed as a pretext. The answers came back soon enough but were scarcely heartening. Each governor readily acknowledged that the seas were infested with pirates, yet none admitted any within their own shores. "Since I have held this government none of the pirates mentioned in your letter have arrived in any of these islands," Governor Codrington of the Leeward Islands wrote in December 1697. "They generally find more remote islands and Carolina to shelter them-

selves in, rather than adventure themselves here." Governor William
Stoughton of Massachusetts likewise reported that "the proclamation
against Henry Every and others was duly published, but after diligent
enquiry and search I cannot find that any of them are in the Government. They find more countenance and better entertainment in other
places. Pirates know they are obnoxious to the Government here." On
this lofty note, Stoughton went on to assure the board that all prizes
had been lawfully taken and lawfully condemned and even provided
the account books to prove it, "so as may wipe off any reflections
unjustly cast upon Massachusetts in that regard." Governor Nicholson
of Maryland went yet further, delivering his own diatribe against the
scourge of piracy and professing love of King William in the same hec-
tic breath:

> I received your commands of 27 August 1696 concerning
> one Henry Every and a copy of the Royal proclamation
> against pirates. I enclose copy of my own proclamation. I
> confess that I always abhorred such sort of profligate men
> and their barbarous actions; for sure they are the disgrace
> of mankind in general, and of the noble, valiant, generous
> English in particular, who have the happiness of being
> governed by so great a King.

Even Governor Fletcher responded to the call. For once he could
truthfully say that his hands were clean; none of Every's men had been
known to reach New York. Fletcher stoutly maintained that all the New
York men were honest and aboveboard, but he allowed one exception,
a man who had received his commission not from Fletcher but from
another who would soon be Fletcher's nemesis:

> One Captain Kidd lately arrived and produced a commis-
> sion under the Great Seal of England for the suppression
> of piracy. When he was here many flocked to him from all
> parts, men of desperate fortunes and necessities, in expec-
> tation of getting vast treasure. He sailed from hence with
> 150 men, as I am informed, great part of them from this
> province.

Fletcher closed with a comment that both was eerily prescient and
revealed a more shrewd understanding of pirate crews than he himself

would have admitted to possessing. "It is generally believed here," he wrote, "that they will get money *per fas aut nefas* [through nefarious deeds], and that if he [Kidd] misses the design named in his commission he will not be able to govern such a herd of men under no pay."

Of all the governors in the Atlantic colonies, only one offered anything more than heated accusations on the one hand and protestations of innocence on the other. This was Jeremiah Basse, governor of New Jersey. Basse received the board's request for information on piracy as a trumpeted summons to action. His colony, due to its proximity to its larger and more powerful neighbor, New York, had suffered much—not the first time that New Jersey would suffer from its relation to New York, and certainly not the last. New York pirates regularly used the shoals around neighboring New Jersey to careen their ships, and many were known to prey on local Jersey trade. Basse was incensed.

There were personal reasons as well. Traveling homeward from the Caribbean earlier that year, Basse's own ship was attacked by a band of German, Dutch, French, and English pirates some twenty miles south of Puerto Rico. After a six-hour engagement the captain of Basse's vessel surrendered. The pirates took Basse and his men to the sea lanes around Hispaniola, where they were kept under guard until it was decided what to do with them. "They used us extremely hard," Basse would later write, "beat us, pinched us of victuals, shut us down at night to take our lodging in the water cask, detained us till they had careened their ship and fitted her for sailing and then, being designed for the coast of Guinea, gave us our liberty." It seems not to have occurred to Basse, given this abrupt end of the narrative, that he had been extraordinarily lucky.

Governor Basse now took his revenge. In his lengthy answer to the board, received in London on July 18, 1697, he wrote: "You cannot be insensible of the dishonor as well as damage suffered by this nation through the increase of piracies under the banner of England in any part of the world." They might be aware of Henry Every's depredations, he went on, but did they know that scores of pirates were already following his example and sailing with illegal commissions from almost every Atlantic port? Unlike Fletcher and the others, Basse did not try to hide the fact that some of these men were from his own colony, nor did he make specific accusations—yet. Instead he offered an indictment of the entire Eastern Seaboard, which must have landed on the Board of Trade like a lead brick:

> The Colonies in the Islands and Main of America have not a little contributed to this increase [he wrote]. In my time several vessels, suspected to be bound in this design, sailed from one province or another of the continent . . . which have on board them men belonging to New England, New York, the Jerseys, etc. They will be emboldened thereto by the good entertainment that they have formerly met withal in those provinces. . . . The people make so much advantage from the currency of their money that they will not be very forward to suppress them, unless it be enjoined on them by a power that they dare not disobey.

In every line of this extraordinary document, Basse reveals himself as a conscientious administrator with a keen understanding of the governor's unique role. The willingness of crown-appointed governors and their adjutants to grant knowingly false privateering commissions simply boggled him, he admitted. "No person," he declared, is "capable of acting without his Majesty's approbation, which indeed seems to render them almost as much the choice of the Crown as of the proprietors." Should the interests of crown and colony conflict, the governor had a sworn duty to obey his sovereign: "If I were so foolish as to act in contradiction to that which it is believed the interest of the Crown doth consist I see not much probability of my having opportunity so to do." Basse closed by throwing the problem of piracy back at the board itself: "I would ask your advice as to what is best to be done (1) with those who have formerly been pirates and are now settled in New Jersey, and (2) with those that enter the country later, in order to suppress them in time to come." As if this were not enough, Basse sent a following letter several weeks later that demanded their immediate reply.

The Board of Trade was being browbeaten, probably for the first time in its history. An enterprising and outraged governor had turned the tables on it and in effect demanded instructions to deal with the very problem of which the board was only just now becoming aware. Yet here, too, was an opportunity that seemed heaven-sent: a man in charge who had not only a grudge against the pirates but firsthand knowledge of them. Governor Basse could be a willing gold mine of information. Secretary William Popple, whom Basse had addressed directly, wrote back to him on July 22, one week to the day since Basse's letter had been read aloud. Things were moving very fast indeed. The governor's letter had been eagerly circulated, Popple told him, but the problem of pirate sponsorship that Basse outlined was still so novel that they could offer no instructions at the present time to deal with it. "While approving your zeal for the suppression of piracy," Popple wrote warmly, the board "desires a fuller explanation of certain matters which you hint at upon that subject." One can almost hear in the queries that followed the scuffling sound of men groping in the dark:

> Which are the provinces that have been most blameable in their conduct towards the pirates? What particular facts do you know about the pirates or their abettors? Who are the pirates now expected to return, and to what particular place? By whom were you yourself taken and ill-used? What methods do you think best for the suppression of pirates, and how do you wish to go about the work? What court is there in New Jersey which can or ever did try pirates, and what law have they there to do it?

Basse was eager to oblige. His response was stunning in its breadth, for in several short paragraphs the governor managed to indict the entire western half of the British Atlantic world of pirate sponsorship. All the veiled hints of the Every trials and cautious obfuscations of the governors were stripped away, revealing the pulsing, quivering mass beneath. For the first time the Board of Trade received a complete account of all the illegal activities undertaken in the last decade, from a man who was in a better position to inform them than almost anyone else in the colonies. Like Homer, Basse chose to begin his epic in medias res. "As to which of the Colonies have been more blameable in their conduct towards pirates," he began, "I think that most of them, both in the Islands and on the Main, have been to blame, some through ignorance of their duty, some from powerlessness to suppress the evil, and some no doubt from the prospect of gain."

Lest they think he was merely an alarmist, Basse went on to present his indictment in detail. The Board of Trade was probably not surprised to learn that Rhode Island, New York, Carolina, and the Bahamas were the most egregious offenders, but eyebrows must have raised as Basse continued: "I have known several persons suspected of being settled in New Jersey, Pennsylvania, Maryland and Virginia." The governor was honest but no fool. "Those in New Jersey have received a pass from the Governor of New York which obstructs any further enquiry by us," he hastened to add. Moving from the general to the particular, Basse offered the board a quick glimpse of the current state of piratical commerce. He was informed, he wrote, that there was now "out on a piratical voyage the ship *Kent*, formerly commanded by one Ball and now by Thomas Day." She was reported to have put in to Carolina, sold all her lading at cutthroat rates, taken in men and provisions, and gone privateering. Then there was Thomas Tew, "of whom you have doubtless heard," who arrived in Rhode Island briefly and then sailed for New York, fitted out his pirate vessel again, and carried with him "one [Captain] Want in a brigantine and another vessel." The two had added a third captain, Glover, to their ranks, in a ship "belonging to the merchants of New York," which probably meant Frederick Phillipse. Another Captain Glover (in fact, the same one) "took a rich prize from the French, went afterward to the Coast of Guinea, and joined the rest on the coast of Arabia."

The list went on and on, with nearly every colony contributing a name, a ship, or a patron. "In all," Basse concluded, "I am told that there are gone from Boston, New York, Pennsylvania, Carolina and Barbados, from each one ship and from Rhode Island two." But Basse did not just provide a catalog of wrongdoing; the Board of Trade had asked for his advice, and he took them at their word. The chief problem, he lectured them, was that there was simply no oversight for governors' activities. In the absence of any such accountability, they acted as they pleased. Moreover, even those conscientious few like himself who had "formed schemes for the suppression of piracy" found themselves thwarted at every turn by a similar dearth of enforcement mechanisms. Governors thought it much easier to condone piracy because the alternative—suppression—was virtually impossible considering the archaic state of legal jurisdiction.

Admiralty law dating from the century before required that all pirates captured in the colonies be remanded to England for trial, a hopelessly outdated piece of bureaucratic obstructionism that made the capture and prosecution of pirates well-nigh impossible. Aside from the expense and hassle of shipping them across the Atlantic, the law gave sympathetic governors, sheriffs, and deputies ample time to effect "prison breaks," just as Markham had done for Every's men. Under the current system, Basse wrote, "I know of no Courts at present in the province with the powers sufficient to try pirates, it being the declared judgment of the Attorney General that we have no Admiralty jurisdiction. . . . This defect will I hope be supplied by the King's Commissionary Vice Admirals in every province." In other words, give us the tools and we will finish the job.

Such impertinence was unprecedented; the Board of Trade, having only just learned of this rising menace, was now accused of being at least partly responsible for it. Yet the problem of jurisdiction was a specific one, with a practical solution. Basse was not asking for a navy, nor (like Snead) a special commission, nor even for more money—just the legal power necessary to put pirates in the dock and at the rope's end. Nevertheless, it was a momentous decision to make, for it would in effect give the wayward governors even more prerogative than they currently enjoyed.

Such a step could not be made without further counsel. Governor Basse had opened the eyes of Board of Trade members, but his information, for all its pungency, remained incomplete. What was needed was a man "on the ground" who could travel through each colony and provide firsthand reports on the state of things; an unbiased bureaucrat, with no particular axe to grind. Yet how could the Board of Trade find such a man within the confused and serpentine tangle of interests, alliances, and factions both in England and in the colonies?

The Board of Trade Strikes Back

The answer was quite literally beneath their collective noses. Among the papers recently submitted to the board for consideration was a comprehensive report on the colonies, written the previous year by a colonial surveyor named Edward Randolph, who had been diligently following the snared threads of smuggling and illegal trade for more than a decade. In bullet-point style it confirmed many of Basse's charges and added a few of its own. "PENNSYLVANIA," one entry began. "William Markham is Governor. . . . The Governor entertains several pirates who carry on an illicit trade with Curacao and other places." Nor were the other colonies spared. Rhode Island was "a free port to pirates and illegal traders from all places. . . . The people are enriched by them." Even austere Massachusetts, which had recently protested its total innocence, was tarred by the same brush: "Though the King has the appointing of the Governor," the report read, "yet illegal trade is carried on as much as ever."

In his report Randolph was very clear on where he felt the blame lay. "It cannot therefore be expected," he concluded, "that the frauds and other abuses complained of in the Colonies can be prevented unless duly qualified men, of good estates and reputation, be approved by the King as Governors."

This was just the sort of language that the Board of Trade wanted to hear. They summoned Randolph and presented him with a unique commission: he would travel the length and breadth of the British Atlantic world, inquiring extensively as to the execution of government in each colony. The list of questions read much like those given to Basse: Were the governors countenancing illegal trade or piracy? Who were the most flagrant offenders? How could this menace best be curtailed?

In the meantime, events of another sort combined to give added impetus to the board's charge. The War of the Grand Alliance, also known as King William's War, was not going well for any of the parties. English and Dutch commerce was in shambles from the constant raids, and France was suffering as well. Its king, Louis XIV, now had other concerns. The war had been engaged partly to check France's expansionism on the continent, a prospect that had largely failed. Despite waging war against an alliance composed of England, Spain, the Netherlands, and the Holy Roman Empire, France had solidified its military hold on the territories in dispute. With Charles II of Spain hovering near death, a new crisis arose. Having dealt handily with his eastern neighbors, Louis shrewdly looked to the west. The death of the Spanish king would offer the chance for a French successor, but not if France and Spain were still at war. Thus, while France was arguably the strongest party at the table, it also had considerable interest in ending this unprofitable and now largely pointless conflict.

The great powers met at King William's palace at Ryswick, not far from the Hague. As with any diplomatic negotiation, each had very different interests. William was primarily concerned with gaining recognition of his claim to the English throne, a point of much dispute since the Glorious Revolution. The French, whose interests were more territorial than theoretical, gracefully conceded the issue. After several more weeks of haggling, the map of Europe was left much as it had been before the war, with a few minor exceptions, and the North American colonies were brought squarely back to status quo. On September 20, 1697, the Treaty of Ryswick was signed. Then all the parties returned to their respective palaces, announced that the war had ended, and busily began laying plans for the next one.

While this diplomatic dance might seem an exercise in futility (as indeed it was; England and France were at war once again within four years), it did have one critical consequence: all privateering commissions granted by colonial governors were summarily revoked, and all privateers were ordered back at once to their port of origin. The power to grant such commissions—which had been the governors' primary justification for sending out men like Tew, Want, Glover, and so on—was gone. Now any commission granted would be, perforce, illegal.

It was during this tidal shift of colonial policy that the Board of Trade determined to send its representative to the colonies to see for himself whether the governors would fall into line. And the man that they chose, Edward Randolph, would prove to be a fateful choice.

-10-

The Most Hated Man in America

NO IMAGE SURVIVES OF EDWARD RANDOLPH, BUT HIS REPORTS from the colonies draw up a compelling picture. By the last decade of the seventeenth century he is in his mid-sixties, which in that era is an advanced age indeed. He suffers from chronic gout, which inflames his joints and makes every step a trial. His sinuses bother him in this climate, and he frequently falls victim to fevers. His stomach has been ill used on this trip, and he detests sea voyages on principle. He is also not the least shy in bringing these facts to the attention of his lords and masters in the Board of Trade. Once he even complains about the lamentable state of his bowels.

We can imagine that Randolph speaks much like he writes: crisply, often caustically, and always very much to the point. Despite deference given his age he can rile an interlocutor to argument in seconds—even the normally unflappable William Markham. He uses adjectives like *licentious* and *hypocritical* when describing the administrators he encounters. Not surprisingly, wherever Randolph travels he leaves behind a trail of resentment and ire. His personality is abrasive, and he cares nothing for the rules of courtesy. He likely believes that such rules would be wasted on the colonists. Despite his many visits to America, his letters from there reveal a man who often feels like a Roman general wandering through barbaric hordes. He is as insensitive to locality as he is to flattery. Crusty and tenacious, morally above both politics and bribery, Edward Randolph is a sixty-four-year-old zealot whose cause is the English state.

Cancer in the Body Politic

Randolph's presence in the colonies was the certain if somewhat tortuous result of the Every trials in 1696. For more than a decade now two trajectories had followed their separate paths, nearing but not yet meeting, but destined to collide. One was the flourishing Red Sea trade. By the end of King William's War illegal trade had become not only a staple of colonial commerce but the primary (and in some cases only) source for many goods and luxuries that colonists from Boston to Charleston now took for granted. It had made the fortunes of men like Frederick Phillipse and provided stable employment for an entire generation of skilled mariners. Piracy had become so interwoven into the social infrastructure of the Atlantic colonies that it helped shape the policies of many colonial governments, most particularly those of New York, Rhode Island, and Pennsylvania. But if those colonies (and their governors) were the most conspicuous, they were certainly not the only offenders. There was no colony on the Eastern Seaboard or in the Caribbean that did not owe at least some share of its revenue to the pirate trade.

Yet this commercial enterprise flourished best in quiet neglect. With scant means of overseeing them, colonial governors had been free to make their accords with the pirates and reap tidy sums for themselves and their colonies in the process. The effect of the Every trials was to bring this gentlemen's agreement ruthlessly into the light of day. The bonds of friendship and commerce would not dissolve at once, but never again would the governors enjoy the same liberty nor obscurity.

This in turn would bring the first trajectory into direct conflict with the second: the inexorable advance of English state building. As the Atlantic colonies had grown in size and strategic importance, so, too, did England's maritime empire. While only of peripheral significance during the late war, the presence of the American colonies was still immensely symbolic: England now bracketed the Atlantic. And while these colonies would never provide the nation with the riches that the East India Company could, they did produce three vital crops: cotton, tobacco, and sugar cane. Moreover, and critically, the colonies were an inexhaustible market for English goods. Thus the politicians of England at the end of the seventeenth century seemed to have produced in state-craft a machine that would forever elude their scientific cousins: the first self-sustaining engine. Atlantic colonies were perennial markets and, as extensions of the state, could be regulated to accept whatever trading terms were most favorable to England. The colonies, in turn, would have the security of knowledge that their own crops would find steady purchase in the mother country. As the colonies expanded, so, too, would their demand for English goods, which in turn would enrich the state, and so on ad infinitum. It was economics of brilliant simplicity, eventually to be termed *mercantilism*.

The lynchpin of this policy was the elimination of all external competition. England must preserve a favorable balance of trade with all other countries, which meant exporting a greater share of goods than it imported. The colonies, inextricably connected to the mother country and in constant need of all manner of finished goods, were the mainstay of England's export market and thus could not be allowed to truck with any other nation than their own. From this truism came the Navigation Acts of 1651, which effectively limited colonial trade to English ships alone. Virtually all subsequent crown policy regarding its colonies sprang from the same impulse as these acts, from the establishment of the Dominion of New England in 1686 to the dissolution of the American colonies ninety years later. While subsequent generations might speak of the British empire in broader, more nationalist terms, in the seventeenth and eighteenth centuries it was first, foremost, and almost exclusively a commercial relationship.

Piracy was therefore a cancer to the body politic in more ways than one. Aside from its traditional menace to the peace and good order of trade between England and foreign potentates, it now posed a critical threat to England's own internal trade with its colonies. Pirates became the middlemen by which foreign goods were brought into American ports, and the pirate trade itself took its place alongside smuggling (another bane of the Lords of Trade) as a viable and reliable alternative to English goods. In sum, while the external threat of piracy for foreign trade had been brought brutally home by the outraged letters from Bombay following Every's raid, the internal threat was equally and uniquely exposed in the trials that followed.

Other factors contributed to a heightened sense of piratical encroachment that would, by the turn of the century, border on paranoia. The growth of piracy and its transfer from the Caribbean to the Red Sea coincided (and contrasted) with efforts by the crown to solidify its grip on the colonies and the concomitant fostering of a new and ever more intricate bureaucracy to further that aim. The first impetus was the political fallout of the Glorious Revolution in 1689. Revolts in Boston, New York, and Maryland led to the establishment of revolutionary governments, all declaring their unswerving allegiance to King William yet in the same moment taking a pickax to the carefully constructed network of obligation and reward that had allowed colonial governments to function since their inception. Among the first tasks of the new king and his ministers was to reimpose some form of order over these wayward subjects, a task that was not aided by the precarious nature of William's own claim to the throne.

The response of the crown was swift and remorseless. Jacob Leisler of New York was caught and hanged, replaced by a man who proved distinctly unfriendly to those Whigs who had seen in the revolution a means of cleansing the Augean stables of political corruption both in England and New York. If King William showed scant loyalty to the men that had so enthusiastically championed his cause, it was no more than necessary: whatever their loyalties, they had overthrown crown-appointed governors and replaced them with ones of their own choosing. Such rebellion could not be countenanced. Perversely, loyalty to the king might well mean disloyalty to the monarchy and as such must be punished by the king—a twist of logic that Lewis Carroll might have envied. Elsewhere, however, William was more circumspect. Maryland, which had overthrown its founder, Lord Baltimore, was allowed to keep its newly elected legislature but received a governor by personal appointment of the crown. A similar arrangement was imposed on Massachusetts, which received a new charter with a greatly enhanced Puritan legislature but yet again a royal governor appointed to act as counterweight. Virginia received shorter shrift; there the unpopular Governor Effingham was sent an even more unpopular deputy, Francis Nicholson, whose previous employ had been with Governor Andros of Massachusetts. Finally, in a similar display of crown prerogative, William Penn of Pennsylvania was divested of his office and replaced by William Markham. The pattern of response in each colony was thus replicated: in most cases the legislatures were allowed to remain intact in their postrevolutionary forms (a concession to those among them who had supported the revolution), but the crown appointed its own royal governor to act as a check and keep the colony firmly under royal purview. It was this political climate that launched the careers of Fletcher, Markham, Cranston, Trott, and nearly all the governors who would later figure so prominently in the pirate trade.

This exercise of royal prerogative in the colonies soon found its expression in the law. The Navigation Acts were reaffirmed and strengthened, articulated once again to the colonial administrators charged with their implementation. The period of 1689 to 1696 was one of consolidation and expansion. The colonies, which until that time had been managed at arm's length and given cursory consideration at best, now moved to central stage. As if to mark this transition, the bureaucracy responsible for colonial affairs was radically transformed. For the last twenty years the entire task had fallen to the Committee for Trade and Plantations, otherwise known as the Lords of Trade. They were all that their name implied: stodgy, aristocratic, chronically ill-informed amateurs. Membership in the committee was based on breeding rather than merit, and members regarded committee meetings as unwelcome (if brief) intrusions on the serious business of grouse hunting and court intrigue. The real work of the Lords of Trade was left to secretaries, among them the gruff and industrious William Popple and the brilliant William Blaythwayt.

Fissures in this relaxed arrangement were already appearing well before 1696; the revelations of the Every trial widened them into gulfs. Colonial affairs had expanded beyond the competence of a few indifferent amateurs; governing them and managing the myriad financial arrangements was now a full-time job requiring skilled professionals. In recognition of this fact, Parliament in late 1695 began laying plans for a new committee, tentatively—and significantly—titled the Board of Trade. The nomenclature was revealing: in the transfer from lords to a board, the business of the Atlantic colonies would pass from the hands of the king and his ministers to those of Parliament. This touched off a brief but fierce political firestorm between William and his Parliament, as both vied for control.

Finally, in early 1696, just as the manhunt intensified for Every's crew, the new Board of Trade appeared. From a distance its membership looked scarcely different than its predecessor's: the first rank of board members were all born of the purple, including its president, the Earl of Bridgewater. Farther down the list, however, the real sinews of the new arrangement appeared: William Blaythwayt was now a full member, and the committee minutes of the inaugural meeting called for the immediate formation of a permanent advisory council whose sole purpose would be the accumulation of fact-finding reports on nearly every aspect of colonial affairs. The Lords of Trade had been crippled by ignorance; the Board of Trade would not be.

Even as these plans were laid, the London trials of Every's crew, compounded with reports from the colonies on the widespread protection given them, presented the board its first major challenge. Their position was much akin to that of someone who has just inherited a property sight-unseen and learns to his chagrin that it is infested with vermin. A January report from the commissioner of customs grimly informed them that the Navigation Acts were neither obeyed nor enforced and under threat of reprimand for negligence proceeded to outline a list of proposals for compelling compliance. The suppression of the pirate trade was first among them. Worse still, the charge that the Navigation Acts were languishing found particular voice among the seaport communities of Bristol and Liverpool. If piracy and smuggling were a boon for cities on one side of the Atlantic, they were an equal drain for those on the other. Merchants from the English port towns petitioned Parliament frequently in the 1690s, citing piracy as one of the chief detriments to their livelihood. The dichotomy between their position and those of their erstwhile colonial brethren was revealing: while the English public as a whole might be sympathetic to the exploits of Henry Every, piracy itself was viewed as a scourge—most especially so by those whose trade was worst hit by its effects.

The King's Man

Accordingly, the members resolved to send their own man to the colonies and prepare a systematic survey of illegal activity therein. The choice of agent was a crucial one, for the task was singular: he would be a human ferret, diving into holes and rooting out corruption wherever he found it. The agent must be industrious, ferocious, and, above all, honest. Ultimately there was only one choice: the author of the 1695 report that had roundly condemned the governors for illegal conduct, former collector of customs Edward Randolph.

Randolph was an acute observer; his reports were compendiums of meticulous research. He was also arrogant, stubborn, irascible, and abrasive—traits that increased rather than lessened over time. His first dealings with Massachusetts as customs collector, long before his appointment by the Board of Trade to investigate piracy in particular, set the tone for the next two decades. Loathing all colonials and Puritans in particular, he burst in upon a closed meeting of the Massachusetts Council and demanded why it had not answered His Majesty's letters. The council ordered him out at once and thereafter treated him with iciness bordering on contempt. Randolph's own prejudices also found their way into his letters to the Lords of Trade: dismissing all evidence to the contrary, he decided that the Puritans represented only a small modicum of the Massachusetts colony and that most subjects wanted nothing more than to break free of this "subjection and slavery." His reports were a direct contributory cause to the establishment of the Dominion of New England by James II several years later.

The first such report, titled "The Present State of Affairs in New England," was dated October 12, 1676. Focusing on Massachusetts (though Randolph's travels had taken him to neighboring colonies, albeit briefly), it was a twenty-five-page indictment of the colony and its proprietors. Massachusetts law, he charged, was starkly divergent from its English precedent (which was scarcely a surprise, as it drew its inspiration not from the Magna Carta but from the Old Testament); it denied the supremacy of English law, and colonists refused to take the oath of allegiance. Most disturbing of all, Randolph accused the colony of gross violations of the Acts of Trade and Navigation, "by which they have engrossed the greatest part of the West India Trade, whereby his Majesty is damaged in his Customs above £100,000 yearly and this kingdom much more." The report was the first to suggest that the colonies were beginning to follow their own course and received much attention. Among those called upon to testify before the lords as to its verity was none other than Sir Thomas Lynch, the pusillanimous former governor of Jamaica who had been Henry Morgan's nemesis.

If Randolph seemed at times almost hysterical in his condemnations, the circumstances of his commission made him more so. In 1677 he was given the post of collector of customs; by 1680 he was personally charged with the enforcement of the Navigation Acts throughout the Atlantic colonies. It was a vast responsibility, far beyond the ability of one man, and typical of the bureaucratic myopia that characterized the Lords of Trade. Nevertheless, Randolph did his best. Between 1680 and 1682, he personally seized a vast collection of ships and masters on charges of smuggling and piracy. The ships—some thirty-six vessels in all—ranged in size from ketch to sloop to brigantine, and nearly all were owned by local merchants.

All but two were acquitted. Magistrates throughout Massachusetts and New York (the two colonies that controlled the lion's share of trade between them) either refused to recognize Randolph's commission or gave it such narrow interpretation as to render it unworkable. The magistrates, allied with local merchants and, as often as not, colonial governors, accused Randolph of harassment and generally made things as unpleasant for him as possible. They not only acquitted those he brought before them; they charged him court costs.

The situation had reached a breaking point by 1689. Randolph by this time was widely despised as a snitch, a prig, and a lackey of the Board of Trade—all of which he was. The downfall of the Andros government in the wake of the Glorious Revolution removed the last pillars of support for his commission, and Randolph suddenly found himself jailed in Boston on charges of sedition and treason. Having arrived in New England as a harbinger of crown prerogative, he was shipped unceremoniously back in 1690, under guard, in a brutal display of colonial independence. The charges against him were quickly dismissed by Parliament, and his relations with the Lords of Trade were still cordial, but the fact remained that Randolph's tenure in New England had been a catastrophic failure.

Just as his fortunes seemed at their lowest ebb, the influence of a powerful patron rescued him. William Blaythwayt, who had known Randolph for many years, had in mind an ambitious project: the first ever complete survey of the American colonies. Randolph would be appointed surveyor general, a title resurrected solely for this commission, and sent as a roving inspector with purview over every customs house in America. He could interrogate witnesses, examine record books, even search for contraband. His unenviable assignment was to bolster the crown's grasp on its colonial finances and bring the recalcitrant colonies firmly into line.

It was a recurring theme in the early-modern phase of English state building. The crown selected a single man, gave him extraordinary powers and purview, and entrusted him with the Herculean task of bringing order to the entire Atlantic world. Between 1680 and 1700 several men were thus installed: Edmund Andros, Benjamin Fletcher, Lord Bellomont. In each case the task given them proved well beyond the ability of a solitary administrator and ended in rebellion, disgrace, and death, respectively. Edward Randolph's fate was somewhat kinder, yet none had as difficult a time as he: the title of surveyor general was synonymous with auditor-in-chief, and thus Randolph would be just as welcome in the colonies as auditors have always been everywhere.

His reception in Maryland in May 1692 set the tone. Governor Copley denied the validity of Randolph's office; when Randolph produced a letter from Blaythwayt, Copley denied Blaythwayt's as well. So began a war of words between the two men that would characterize Randolph's relations with the colonies for the rest of his life. Copley and his council were "silly animals"; Randolph was "scurrilous and haughty." When Randolph attempted to fulfill his commission, Copley blocked him at every turn. Not one single vessel or master was ever successfully brought to justice—Randolph prosecuted the sloop *Providence* three times without a conviction.

Though based in Maryland, Randolph traveled throughout the colonies. What he found there was scarcely heartening. It is hard to read his communiqués from this period without a certain skepticism, particularly given his own irascibility and prejudices. Over time, his letters to Blaythwayt became increasingly bitter and even frenzied. "New England is worse than Bedlam," he wrote, referring to the infamous insane asylum in South London. "Every place full of horror and confusion. Connecticut [is] overrun with fraud and hypocrisy; Rhode Island with folly and Quakerism. New Plymouth is as poor as a church mouse, Boston over spread with fantastical delusions. Horrid murders, cruel slavery and oppression rampant."

In fact Randolph was not far wrong. In 1692 Massachusetts was convulsed by the horrors of the Salem witch trials, Indian raids were at an all-time high in New York, and the revolutionary sentiments brought to boil during the Glorious Revolution still writhed under the surface throughout. Everywhere, it seemed, the fragile communities that had only just secured their hold on the landscape were in constant danger, both along their frontiers and within their own homes. Yet it is likely that Randolph's ire had a very different cause. Not long after his arrival in the colonies, influential men including Governor Copley began laying plans to discredit and remove him. By the end of 1692 the campaign had matured, and the Council of Maryland accused Edward Randolph of "oppressing and tyrannizing over the Subjects; commanding and abusing their Persons; pressing, taking and employing their servants, etc., without pay by color of his office." They also accused him of taking bribes. These charges and others were duly posted to the Lords of Trade, along with a vehement petition demanding his withdrawal.

Randolph had naive faith in his masters in Whitehall. "I expect letters from England which will end all disputes," he wrote confidently to his friend Sir Thomas Lawrence. Perhaps they would have come, in due course, but Governor Copley was taking no chances. Allegedly incriminating letters from Randolph were found concealed in Lawrence's pockets (much in the same way that overzealous police sometimes "find" evidence conveniently planted on a suspect's person), and Lawrence was thrown in jail. An arrest warrant was ordered against Randolph; warned just in time, he fled across the bay and lay concealed in the Maryland swamps—no easy feat for a man in his sixties.

A reprieve of sorts came several months later, when Governor Copley suddenly died. But by this time Randolph knew his commission, in fact if not in word, was at its end. The post of surveyor general had been no more successful than that of collector of customs—indeed, less so. Even without Copley at its head, the Council of Maryland continued to block and thwart him. Though he soldiered on for another year, Randolph admitted to himself and to his superiors that the persistent deviousness of the colonies overwhelmed his efforts. In the summer of 1695 he returned to England, weak and close to nervous collapse, believing himself to be an utter failure. His only tangible legacy was a sheaf of reports, dating back four years, which outlined in comprehensive detail the iniquities he had observed: smuggling, bribery, piracy, corruption of every sort. Leaving aside the hyperbole and antisectarian fervor that colored much of his writings, they were astonishingly comprehensive: it was as though Randolph, powerless to affect these events, resolved to expose them as much as possible. Among the many papers filed with the Lords of Trade on his return was the 1695 report that accused the governors of five Atlantic colonies of pirate brokering.

Having brought Edward Randolph's narrative up to date, we can now turn again to the cataclysmic events of 1696 and 1697 that would pit him once more against the recalcitrant governors. Among the recommendations Randolph offered to the new Board of Trade in July 1696 was a "Proposal humbly offered . . . for preventing frauds." It was clear in the ensuing paragraph whose frauds he had in mind. Governors, Randolph wrote, should be compelled to take new oaths of allegiance to the crown, and unsuitable governors (including those of Maryland, Carolina, and Pennsylvania) should be replaced. Admiralty courts should be convened in the colonies for the purpose of effecting swift justice for smugglers and pirates, and customs officers with questionable dealings should be removed from office after review by a crown-appointed commissioner.

Randolph's proposals were tendered in a new climate of bureaucratic zeal. The Board of Trade, deeply concerned about accusations of pirate brokering from Randolph and Basse, had already resolved to create the very admiralty courts that he advocated. The last of the Navigation Acts appeared in April 1696, bearing the imposing title "An Act for Preventing Frauds and Regulating Abuses in the Plantation Trade." When Randolph suggested a new oath for governors, Blaythwayt and the Board of Trade not only adopted the suggestion, but they also gave the job of administering it to Randolph himself. Then they went further: Randolph was reinstated as surveyor general (a post that he now detested), his salary was raised to a handsome £365 per annum, and his instructions were the broadest yet. Randolph was to travel throughout the colonies, ensure that the Navigation Acts were being properly imposed, and "from time to time give them an account of whatsoever he shall judge proper." Special instructions further commanded him to look specifically into the matter of pirate patronage by governors.

So it was that Edward Randolph set across the Atlantic for a third and final time, in October 1697, once again to attempt to impose the royal will on the colonies. But if the mission had not changed, the political circumstances certainly had. The Board of Trade finally invoked the dread threat, which its predecessor never dared do. In April the governors of Rhode Island, Connecticut, and Pennsylvania received terse letters threatening them with forfeiture of their charters. The governors of Maryland, Jamaica, Barbados, the Leeward Islands, Bermuda, and Virginia were informed that unless they complied fully with crown instructions, they would be removed from office. "Very great abuses have been and continue still to be practiced," the board wrote one governor, "[and] if we shall hereafter be informed, we shall look upon it as a breach of the trust, [and] we shall punish with loss of your place in that government and such further marks of our displeasure."

Edward Randolph's second arrival in Maryland, in December 1697, was scarcely more auspicious than his first. But the situation was transformed: the war—which had obscured all manner of illegal dealings—was over. The crown's attention, hitherto distracted by military matters, had shifted back to its colonies, and the colonies themselves were put on notice. Thus, while the colonists certainly had no reason to like Randolph any more than before, they had much greater reason to fear him. Randolph quickly found he had an unlikely ally. Governor Nicholson, who had replaced the deceased and unlamented Copley, brought Randolph to his house and entered eagerly into plans for suppressing the pirate trade. "I am heartily disposed to Governor Nicholson," the surveyor reported back to the Board of Trade. "He is really zealous to suppress piracy and illegal trade and was formerly very severe to those who were even suspected of countenancing pirates, so that not one of Every's men came to Maryland." Later, Randolph would also find support from his old friend Governor Andros, now governor of Virginia.

The Hydra of Pennsylvania

Those were exceptions, however. The remaining colonies continued to obfuscate, and among them Pennsylvania and New York were the worst. The former had long been marked as a pirate haven, stemming directly from the revelations of Every's crew that several had found safe haven there. The accusations became so heated that William Penn wrote personally to the House of Lords on March 1, 1697, assuring members that the charge "that the Governor [Markham] favors pirates is both foul and false." Clearly William Penn was not as easy in his mind as this denial suggests, for in the following month he informed the Pennsylvania Council of rumors that "you do not only wink at but embrace pirates, ships and men." Surely there could be no truth in it, he went on hurriedly, but as Governor Nicholson of Maryland was making a great noise about it downstream, "I do therefore desire and charge you, the Governor and Council for the time being, to issue forth some act . . . to suppress both forbidden trade and piracy." Though Markham was governor, Penn was still proprietor of the colony, and the council did as instructed.

Markham wrote Penn to answer the complaints. His letter had a refreshing candor that was markedly absent from his communications with the Board of Trade. The villain of the piece was quickly identified. "As to the privateers," which Governor Fletcher had commissioned, "they might have been pirates for any thing I know to the contrary." Fletcher, Markham reported, "fleeced them at New York . . . not by any violence, but blind signs which made them make a purse of gold to present him." The New York governor had also given them written and verbal offers of protection, in return for remuneration paid to his clerk. Finally, Markham admitted, he, too, had been the recipient of a few pirate trifles. "Some of those men gave me a small present," he wrote, "and one of them dying left me fifty pounds, but that they were pirates I can safely declare I never saw nor heard."

Even as Governor Markham penned these words, another, more serious scandal was brewing. In 1696 Markham had entertained a young mariner named Captain John Day and granted him a privateering commission to harass the French offshore. Day at once set off for Curacao and a piratical career. In November of that year Day arrived in Maryland, where—expecting a hearty welcome from Governor Copley—he found instead an outraged Governor Nicholson. One of Day's men wrote furiously to Markham: "A strange invasion happened in this town yesterday. The Governor of Maryland sent over sixty men in a hostile manner to invade our liberty, and to seize Captain Day." Describing the iniquities at some length, the respondent closed icily, "If you will suffer this gross affront from the Governor of Maryland I shall hold my hand on my mouth and say no more."

Markham would not. He wrote a furious letter to Nicholson, demanding the release of Day and his men. Nicholson refused and sent a copy of his reply to the Board of Trade. Day and his crew were held by Captain Josiah Daniell of His Majesty's hired ship *Prince of Orange*. Governor Markham wrote a chilly note to the captain commending him for his zeal but remarking that "sixty armed men marching into a town with colors flying . . . was a most irrational achievement, to say nothing of the abuse of government."

Having started on this dangerously belligerent note, events rapidly devolved into farce. Not long after Day's capture, several of Daniell's men stole a longboat and deserted, purportedly heading to Philadelphia. This prompted a furious letter from the captain to Governor Markham, which must have given the governor a great deal of amusement. Daniell began by demanding that Markham "give [himself] a little trouble on his Majesty's account and cause strict inquiry to be made" regarding the deserters. He went on to insult his recipient at great length: "The worst sailors know how ready you are to entertain and protect all deserters," he fumed. Then, in a rambling manner that showed more indignation than caution, the captain laid all his cards on the table:

> It is ruin for any ships to lade here so long as they have
> such encouragement to run in your parts, whence they are
> allowed to go "trampuseing" [pirating] where they please. I
> read in last July's Gazette a proclamation to apprehend
> Captain Every and his crew, and hear that some of them

are in your province. . . . I wonder that you prefer to grat-
ify them rather than have regard for the King's service.

Daniell closed his missive with a thinly veiled challenge to duel. "If
you fall my way," he growled, "I will endeavour to treat you as well as I
am capable."

Markham, in the face of these threats and imprecations, chose to
see the humor in them. "Yours of the 9th inst. is so indecent that it
seems rather penned in the cook-room than the Great Cabin," he began
in reply. Leaving aside the charges of pirate brokering and encouraging
desertion, he promised to employ his best efforts to secure Daniell's
men, "and do all things else for the King's service, not withstanding your
vilifying of us." Then he allowed himself a little playfulness:

> I know not what you mean by "trampuseing," unless you
> aimed at French to show your breeding, which you have ill
> set forth in your mother tongue. . . . I hope I shall not fall
> in your way, lest my treatment be such as I find in your
> letter. I wish you a good voyage and a better temper.

Writing some months later to the Board of Trade in response to
Nicholson's charges of pirate brokering, Markham downplayed the
whole incident. He freely admitted giving Day a commission to hunt
the French and professed astonishment that Governor Nicholson would
apprehend a man engaged in this good work. His reply was an ironic
barb: "Governor Nicholson, on hearing that such a vessel as Day's was
in this river, sent Captain Daniell (who is an easy, good natured man)
upon a project of getting Day's men." Having made the whole affair
seem faintly ludicrous and a waste of time, he closed with the gentlest
twist of the knife: "I have told you that there is suspicion of him
[Daniell] in some quarters that he had conspired with Governor Nicholson to subvert your Government; but this I never believed."

Assuredly, when Randolph arrived on the scene several months later,
Nicholson wasted no time in communicating the entire affair, as well as
his belief that many of Every's men were still inhabiting Philadelphia.
Randolph decided to see for himself. What he found not only confirmed
Nicholson's charge but in fact was far worse than he had said: "I saw
Stephen Claus, one of them, living within twenty rods of the Gover-

nor's house, and another of them married to his [Markham's] daughter. . . . I enclose a copy of the examination of two of Every's men who were living in Philadelphia, though the Governor had received the King's circular ordering them to be arrested. I saw them walking about the streets of Philadelphia for three weeks [during] my stay."

Randolph also encountered Robert Snead, the embittered customs agent whom Markham had humiliated the year before. Now out of work and almost penniless, Snead looked upon the surveyor general as his long-awaited messiah. He willingly wrote a long and detailed report of the affair of Every's crew, spelling out in detail how Governor Markham had blocked him at every turn. This time Snead's report, with all its accusations, was included in the packet with Randolph's own and sent directly to the Board of Trade.

Things were becoming serious for Governor Markham. Snead had written how he was prevented from arresting Every's men Lassells, Clinton, and Claus; Randolph now reported seeing them walking about the streets. Worse still was the matter of Every's crewmate James Brown, who had married Markham's daughter. When the board wrote to Markham demanding his explanation for the affair, he was stung into admitting that "Clinton, Lassells and some others supposed to be of Every's crew" had "happened to sojourn here," but he insisted that the men were arrested and made their escape to New York, after which time he had no idea of their whereabouts. "As for pirates or pirates' ships," he went on, "we know of none that ever came or were harbored here, much less that were encouraged by the Government and people, who are sober and industrious and have never advanced their fortunes by piracy or illegal trade." Still, Markham must have wondered what other accusations Randolph might have up his sleeve. He chose the preemptive strike, much as he had with Governor Nicholson, attempting to turn the tables and cast aspersions on Randolph himself: "As for the persons who came here as travelers about seven years ago and were supposed to be pirates, though they settled and claimed the liberties of English subjects among us, they were encouraged thereto by Edward Randolph, who gave expectation of pardon to some of them, as his enclosed letters show."

It was skillfully done, but little could turn the tide at that point. Markham must have realized that his situation was growing acute, for, venting his rage against Randolph in a letter to William Penn, he allowed some of his own desperation to show:

> I wish any that had been acquainted with Randolph's huffing and bouncing had but seen him when I called him to account for his affronts here; they would have seen him truckle & as humble as any spaniel dog, but no sooner got out of the town but fell to abusing and reviling me after his base manner. Had I not been so lame at that time I would have been after him & made him have known what wood my cudgel was made of.

Edward Randolph, whose nose for scandal was among the most acute of his senses, closed in. Report after report left Maryland, detailing Markham's relations with the pirates. Nicholson and his deputy Robert Quarry delighted in supplying witnesses who would testify to having been threatened or imprisoned or even beaten by the governor and his men for their attempts to collect His Majesty's due customs. Indeed, Nicholson's animus against Markham seems at times so fierce as to be pathological. Governor Markham, who was no stranger to guile and deceit, boggled at the Judas kiss he received during Nicholson's last visit: "He embraced me with a kiss, and on a ride through the country would call at poor people's houses and enquire after miscarriages in the Government, and what the poor ignorant people could say he put down in his memorandum book. Who can escape complaints when there are such diligent informers?"

The reasons for this hatred are not entirely clear. Certainly Nicholson had cause for grievance: pirates bound to and from Philadelphia made regular stops at nearby Baltimore, to his chagrin. It appears also, if Randolph's impressions are correct, that he was genuinely committed to stamping out the pirate menace. Yet neither of these factors can account for the wrath vented northward across the Chesapeake. Whatever its cause, Randolph was quick to make use of it. Governor Markham was now an easy target. "Five or six vessels," Randolph reported in a routine dispatch, "are come in from the Red Sea; some are gone southward towards Carolina and Providence. I doubt not to hear later that some of them have touched at Philadelphia, where Mr. Markham continues their steady friend."

Nor were the reports confined to Markham himself. All of Pennsylvania was to blame, according to Randolph. He related a tale communicated to him by an anonymous informer, who claimed that during the last pirate raid on the grimly named town of Whorekills a call was put out in Philadelphia for volunteers to capture the miscreants. There were none, not even after a substantial reward was offered. It was clear—to Randolph, at least—that the government itself was responsible for this widespread indifference. If anyone had volunteered, he wrote, the council would be forced to provide them with arms, which they were quite unwilling to do.

Randolph's reports, like water on stone, finally had their effect. In 1699 Governor Markham received a terse letter from the Board of Trade that in four sentences stripped him of his office and hinted at possible trial for gross corruption. The Pennsylvania Council received a letter to the same effect, along with instructions to reinstate the proprietor William Penn as governor of the colony. On the one hand it was a singular victory for crown prerogative, as it marked the first time that a sitting colonial governor was brought down not by internecine politics but through the diligence of an external and objective review. On the other, it was a severe embarrassment for the board, which had (in its previous existence as the Lords of Trade) instructed the equally disgraced Governor Fletcher to appoint Markham for precisely the opposite reason: to stymie Penn's overreaching proprietary power.

It was an unalloyed victory for Edward Randolph, however. After decades of suffering indignities and worse at the hands of the colonial governors, he had finally put his own mark on the board. By that time, however, Randolph had set his sights upon a much greater and more formidable target. Governor Markham might be disgraced, but the man who was still Markham's nominal superior—the same man who sat at the head of the greatest pirate cabal in the Atlantic world—had thus far eluded his grasp.

In April 1698 Edward Randolph arrived in New York.

-11-

Nemesis

SPRING HAD COME TO NEW YORK, BUT IT BROUGHT LITTLE CHEER for Benjamin Fletcher. The Albany frontier was still insecure, rumors had reached him that the natives had perpetrated some new atrocity just fifty miles north of the city, and the Connecticut Council was still being obdurate in the matter of fresh troops to man the garrisons. Worse still, his political fortunes had reached their lowest ebb. His old friend William Markham—the man he himself had appointed—was removed in disgrace. And Markham had apparently tried to take Fletcher down with him; there were nasty rumors that the late governor had spoken of Fletcher's favor among the pirates.

A Confederacy of Whigs

Piracy, indeed, seemed to be an albatross around his neck. As long ago as 1695, he was already withering under damning reports from Peter

Delanoy and other enemies that he had countenanced and even financed piracy in New York. By spring of 1698, when Edward Randolph arrived in the colony, matters had degraded still further. The Leislerians had formed an alliance with their Whig confreres in Massachusetts and began pressing their case at Parliament for a new governor with purview of both New York and New England. Prominent Whig businessman Robert Livingston arrived in London as their spokesman. The timing of his appearance was crucial: February 1697, coinciding with the creation of the new Board of Trade and its sudden interest in pirate brokering. The board naturally looked to Livingston, a leading colonial merchant, as a potential source of hard evidence.

Livingston was happy to comply. Testifying before Lord Shrewsbury and the board, he outlined in detail Fletcher's support for the notorious pirate Thomas Tew, as well as others. Peter Delanoy's letters, dated two years earlier, were reintroduced as evidence of corruption. Livingston even paraded a half dozen New York merchants now residing in London (Whigs to a man) who concurred and added their own condemnations: Governor Fletcher rigged elections, Governor Fletcher stole public funds, Governor Fletcher drank his own bathwater.

Robert Livingston's testimony before the Board of Trade, seemingly conducted in apolitical sterility, did little to conceal increasingly caustic party factions. Just as New York was divided within itself between Whig and Tory, so, too, was King William's court—and the Board of Trade. Livingston immediately began cultivating key Whigs, including the influential Shrewsbury. But Fletcher had his friends as well among the Tories, most notably Gilbert Heathcote, director of the Bank of England, and William Blaythwayt. Yet political tides had turned. In 1694 the Tory ministry, which had granted Fletcher his commission, collapsed, to be swiftly replaced by one composed almost exclusively of Whigs. This "second Glorious Revolution" meant more than a political housecleaning: it presaged several radical bureaucratic reforms, including the creation of the Board of Trade.

Hence the board, already suspicious of Atlantic governors in light of revelations from the Every trials, was only too ready to accept Livingston at his word. It also listened very carefully to his proposal: not only should Governor Fletcher be removed from office, but the entire government of the northeast colonies should be transformed. A single governor would assume control of both Massachusetts and New York, a prospect disturbingly similar to the Dominion of New England under James II. Livingston hastened to press his case. Governor Stoughton of Massachusetts was well intentioned but weak; Governor Fletcher was debauched beyond all redemption. Only a single, firm hand could sweep away all the festering corruption in both colonies.

Robert Livingston knew just the man. His choice (or, to be more accurate, the choice of the Massachusetts Council, from whom he was receiving his instructions) was Richard Coote, Lord Bellomont. The two men had first met in August 1695, during an earlier visit by Livingston to London. That their fortunes should eventually be entwined was almost inevitable. Livingston was the self-appointed spokesman for all American Whigs, and Bellomont was among the most fervent Whigs in court. Almost from their first meeting the two men shared a single goal: the removal of Benjamin Fletcher. Meeting clandestinely in Chelsea, Livingston and Bellomont began laying schemes to disgrace the governor and embarrass his powerful sponsor, William Blaythwayt.

At this point a third figure entered the conspiracy. Among Livingston's friends in London was an out-of-work privateer named William Kidd. The two had traded favors for one another in New York (Kidd serving as foreman on a jury that acquitted Livingston on charges of trading with the enemy, for example) and shared certain political affinities. Livingston and Bellomont arrived at what they believed was an ingenious means of ensnaring Fletcher: William Kidd would be granted a commission to intercept pirates on their way into New York. Thus not only would Fletcher be embarrassed (and impoverished), but the coin meant for him would pass into the greedy hands of Bellomont and Livingston. Bellomont, acting in secret, received King William's approval for the commission and then quickly raised the necessary funds from his fellow Whigs. The only snag proved to be Kidd himself. The captain, whose ignorance of political matters made him cautious, balked at being made a tool of the Whig party. Bellomont then "added threats to his wheedles," according to Kidd, promising to hold Kidd's ship, the *Antigua*, under arrest. "I thinking myself safe with a King's commission and the protection of so many great men," Kidd later testified, "I accepted, thinking it was in my Lord Bellomont's power to oppress me if I still continued obstinate." Captain Kidd, departing London in

March 1696, was poised to strike a blow for the Whig party that would set the colonies reeling.

Now it was one year later. There had been no word from Captain Kidd, but Livingston felt it was time to put the plan into action. He presented his case against Fletcher to the board and offered as replacement that great gentleman Lord Bellomont. There could be no question that Bellomont looked the part. Just over forty years old, strikingly tall and handsome, the earl seemed every inch a man of unimpeachable rectitude. A painting done after his arrival in the colonies reveals a sharp nose, deeply set eyes, and a determined chin. Not quite so apparent were the earl's great love of money, spendthrift habits, and constant debt.

Lord Bellomont Takes on the Pirate Brokers

The Board of Trade ultimately approved both Livingston's plan and his choice of successor. Lord Bellomont was named governor of New York, Massachusetts, and New Hampshire; he was also given command of the militias of Rhode Island, Connecticut, and New Jersey. As such, he would have nearly all the powers once given to Edmund Andros and all the responsibility as well. "The subjects upon which you are to make more particular inquiries," the board instructed him, "are the officers in any part of the administration of the government, and the legality of their qualification for the execution of their respective offices."

This careful language was echoed in a letter to Fletcher himself, breaking the news of his removal in the gentlest way possible. He should not think, the board told him, that this action was motivated by any animus against him personally. King William himself had written to Shrewsbury that "His Majesty, having found no fault with Colonel Fletcher during his government, is pleased to allow those favorable words, of taking care of him, and otherwise employing him, which are not unusual in letters of revocation."

However delicately the Board of Trade chose to couch its actions, there could be no doubt as to Bellomont's intentions. Arriving on April 2, 1698, the new governor was met by his outgoing predecessor, Governor Fletcher, in a great and well-rehearsed display of feigned good feelings. The city elite (including Frederick Phillipse) met him at the pier, and the council (including Nichols, Bayard, and others of the infamous cabal) welcomed him at their homes. Bellomont responded by issuing an edict that summarily outlawed drinking, cursing, womanizing, licentious displays, and neglecting the Sabbath. The obvious implication was that all this and more had been condoned by former governor Fletcher. Within ten days the two men were no longer on speaking terms. As Robert Livingston passed Fletcher on the street and raised his hat mockingly, Fletcher lost his temper. He reached out, grasped Livingston's nose between his thumb and forefinger, and tweaked hard.

One week later, Edward Randolph arrived.

It was as though two hurricanes, one from London and one from Pennsylvania, had crossed paths over New York. Each gained strength from the other, and both combined to sweep through governor and council with epic force. As early as February, Randolph had warned the Board of Trade that "these villains," the pirates, "frequently say that they carry their unjust gains to New York, where they are permitted egress and regress without control." Now in the colony, Randolph found events moving even quicker than he imagined. Within hours of his arrival he was ensconced as a guest of Governor Bellomont. As for Governor Fletcher, whom he had come to expose, he saw nothing but heard much. Bellomont, he understood, was in a delicate position. Charged with administering two colonies and four militias, stamping out piracy, and cleansing the customs service, the new governor had to reckon first with a seat of governance that was rife with dissension. Piracy was good business for the colonies, a fact that Fletcher had appreciated only too well. Fletcher still had many friends both within the colony and in the Board of Trade. If things soured too much—if the Whig government fell or if Governor Bellomont made a hash of things—Fletcher might well find himself back in power again. Bellomont had to move quickly to disgrace his opponent past all hope of resuscitation.

He began on May 8. At the first meeting of the Council of New York, with Edward Randolph sworn in as honored guest, Bellomont ascended the podium with a sheaf of papers in his hand. The first was a letter from the Duke of Shrewsbury condemning piracy, followed by a memorial from the East India Company reiterating piracy's dire effects on English trade. Then Bellomont turned innocuously to the council members and asked if they had any thoughts on the matter. When no one spoke, he went on in a chilly, remorseless voice that he "had received information that Colonel Fletcher had admitted notorious pirates to bring their spoils to New York, receiving considerable rewards for the same, and that Mr. Nicholls [another member of the council] had been the broker in making the bargain between them." Nicholls, who was present, replied hotly that he had never even met a pirate, at which time Bellomont flourished a deposition by one Edward Taylor that confirmed Nicholl had taken eight hundred pieces of eight off of him. Nicholl was reduced to silence.

Bellomont pressed on. A local captain named Evans, who had allegedly promised to "man his ship with pirates," was brought forward. Evans, like Nicholl, denied the charge and, as the record tersely states, "he and Mr. Nicholl then withdrew." By this time the council was thoroughly alarmed, so much so that when Bellomont suddenly produced a proclamation against piracy, it was passed without dissent. But Bellomont was far from finished. He demanded to know what action would be taken against the notorious pirate brokers Fletcher, Evans, and Nicholl. Fletcher's close friend Chidley Brooke was stung into answering "that the giving protection to pirates had not formerly been looked upon as so great a matter, and that all the neighboring governments had done it commonly." But Bellomont would have none of that. Brooke might think it a "peccadillo," he replied icily, but King William and his ministers regarded it as "a high offense." Brooke was cowed into muttering that he "did not excuse it, but only stated what had been done."

Lord Bellomont had bludgeoned his council into submission. From the sidelines, Edward Randolph could only sit and marvel. What came next was even more extraordinary: Bellomont demanded that both Fletcher and Nicholl be arrested and tried for gross corruption, and the council members (who by now must have been fearful that their own "peccadilloes" might come to light) agreed unanimously. The evidence against Fletcher was sealed in a packet and marked for the king, to be sent along with the disgraced governor on the first eastbound sloop to London.

This stunning reversal of fortune was compounded one day later. Standing on the steps of Fort William, the same embattlement that just ten years before had been the site of Jacob Leisler's downfall, Bellomont announced that henceforth "all pirates and sea rovers that shall come within the jurisdiction of this province should be suppressed, and that effectual care might be taken to arrest, seize and secure all such pirates and sea rovers, as the laws in such cases do direct." The consequences were swift and brutal. Writing three days later, Randolph observed that while he had known of forty pirates recently arrived in New York and had seen for himself one of them, all were arrested within hours of Bellomont's proclamation—though most eventually escaped to other nearby colonies, where the governors were "afraid to meddle with anyone lest the people that live by the seaside . . . choose another Governor for the next year." It might have amused Randolph to see that Bellomont was now even more despised in the colonies than himself. "Lord Bellomont has highly displeased the trading men in New York," Randolph reported, "who have all along encouraged privateers."

From Randolph's glowing accounts we find an image of the new governor in almost saintly garb, wielding a shining sword of justice through the slough of venality that was New York. Edward Randolph naturally looked upon Lord Bellomont as an ally, a fellow crusader against the scourge of piracy and staunch defender of the monarchy against incipient colonial independence. A more astute man, however, would have perceived that while their aim was certainly shared, their motives could not have been more different. The earl may genuinely have loathed pirates and privateers, but he also consorted with them. His own protégé, William Kidd, was currently somewhere in the Red Sea, and the reports filtering back were not encouraging. Bellomont was, first and foremost, a politician. His depiction of New York as a den of pirate brokers was accurate—as other witness testimony proves—but it was no less politically motivated. The best evidence of this is his letters. On May 18 he composed his first missive to the Board of Trade, claiming that "since my arrival I have received many complaints of the maladministration of the late Governor. . . . There is a great cry that Governor Fletcher has embezzled and converted to his own use large sums of money." Cannily, he added a postscript that included a letter from Fletcher himself, "declaring his justice, good government, the current of the laws and the increase of trade, which he designs for absolving him from the complaints made against him." Bellomont had not yet seen the list of subscribers, he admitted, but he had no doubt whom it would include: the very men "who have grown rich together with him by fitting out pirate ships and trading with Madagascar, Scotland, and Curaçao. Being instruments of his maladministration, they now justify him and thank him for that which will probably be censured by the King." Thus by including Fletcher's letter in his own packet and providing a negative spin on its contents and supporters, Bellomont neutralized both.

Moving from the specific to the general, Bellomont also provided the first of many accounts of the soon-to-be infamous pirate brokerage by Phillipse and others:

> There is a great trade managed between this place and Madagascar from whence great quantities of East India goods are brought, which are certainly purchased from pirates. I do not know what to do herein, and beg for your directions. This practice is set up in order that the spoils taken by the pirates (set out from New York) may be brought here in merchant ships whose owners are also owners and interested in the pirates' ships.

Bellomont's charges were astounding. New York not only countenanced piracy; it operated a sophisticated form of money laundering two centuries in advance of the *Cosa Nostra*. In the following week he moved in two directions at once. First, he called a special session of the House of Representatives to lay before them the charges against Benjamin Fletcher. This was ticklish ground: aside from the Leislerians, who had neither wealth nor numbers in the colony, Fletcher had been widely admired and even loved. His unflagging efforts to secure the Albany frontier from Indian raids were well known and yet another mark in his favor. Bellomont, on the other hand, was an English aristocrat whose brief tenure in the colony had thus far been marked by arrests, seizures, and massive disruptions of trade. He began on a plaintive note: "My voyage was long and tedious, but I have endeavored by industry to make up the loss and time. I find that my predecessor has left me a divided people, an empty treasury, a few miserable, naked, half starved soldiers . . . in a word, the whole Government out of frame."

This was arrant nonsense. New York was among the wealthiest colonies in the Atlantic world, thanks in no small part to Fletcher's amicable relations with the pirate brokers. The treasury was burgeoning, in

spite of the admitted strains imposed by maintaining fortresses and garrisons along the frontier (Bellomont's arrival in New York had, in fact,
interrupted an ongoing feud between Fletcher and the acting governors
of Connecticut and Massachusetts to equip the forts). That the colony
was divided, however, was an undeniable truth. It was precisely those
divisions that Lord Bellomont intended to exploit. "It has been represented to the Government in England," he told the House, "that this
province has been a noted receptacle of pirates and seat of illegal trade.
I hope that you will discountenance to the utmost piracy, which is the
worst form of robbery." The reaction to this was mixed. Leislerians
cheered, naturally (forgetting that Jacob Leisler himself had commissioned many of the same men Bellomont now named as notorious
pirates); Tory merchants looked worried. Bellomont hastened to reas-
sure them. While he saw it as his foremost duty to stamp out the pirate
trade, he said, "I shall encourage a lawful trade by all means in my
power." That these two aims might not be mutually compatible was
apparently not considered.

Second, the same afternoon, Bellomont sent a long and comprehensive report to the Board of Trade. Having shored up his position in
the colonies, he now sought to consolidate it at Whitehall. The whole
of Benjamin Fletcher's alleged perfidy was laid before them. Going as
far back as 1691, Bellomont echoed almost verbatim Peter Delanoy's
charges regarding Thomas Tew, that "although a man of infamous character, he was received and caressed by Governor Fletcher, dined and
supped often with him, and appeared with him publicly in his coach."
But Tew had gone to the Red Sea four years ago and never came back:
his scandal, like his corpse, had desiccated. Bellomont added the names
of Moston, Glover, and Hoar, three pirates who had sailed with Tew
and then returned to collect additional commissions in 1695 and 1696.
Then there was "one Raynor, said to be one of Every's crew, who landed
at the east end of Nassau Island [Long Island, New York] with a treasure valued at £1,500." This was a new charge: as far as the board knew,
none of Every's men had reached New York. A sharp-eyed sheriff spot-
ted the loot and arrested Raynor, but the pirate appealed to Governor
Fletcher and in exchange for a bond was allowed to depart. "I have heard
also of several other protections purchased from Colonel Fletcher, but
I am assured that no pirate was prosecuted during his term of office."

Lest the board think that Fletcher's iniquities were past tense, Bellomont brought them ruthlessly up to the present. His arrival in the colony had caused great confusion for the evildoers, as he exulted:

> I have further information that five sail, supposed to be pirates, were seen hovering round the coast since my arrival, and that one of them landed some men in the Jerseys to ask who was Governor here. On learning that I was come they departed, not daring to come to this Government, so that my coming is reputed to have caused Governor Fletcher great loss.

It is well to read these extravagant charges with a skeptical eye. As already noted, Lord Bellomont had a vested interest in making the colony under his care seem as degenerate and impoverished as possible, so that the transformation under his governance appeared all the more miraculous. This accounts in part for the demonization of Benjamin Fletcher; the rest, of course, was politics. Yet while Bellomont may well have inflated his claims, the base truth of them was well documented. Included in the packet sent to the Board of Trade on May 19 was a series of signed depositions. In the weeks following his arrival, Bellomont had scoured the town for all the miscreants he could find. In most cases it was an easy task: the pirates were far from a clandestine lot. Most lived ordinary, respectable lives within the community.

Samuel Burgess was a case in point. Burgess, the pirate that Frederick Phillipse had entrusted with the task of bargaining with Adam Baldridge in 1695, had since made several trips to the pirate colony at St. Mary's. He was as well known and well respected as any other local—drawn, in fact, from the same class and social circle as Bellomont's own protégé, Captain Kidd. His voyages to Madagascar in Phillipse's ship *Margaret* were routine, and the cargo he carried seemed equally mundane; its only distinction was that it was to be sold to pirates.

Seized and interrogated by Lord Bellomont on May 3, Burgess cheerfully admitted that he and another pirate had returned from a voyage in the Red Sea in 1695 and sought permission from Fletcher to enter the harbor. After five days it was granted, in return for several hundred gold pieces collected from the crew. Burgess noted, "I gave Mr. Honan two gold sequins for Governor Fletcher's protection." Captain Edward Taylor, another pirate whom Edward Randolph had earlier seen walking about the town, also testified to Fletcher's venality. He had been fleeced to an even greater extent than Burgess: Fletcher and Nicholls had demanded £700 to enter and discharge his cargo. "The promise of £700 could not be fulfilled," Taylor admitted ruefully, "because the crew had dispersed, so the owners made the Governor a present of the ship."

While Bellomont was chiefly interested in evidence of Fletcher's misdeeds, other names cropped up in the depositions. Leonard Lewis, for example, named one of Frederick Phillipse's closest friends:

> My brother, who had sailed with the pirate Tew in the Red Sea, asked for my advice how he should escape trouble on that account. I went to Mr. Nicholas Bayard, of the Council, who advised me to go to Governor Fletcher; upon which I asked him to apply to him on my behalf, when he answered that a protection could not be obtained for less than 100 dollars. I replied that my brother was poor, and offered 75 dollars, which Colonel Bayard took, saying he would try what he could do.

In one month Lord Bellomont succeeded in shaking the colony of New York to its core. He would later proudly claim that he had kept more than £100,000 of illegal trade out of the city, a figure that his enemies would seize upon in their charge that he was driving New York into the ground. Either way, Bellomont's pogrom seemed destined to quash the pirate trade in New York, perhaps even piracy itself. Yet appearances were deceiving. The same pirates that had complacently testified to bribing Governor Fletcher still flourished under the protections granted by him—a fact of which Bellomont was well aware but could not change. His fiery proclamation from Fort William against the pirate trade carried a small but crucial addendum at its end: "Provided always that nothing herein shall be construed to extend unto any person or persons that have surrendered themselves and obtained protections from the late Governor."

Bellomont shared his frustration over this fact with the Board of Trade. He knew where the pirates were, he told them, but "I have not proceeded against them, since I could not violate the protections, being an act of public faith, without the King's orders." This lack of enforceability made a mockery of the governor's ambitious plans. Business, having received a short and salutary shock, went on as usual. In June 1698, exactly one month after his deposition, Burgess was off again in the *Margaret*, carrying another load of Phillipse's goods to the pirates of St. Mary's. The manifest gave eloquent testimony to the depths of their bellicosity and thirst:

> Six chests and seven casks sundry merchandise
> Thirty half barrels of peas
> Sixty half barrels of salt
> Forty-five barrels of beer
> Twenty-six casks Madeira wines
> Sixteen casks of Rum
> One barrel lime juice
> Three hundred fifty weight of gun powder

The Board of Trade commiserated with Bellomont's predicament and offered all the help it could. "We have been much troubled to hear of your difficulties," it wrote him in October, "and commend your zeal. Your advices as to pirates and illegal trade are very useful; we entreat you to continue them." He could pardon Burgess and Taylor if he wished, and as for Governor Fletcher's protections, "which extend only the protection of the law," Bellomont should interpret them narrowly. "Wherever the law enables you, proceed against pirates and suspected pirates." The board also showed itself well aware of the trade between Phillipse and Baldridge and no less diligent in obtaining depositions than Bellomont himself. Enclosed in the packet was the testimony of Humphrey Perkings, "master of the ship *Frederick*, belonging to Frederick Phillipse of New York and lately employed in trading with pirates, and he is said to have been himself a pirate."

The Board of Trade had given him all the power and incentive it could, but the underlying message was clear: this was Bellomont's job, and his reputation lay with its success. The board closed with expressions of goodwill and two letters, still sealed in their envelopes, for the governors of Rhode Island and Connecticut. The letters, as the board candidly told Bellomont, accused both men of harboring pirates in their colonies. He must see what he could do about that problem, as well.

-12-

"Your Loving Friends"

CAPTAIN SAMUEL BURGESS HAD SUFFERED A VERY CLOSE SHAVE. His recent history was enough to give even the stoutest mariner dyspepsia: interrogated by Lord Bellomont in New York, threatened with imprisonment and even execution, and finally—inexplicably—set free. Even afterward his luck held. Phillipse, whom Burgess had implicated as a pirate broker, still seemed inclined to trust him. He had outfitted the *Margaret* for yet another voyage to St. Mary's, and Burgess had left New York (probably with great relief) in the summer of 1698. The prospect ahead seemed promising. Whatever strange chill seemed to have descended over the Eastern Seaboard, and its administrators, would certainly dissolve once he reached Madagascar.

But things had changed there as well. Arriving in St. Mary's two weeks after the new year in 1699, Burgess discovered that King Baldridge was gone. The native tribes that built his castle and suffered his frequent slaving forays finally rebelled, and Baldridge was driven right off the island. The crumbling remains of his fortress still stood, the taverns of St. Mary's were still open for business, but Burgess could sense that the fragile unity that held the pirate colony together was disintegrating. He offloaded his stores—scissors, knives, and liquor—and received ten thousand pieces of eight from the pirates in return. Burgess stayed in St. Mary's for just a few weeks, careening his ship and taking in stores. More surprisingly, he also received nineteen bedraggled pirates desperate for passage home. This was a first, and Burgess began to feel uneasy. An English man-of-war had passed through not long before offering pardon for those pirates that would accept it and abandon the colony. A great number of them did. Rumors had reached them of pirate hunters sailing out of London, and reports came that many of their old associates were turning coat and hunting down old friends.

Burgess was anxious to leave and did so in early February. He made first for St. Augustine's Bay on the island of Madagascar, where he took on meat and slaves and fresh rumors of English pirate hunters nearby. These were not ordinary navy vessels, he learned, but private captains hired by the East India Company to protect its trade. Some had a fierce reputation, and it was widely acknowledged among the pirates of Madagascar that the Red Sea trade wasn't what it used to be. Captain Burgess remained at St. Augustine's Bay longer than he had at St. Mary's, but by November 1699 he was ready to make the long voyage round the Cape of Good Hope and home to New York. Frederick Phillipse would be anxious for his payment and his slaves.

The storms began just days after they left Madagascar, and after one week the *Margaret* was battered and leaking badly. As they rounded the Cape of Good Hope the seas worsened, and Burgess knew his ship must either find safe harbor or founder. It was a difficult choice, but he finally turned north and brought the *Margaret* into port at the cape. He intended only to stay long enough to ride out the storm, revictual hurriedly, and pump out the hull. Yet a sharp-eyed agent, Captain Matthew Lowth, spied the *Margaret* in the harbor and did not recognize her.

Unfortunately for Burgess, Lowth was one of the men hired by the East India Company to hunt down the pirates. Lowth summoned Burgess to his own ship, tellingly named the *Loyal Merchant*, and began interrogating him. The unfortunate pirate must have felt a sense of déjà vu. This time, however, Lowth ordered him chained and confined on suspicion of trading with pirates and seized the *Margaret*. As Burgess's boat returned to the ship without him aboard, several of the passengers and crew panicked and threw themselves overboard. Rightly interpreting this as evidence of guilt, Lowth took the *Margaret* in tow to Bombay and disposed of her cargo. From there they headed north, where Burgess and his crew would face trial before the High Court of Admiralty, on the charge of piracy.

Trouble in the Colonies

These incidents were repeated with increasing frequency. Almost as if Edward Randolph had driven a wedge into the solid wall of colonial governance, cracks suddenly appeared everywhere at once. From India came the reports of another colonial agent who, having lived with the pirates himself, claimed to have firsthand knowledge of pirate sponsorship. Among his earliest communications was this startling piece of news: "During my residence with the pirates," he wrote the Board of Trade, "I understood they were supplied with ammunition and all sorts of necessaries by one Captain Baldridge and Lawrence Johnson, two old pirates that are . . . factors for one Frederick Phillipse, who under pretense of trading to Madagascar for negro slaves supplies these rogues with all sorts of stores."

Baldridge, who by late 1699 had returned to New York, was now a respectable city merchant. He was happy to confirm all the colonial agent's charges and provided a detailed deposition that named every pirate that had visited St. Mary's from 1691 to 1699. There, in bold type, were all the men whose names had graced privateering commissions for the last decade: Raynor, Tew, Churcher, Glover, Hoar, Wake, Burgess, Coates, and so on. Baldridge also confirmed, albeit more reluctantly, that his ready supplier throughout had been Governor Fletcher's great friend and councilman, Frederick Phillipse.

The industrious colonial agent had made other charges as well. Of Glover and Hoar, two pirates named by Baldridge (and earlier by Bellomont), the agent confirmed what the board already knew: "They had a commission from the Governor of New York to take the French. They fitted their ship from Rhode Island, and the then-Governor of New York knew their designs, as also the Governor of Rhode Island."

Fissures appeared in unlikely places. Governor Codrington of Antigua, who had thus far been untouched by scandal, suddenly surfaced in one of Randolph's reports. Hearing rumors that several navy captains had traded with pirates in the Leeward Islands, Randolph inquired of the lieutenant governor, John Yeamans, why Codrington (who had been apprized of the affair) did nothing to stop it nor prosecuted the men afterward. "Mr. Yeamans replied," Randolph related, "that he had advised the Governor to prosecute them and that he drew a general warrant for their apprehension, which Governor Codrington promised should be executed. But he never did so." In this particular instance the matter was moot; just as Randolph began turning his cannons to bear on Antigua, Governor Codrington died.

Sometimes even an oblique charge in one of Randolph's reports provoked a furious response, so heated as to raise new suspicions. "About ten days ago," Randolph wrote in a routine dispatch, "it was discovered that five or six ships from the Red Sea were on the coast. One of them was at Connecticut, and delivered part of her goods." It was not much of an accusation, but the governor and Council of Connecticut protested inordinately:

> All reports of our harboring pirates and carrying on illegal
> trade are utterly false. Our trade at the most is so inconsid-
> erable that it would be impossible for illegal traders to pass
> undiscovered; and as to our being a receptacle for pirates,
> not one vessel, belonging or reported to belong to any
> pirates, real or supposed, has come or been admitted to
> any of our ports, bays or any other place.

Similarly, the charge of pirate brokering had finally been enough to bring down a third governor, John Goddard of Bermuda. Here, however, it was not due to the diligence of Edward Randolph but to another collector of customs, ironically named Nicholas Trott (a distant cousin of the governor of the Bahamas). Collector Trott had assembled a sheaf of evidence against Goddard, which he proposed to forward at once to the Board of Trade. As Isaac Richier had once done with another overeager customs agent, John Larkin, Goddard did again: Trott was imprisoned—possibly even in the same horrid cell where Larkin had languished. Goddard attempted to explain the decision to an enraged board. Trott, he said, was "a villain and a rogue" who had "abused me since his return from England with such villainous language that I was forced to remove him out of all his employs and throw him into jail. . . . He is the most factious, seditious and mutinous fellow on the whole island [and] I hope your Lordships will see it fit in your high prudence . . . that he may receive a punishment agreeable to his deserts."

The Duke of Shrewsbury, chairman of the Board of Trade, was skeptical. He ordered Trott to be released at once and Goddard to provide a detailed accounting of all his relations with the pirates. Goddard replied with a précis of evidence against his predecessor, Isaac Richier, particularly with regard to Thomas Tew. The former governor was still very much alive and now, with his brother in London, was angling to succeed Goddard. Attacked on all sides, Goddard lashed out:

> So long as I am Governor, no pirates shall receive protection in Bermuda. I hear from England that Mr. Richier's brother has turned me out of the Government with villainous falsities, scandal and untruths, which the Council of Trade are pleased to believe. I can with confidence affirm that there are not two idler men in the world than Richier and Trott.

The board answered by removing Goddard from office. Yet just one year later, when Edward Randolph arrived to check on things himself, he found Goddard's replacement, Samuel Day, scarcely an improvement. Once again poor Trott had been jailed for his pains. This time the charge was that he had taken possession of a wreck, disarmed its crew, and stolen from the ship the complete contents of its cargo, worth £75,000. According to Edward Richier, who proffered the charge against him, Trott had even charged each of the unfortunate crew members £50 to receive their weapons and depart the island. "I thought I was in justice bound to inform myself what truth there was against Trott," Randolph wrote, "and the cause why the Governors successively imprisoned him." What he found was much as he expected: Richier, Goddard, and Day had all been making tidy sums granting illegal commissions and harboring pirates in Hamilton and St. George's. As with New York, the Bermuda Council was composed exclusively of merchants who derived substantial income from the pirates and saw no reason to constrain good business. Day, Randolph reported, was "a man laden with pride and vanity, more fit for a pasha than a governor." The council was equally tainted, including among its members one William Outerbridge, "who was part-owner of the sloop *Amity*, Thomas Tew master."

The next to fall was perhaps the most inevitable: the customs agent's cousin Governor Nicholas Trott of New Providence. It was Trott, after all, who had been named first and repeatedly by Every's men as the man responsible for giving the *Fancy* safe haven. Because Randolph could not be everywhere at once, the Board of Trade sent another man, John Graves, to investigate. Graves arrived in New Providence on July 19, 1697, at which time the population of the colony still hovered around one hundred persons. Thus it did not take long to verify the truth of Dann's and Middleton's claims. Graves was introduced to seven men from Every's crew, now happily married and living a contented existence scattered throughout the isles. "Governor Trott got considerable out of them," Graves told the Board of Trade, "particulars I cannot certify, but it is reported at least £7,000. This Governor has fleeced those he found here and gives them another instrument of writing for a pardon."

Trott, like Markham of Pennsylvania, Fletcher of New York, and Goddard of Bermuda, was called back to England to face charges. "The Case of Nicholas Trott" appears in the colonial records dated October 25, 1697, one year to the day since the trials of Every's crew. Yet in course and manner it could scarcely have been more of a contrast. Where the former trials had occurred in the awesome and very public splendor of the Old Bailey, the trial of Nicholas Trott would remain entirely *in camera*, conducted not by the lord chief justice but rather by the Board of Trade. In several trenchant pages the whole of the story was retold: Every's arrival in New Providence, his approaches to Trott, the infamous £1,000 in gold presented as "security."

In reply, Governor Trott came out swinging. To the charge of accepting bribes, Trott answered that "the two men upon whose evidence the charge rests were both notorious pirates, one of whom was executed and the other saved his life by turning informer." True enough. But that hardly seemed to resolve the accusation, and in later proceedings Trott's replies faltered. Did he suspect the men who came to him were pirates? "*Answer*: How could he know it, and how could he have secured 113 men on suspicion? Suspicion is not proof." Perhaps the most useful defense was that implied in this reply: even if Trott did know, as indeed he must have, how could one man and a colony of less than a hundred souls—with no navy—secure and hold some 113 pirates with a magnificently equipped brigantine of forty-six guns?

Nevertheless, it was Trott's malfeasances that had brought the board's attention to pirate sponsorship in the first place, and so it was only justice that he should be made an example of. The Duke of Shrewsbury summarily removed him from office, charging one Captain Webb to replace Trott, investigate the matter, and submit his findings. He did not, however, press any criminal charges. The dignity of the crown still had to be thought of.

Samuel Cranston, Pirate Patron of Rhode Island

The spectacular falls of Fletcher and Markham, not to mention those of Goddard and Trott, seemed to presage an end to the quiet accord between pirates and governors. Historical precedent indicated this as well: throughout its history, piracy flourished best in neglect. With the stern eye of the Board of Trade upon them, it appeared as though the Atlantic governors would divest themselves of such questionable friends and the pirates would be left to fend for themselves. Yet this was not the case. In spite of Randolph's efforts, in spite of the constant scrutiny and censure of the Board of Trade, most Atlantic governors went on much as before—and suffered no repercussions for so doing. The removal of Fletcher and Markham in 1698 did not signal the beginning of a complete turnover of colonial governance, much as Randolph and Lord Bellomont might have wished it. Indeed the most extraordinary aspect of this period is not how many governors were disgraced for dealing with pirates, but how many remained in spite of doing so.

Consider the case of Samuel Cranston, governor of Rhode Island. On the chaste white marble of his tomb in Newport's Common Burial Ground is an epitaph bespeaking of breeding, character, and service:

> Here lies the body of Samuel Cranston, Esq., late Gov-
> ernour of this colony; aged 68 years; and departed this life
> April 26, A.D. 1727. He was the son of John Cranston,
> Esq., who was also Governour here, 1680. He was
> descended from the noble Scottish Lord Cranston, and
> carried in his veins a stream of the ancient Earls of Craw-
> ford, Bothwell, and Traquairs. Having had for his grandfa-
> ther James Cranston, clerk, Chaplain to King Charles the
> First. His great-grandfather was John Cranston, of Bool,
> Esq. This last was son to James Cranston, Esq., which
> James was son to William Lord Cranston.

Samuel Cranston was governor of the colony from 1698 to his death in 1727, the longest tenure in Rhode Island history. He was a gentleman, descended (as his epitaph makes clear) from a lineage both aristocratic and pious. He had inherited the title of governor from his father and would pass it to his son. Yet it was this same Cranston who presided over a colony dubbed by one observer "a free port to pirates and illegal traders of all places." From the mid-seventeenth century until well into the eighteenth, pirates enjoyed virtual carte blanche in Rhode Island, basking in the security of an amicable and lenient government. For thirty years, despite numerous condemnations from Randolph and Bellomont (not to mention Cranston's archnemesis, Governor Dudley of Massachusetts), Cranston survived in office—survived and flourished. And long past the bureaucratic reforms of 1698, Rhode Island and its governor continued to harbor the pirates, as did many other governors in other colonies.

Rhode Island is a cornucopia of isles, inlets, sheltered harbors, and bays. With only two major trading cities, separated by Narragansett Bay, it offered numerous safe harbors to any ship that approached its shore. As David Starkey recently pointed out, even if Rhode Islanders had wanted to drive the pirates from their midst, it would have been virtually impossible to do so. Moreover, the colony of Rhode Island was more dependent than any other on mercantile trade. Its entire society—the wealthy merchant upper class, the ship chandlers and tradesmen of the middle class, and the seafaring lower class—all owed their livelihoods to the sea. Thus it was quite likely that they would seize upon privateering with enthusiasm, for the colony had more skilled mariners per capita to undertake such voyages and a surplus of trained seamen to act as crew. When the Navigation Acts effectively deprived the colony of most of its legitimate commerce, privateering offered an easy alternative to employ out-of-work sailors, reactivate dockyards and shipbuilding firms, enrich chandleries, and boost colonial revenue.

The first recorded case of Rhode Island privateering occurred in 1653, when two local merchant mariners, Edward Hall and Samuel Comstock, sailed from Newport in a bark named the *Swallow*, bearing a commission from Governor William Dyer to harass Dutch trade. The bark returned some months later, whereat a prize commission was duly convened. The government received £56 for its troubles—a respectable but not princely sum. Colonial records indicate the prize was purchased by one Christopher Almy, merchant. The next case of privateering, which occurred later that same year, makes for an interesting coda. It was commanded by William Dyer himself. Dyer seized and plundered a Dutch trading post on the Connecticut River and returned to his colony several hundred pounds richer.

The curious career of William Dyer hints at a pattern that would emerge strongly in the later seventeenth century. The first pirates to sail from Rhode Island were local men, usually of the middle or even upper mercantile classes. Most were ex-merchant captains who had earlier earned their livings through trading voyages. In an era when privateering commissions were still legal, they made the transition from one form of commercial enterprise to another with easy grace. There are no records of piracy trials between the years 1653 and 1683, nor is there any mention of piratical activity around Rhode Island in surviving crown records. Yet it is undeniable that it was during this period that the relationship between Rhode Island governors and pirates germinated. Dyer's example is instructive. So, in its own way, is that of Captain Thomas Paine. In 1683 Paine, a native Rhode Islander, returned to Newport laden with captured booty and demanded condemnation of his prize. He produced a commission from Governor Lynch of Jamaica, which was, according to one customs agent, "a more forged than fair and true commission." This same agent also noted that even the governor's titles were not correctly listed. Rhode Island governor Coddington "was of another opinion," however, "and declared the ship a free bottom by virtue of the same."

Yet Paine was not quite free and clear. The customs collector—ironically, William Dyer Jr.—declared Paine an "arch pirate" and ordered him to stand trial. Coddington intervened, and the matter was dropped.

Two years later the records reveal that Paine sat in respectable splendor on a grand jury. A short time afterward, during King William's War of 1690, Governor John Easton sought out the unrepentant mariner and made him commander of the sloop *Loyal Stede*, providing him with a commission to drive off the French raiders from Rhode Island's shores.

By 1690 forty years of legal privateering and a remarkably lenient government had made Rhode Island one of the most pirate-friendly ports in the Atlantic colonies. Massachusetts Puritans began to refer to it as "Rogues' Island," and Connecticut legislatures introduced a bill for the mandatory seizure of any Rhode Island denizen crossing over its borders. Yet the real impetus came in 1691, with the arrival in Newport of Thomas Tew at the completion of his first successful pirate's cruise of the Indian Ocean. Tew, a native Rhode Islander, was greeted like a hometown hero. Edward Randolph reported that Tew brought no less than £100,000 of Red Sea plunder to Rhode Island, a number that is doubtless exaggerated yet indicates nonetheless the incredible riches which Tew displayed. It is a matter of record that each of Tew's shipmates received a princely share of £1,200 apiece. The effect of this ostentatious display was galvanic. A veritable rush of potential seamen, drawn from the highest reaches of the merchant class down to lowly deckhands and even personal servants, hurried to enlist for Tew's next voyage.

Tew's example effected a remarkable change in the piratical practices of Rhode Island. Where previously pirates had been primarily local, usually ex-privateers or merchantmen, the colony now began to attract brigands from every colony. This was due both to its geographic advantages as a safe harbor and to the complacency of its government. Yet 1691 also marks the beginning of Rhode Island's "pirate fever," when the colony became virtually synonymous with piratical trade.

Inevitably, as Rhode Island's reputation became more widely known, complaints began to filter back to the Board of Trade. These surviving documents provide the most lucid picture of the actual state of affairs between the governors and the pirates in that era. In December 1696 the board received a complaining letter from the East India Company concerning one Captain Want, of Rhode Island. He fitted out his ship, *Portsmouth Adventure*, in Newport (the ship's name derived from that of a neighboring town), and then embarked for the Red Sea. Want had allegedly produced a commission signed by Deputy Governor Green; Green denied ever having heard of him, but the fact remained that Want's own wife was still a resident of the colony when the complaint arose. In April 1697 a group of anxious merchants from other New England colonies wrote despairingly to the Board of Trade that they could no longer allow their ships to drop anchor in Rhode Island, for their crews would desert at once for nearby pirate vessels. And in February 1698 a prisoner of the pirate captain Hoar reported that Hoar and his men "fitted out their ship from Rhode Island, and the Governor of New York [the ever-accommodating Fletcher] knew their designs, also the Governor of Rhode Island." Just two years before, the records show that Hoar had condemned a prize in Newport, the *Saint Paul*, which he renamed *John and Rebecca* (named after himself and his wife) and promptly sailed off again to the Red Sea. Hoar, like Want, was a Rhode Island native. Shortly thereafter, in September, the attorney general of New York informed Lord Bellomont that Tew, Hoar, and numerous other pirates had disposed of their cargos in Rhode Island. Lord Bellomont forwarded the letter to the Board of Trade, which concluded, "We are not only assured that they [Rhode Island] have no right to give these commissions but we have reason to believe that they have done so knowingly and for unlawful purpose."

This was perfectly true. The manner in which pirates obtained their commissions from the governor and, later, condemned their prizes reveals much about the relations between the two. The governors granted commissions as a matter of course. Yet sometimes it was good policy to do so quietly or through another channel. When Tew offered Governor Easton £500 for a letter of marque, Easton politely refused. It was not a matter of conscience: Tew's exploits had already made him the most notorious pirate of the age. Easton sensibly referred the matter to Green; Green granted the commission at once. A letter dated some three years after Tew's death indicated that the scandal surrounding his commission had scarcely abated. Having obtained a deposition from ex-governor Easton admitting to the charge, Benton included his own piece of advice: Rhode Island should be required to provide a complete list of all the commissions granted to privateers, as well as the bonds given by the privateers on receiving them. This seemingly innocuous request was made less so by its date: October 1698, several months after Edward Randolph accused the current governor, Cranston, of granting illegal commissions.

The condemnation of prizes was likewise revealing. The question of jurisdiction was already debatable: under the most logical reading of the crown charter, governors lacked the competence to convene their own prize courts. This was, as it would be for the next two centuries, a matter for the Admiralty. Yet the colonial governors were given wide latitude over the regulation of trade; hence, they interpreted the law as loosely as possible and convened the courts ad hoc. It was not uncommon for a conscientious customs official to refuse to condemn a prize, only to be countermanded by direct order of the governor. Superficially, the process by which a prize was condemned seems very legalistic and solemn. The ship arrives at harbor, declares itself and makes an accounting of its voyage to the customs official, and then applies for permission to sell its goods. At this point a court of inquiry is convened to ascertain whether those goods were obtained legally. The governor's commission is produced, the goods are assessed for their value, and the court (presided over by an official of the customs office, but answerable directly to the governor) renders its verdict. If unfavorable, the goods are seized by the crown in entirety. If favorable, the crown subtracts its own cut (usually about 10 percent, or more for a particularly successful cruise) and releases the goods for public sale.

That, in any event, was how it was supposed to work. The reality was rather different. It was manifestly illegal for the governor to personally gain from the crown proceeds, all of which were designated for the public coffers. Sometimes captains could make a small present to the governor by way of a gift of gratitude, but this was to be drawn from the pirate's share, not that of the crown. Yet, as this entire procedure was presided over by the governor exclusively, abuses were common. As William Owen notes, "In lean times the officials were tempted not only to fleece the captors, but also each other." In the late 1690s two pirates, Munday and Cutler, were seized in Newport, and their goods taken into custody. A trial date was fixed, but the two were freed on bail—the bond, of course, being their seized treasure. Edward Randolph described the events:

> Robert Munday and George Cutler were seized, and about
> £1,500 taken from them, which money was retained by
> the Governor. That they were put in prison, and soon after
> by the Governor's order admitted to bail, one of the Gov-

ernor's uncles, Gresham Clark, being their security. They
made their escape, leaving the money to be shared by the
governor and his two uncles, who have been great gainers
by the pirates who have visited Rhode Island.

Randolph also reports that Cranston later returned a substantial
share of the booty to the pirates, though he kept the lion's share for himself. Another pirate, Gillam (a shipmate of Kidd's), was less lucky; his
entire fortune passed into the hands of Governor Cranston. Pirates were
often very canny in steering a course between the greed of the governors, the necessary pretences of legality, and their own ambitions. Three
pirates, Edward Davis, John Hinson, and Lionel Wafer, were seized in
Virginia in 1691. Their arrest warrants were dismissed, but their loot
was seized. Incredibly, the pirates petitioned the crown for return of their
goods. William Noel Sainsbury, chief clerk of the British Public Record
Office in the mid-nineteenth century, writes of the curious bargain that
they eventually struck: "Their final stroke of diplomacy, offering £300
to the College of William & Mary if the King would restore to them
the remainder of their property, was certainly able, and turned out to
be successful." The bishop of London's representative in Virginia duly
declared, "I do humbly certify that the Petitioners have devoted and
secured towards the carrying on the pious design of a free School and
College in Virginia, the sum of £300 provided that the order be given
for restoring them their money." In due course, the king issued the
appropriate command:

> It is this day ordered in council that the money, plate, jew-
> els and other goods belonging to said petitioners and
> seized by Captain Rowe now lying in their majesties ware-
> house or wherever the same may be forthwith restored to
> the petitioners.

The ascension of Governor Cranston and Lieutenant Governor
Green in the late 1690s made the process of obtaining privateering commissions a matter of course. For the price of £300—no small amount
in those days—any ambitious seaman could obtain the necessary papers
from Green, who regarded it as a perfectly legitimate means of increasing crown revenue. In such a manner did Robert Colley, John Bankes,
William Mays, David Wanton, William Farrow, Richard Glover, John
Hoar, and scores of others gain commissions for their piratical activi-

ties. Earlier governors might have persuaded themselves that these men would keep to the letter of the law; Green was under no such illusions. Colley set off at once for Madagascar, Bankes sailed with Tew (as, in fact, he had done in an earlier voyage, rendering false Greene's later protestations of innocence), Mays joined up with Henry Every, and all the rest turned pirate as well. The wording of the commissions was cleverly crafted to give the pirates as wide a latitude as possible, while still maintaining the pretense of legitimate purpose. "In defense of Your Majesties' Plantations," it began, privateers were thus "requested and required" to "annoy the enemy according to Your Majesties' commands those as shall at any time hereafter attempt or enterprise the destruction, invasion, detriment, or annoyance of the said inhabitants or Plantations." In short, the pirates could thus attack anyone who they decided was—or could conceivably be—a threat to Rhode Island commerce. Legally speaking, the document was porous as a sponge. Yet Cranston would later declare to the Board of Trade with no trace of irony that these commissions were entirely defensive (to which the Board of Trade responded, with heavy sarcasm, "Are these defensive commissions? You know better.").

It did not take long for Randolph to uncover much of Cranston's dealings with the pirates. Indeed, they were scarcely concealed. In 1698 Lord Bellomont wrote to the lords of the Admiralty: "Mr. Randolph tells me that the Government of Rhode Island have seized some pirates and claim by their charge to erect a Court of Admiralty, no doubt in order to try and acquit them. Their encouragement of pirates and connivance with breach of the Acts of Trade will make them tender prosecutors."

Randolph's reports touched off a furious war of words—accusation, justification, counter-accusation—between himself, Cranston, and the Board of Trade. The contents of this exchange reveal much about the competing interests and motivations of the authors, and as such it is worth considering in some detail. Randolph's opening salvo was quickly countered by a letter dated May 8, in which Cranston denied the charge of pirate brokering and attempted his own revision of events:

> Several informations have been forwarded to you that
> Rhode Island is a place where pirates are entertained. Thus
> it is said that William Mays, a pirate fitted out at Rhode

Island, and that Thomas Jones was concerned in the old bark with Captain Want. These things have been misrepresented to you. We have never countenanced such proceedings, and we are sure that William Mays had his clearance here for Madagascar and a commission from this government to fight the French.

Eyebrows must have shot up at the Board of Trade as this missive was read; William Mays had been convicted of piracy with Henry Every and executed more than a year before. Clearly Lord Shrewsbury was not impressed. On hand was another letter of Bellomont's, with the following charge:

Deputy Governor Green during the time of the late war granted several sea commissions under the public seal of the colony unto private men of war (otherwise pirates). . . . Nor could he tell by the contents of them who was to execute the same, being directed in an unusual manner to the captain, and otherwise full of tautologies and nonsense. . . . The government is notoriously faulty in countenancing and harboring pirates, who have openly brought in and disposed of their effects there; whereby the place has greatly been enriched. And not only plain breaches of the Acts of Trade and Navigation have been connived at, but also manifest and known piracies, and all that has been done by them on pretense of seizing and taking up of known pirates has been so slender, weak and not pursued to effect as plainly demonstrates it was done more in show than out of any hearty zeal.

Referring both to Bellomont's earlier letter and Cranston's heated denial, the board chairman left no doubt as to whom he chose to believe. "Their [Rhode Island's] favoring of pirates and carrying on illegal trade has been so often complained of and the instances hereof are so manifest that we cannot doubt the truth of it," he declared roundly. "And that having seized some pirates with their money they designed to try them and probably would acquit them. . . . They have frequently granted commissions of war to privateers, which practice has been owned to us, and insisted on as lawful in a letter from the present governor Samuel Cranston, with relation to one William Mays, of whose piracies we were otherwise informed."

The pattern of correspondence was familiar. Here again, a zealous commentator (actually two, Bellomont and Randolph) denounced a colonial governor, the governor replied weakly, and the Board of Trade intervened. Cranston's own letters did him no credit. His answers to Bellomont's charges were a cloying combination of groveling, deceit, and self-deprecation, so transparent as to be almost comical. "We shall not justify ourselves, wherein we have been remiss or negligent in that affair," he began and then proceeded for some length to do exactly that. His conclusion was worthy of Uriah Heep: "We being a plain and mean sort of people, yet true and loyal subjects to his most excellent majesty King William, and we hope time will make manifest the same to your lordships, we being not insensible of the many enemies we have, who hath and do make it their business to render us as ridiculous as they can."

The Board of Trade was not amused. In June 1699 it sent its most scathing letter yet, couched in terms stronger than anything Fletcher or Markham had ever received. Anyone reading it would surely conclude that Governor Cranston was destined not only for disgrace but possibly even for charges of treason as well. "We observe what you say upon the subject of privateering commissions granted," the board told Cranston. "We cannot but esteem this willful neglect, and we must tell you, that unless you reform all such shuffling in your correspondence with us, you will unavoidably find it turn no less to your prejudice than the miscarriages themselves that you would conceal. . . . Your answers are so contrary to truth and to your duty that we wonder how you could write them."

It was signed, "Your loving friends."

Evidence was piling up. Yet Cranston continued on as before, evincing almost complete disregard both for Bellomont and the Board of Trade. One story is illustrative. Colonel Byfield, a customs official, found himself in serious trouble when he refused to condemn a pirate vessel that had returned to Newport laden with plunder. His letters to the Board of Trade reflect, if nothing else, the incredible audacity of Governor Cranston. Having endured several years of fierce scrutiny from the Board of Trade, numerous accusations of pirate brokering from no less than four different colonial governors, and countless scathing letters from the board itself, the governor was as unrepentant and unreformed as ever. "I humbly take leave to inform your honor," Byfield wrote grimly, "that it is now a year since his Excellency Joseph Dudley, Captain General and Governor of the Massachusetts Bay, sent me Her Majesty's letter referring to the irregularities practiced in the proprietary colony of Rhode Island. . . . Yet upon the 7th of November last, the said governor Cranston granted a commission to Captain Halsey of the brigantine *Charles*, a private man of war. When Byfield angrily refused to condemn the ship on its return, Governor Cranston sent him a personal note: "Since the said prize was taken by my commission, which has been deemed a lawful and good commission by yourself, and is now as good as ever . . . I can do no less than require a condemnation of said prize, according to law." Byfield himself relates what happened then:

> The next morning I proceeded to Newport, contrary to
> the advice of many of my friends, who told me there was
> talk that if I do not condemn the prize upon Governor
> Cranston's commission, my life was threatened—however,
> I proceeded. And when I came to Newport the governor
> came to me, who I acquainted with what I had heard, and
> proceeded to hold a court of admiralty. . . . The *Charles*
> was thus condemned.

If there were any point at which the accusations against Governor Cranston should have culminated with his removal, it was surely then. Governors Bellomont and Dudley had condemned him, Edward Randolph had provided clear testimony of his guilt, and now here was an officious customs agent (following the same hard path as Larkin and Trott of Bermuda) providing his own account. And yet Cranston remained. As late as 1705, Governor Dudley of Massachusetts was again writing the board concerning Cranston's dealings with the pirates. Now his complaint was rather different. Pirates Peter Lawrence and Jonathan Blew had obtained commissions from Dudley to attack French trade— the War of the Spanish Succession had again made such activities legal— but returned with their prize not to their home port of Boston but to Newport. Cranston gleefully agreed to condemn them and take the crown's share of the proceeds for himself. Governor Dudley was beside himself with rage. He sent a long list of accusations to the Board of Trade, only revealing his own personal animus at the very last:

1. That the government of Rhode Island does not observe the Acts of Trade and Navigation; but countenances the violation thereof, by permitting and encouraging of illegal trade and piracy.

2. That Rhode Island is a receptacle of pirates, who are encouraged and harbored by that government. . . .

18. That two privateers, Lawrence and Blew, commissioned by Colonel Dudley, took a Spanish ship upon the coast of Cuba, which they brought into Rhode Island, where the men were debauched by that government and prevented from sailing to their commissioned port, where they would have been made accountable for Her Majesty's dues and the rights of the lord high admiral.

The dichotomy between the dubious legality of the privateering commissions and the reality of Rhode Island piracy became painfully apparent during the War of the Spanish Succession. Commissions were once again lawful, and Cranston gave them out readily. The recipients, which included the aforementioned Want and Lawrence, were pirates without exception. Thumbing their nose at the Board of Trade, the Rhode Island Assembly declared in June 1705 that they "have had, and still have the power and authority to grant commissions to privateers, provided that they take bond, and do other things as the law directs." Yet these bonds were a legal fiction of the flimsiest sort, as Customs Officer Peleg Sanford testified:

Such men are here [in Rhode Island] countenanced, entertained, and concealed, as will appear by the evidence enclosed, that for such as are seized and committed, bonds to the amount of £2000 or £3000 are forthwith given for them; and having thus obtained their liberty, they gave notice unto their wicked companions, whereby they know how and where to secure themselves.

Crown Governors vs. the Crown

In sum, the case of Samuel Cranston poses two questions. First, how can we account for his fierce and at times illogical favoring of the pirates, even in the face of constant scrutiny and accusation? Second, and related, how did Samuel Cranston survive? Neither Fletcher nor Markham nor even Trott had the same degree of animosity directed against them, nor did they have the same weight of evidence proving their culpability. Yet they were disgraced, while Cranston lived on to a happy and unrepentant sixty-eight years of age, presiding over his colony well into the eighteenth century.

The first question is the more facile. The relationship between the pirates and the governors of Rhode Island persisted because it was enormously profitable to both, as well as to the colony entire. The exact extent to which the colony of Rhode Island profited from the pirates can never be known, but an approximation can be made based on the surviving records. A successful pirate voyage on the Red Sea might yield a treasure between £5,000 and £20,000; a spectacular voyage like Tew's might net five times that amount. Buried treasure and pirate hoards are largely an invention of Robert Louis Stevenson; in reality, the pirates wanted to offload their booty as fast as possible, so that they might obtain a new commission and return to sea forthwith. Thus, auctions took place on the wharf, where local townsmen obtained priceless commodities on the cheap, while the pirates themselves gained liquid cash in exchange for goods and valuables. It was, in short, good business all around. While the exact commercial gains for the colony are hard to estimate, the overall effect of piracy on Rhode Island commerce is undeniable. In 1700 Lord Bellomont noted sadly, "The Government is notoriously faulty in countenancing and harboring of pirates, who have openly brought in and disposed of their effects there; whereby the place has been greatly enriched."

Locality also played a role. Three decades of privateering fostered an open amity between administrators and seafarers, as well as a certain fluidity between the titles of merchantman, privateer, and pirate. As we have seen, the early pirates were almost entirely local mariners; these were later joined by numerous others from throughout the colonies, yet as late as the 1700s there continues to be a preponderance of native Rhode Islanders—men like Want, Hoar, and Lawrence—sailing from Rhode Island ports. This accounts also for the continued good relations between the pirates and the government; they were drawn, frequently, from the same classes of Rhode Island society. Thus could a wealthy

Rhode Island merchant captain like Tew easily transfer from privateer to open pirate and still be sure of the continued good graces of his governmental sponsors. The legal mechanisms of commissions and prize courts facilitated rather than hindered men like Tew, by giving legal pretense to patently illegal actions. Cranston, Easton, and Green were quite content to openly confound crown law, in the interests of preserving the commerce of their colony. The legal and social means by which they did so, as well as the men whom they aided and protected, are comparable to almost every Atlantic colony under British jurisdiction.

By the dawn of the eighteenth century, however, this pattern of passive noncompliance seemed to indicate something far more portentous: the germination of an independent colonial identity. This was seen most clearly both in the manner that Cranston and other governors willingly flouted the Board of Trade, and as well in the behavior of the colonists under their purview. The legal relationship of crown and colony was a tenuous one: crown law was really nothing more than crown policy, articulated to the governors and left to them for implementation. With no external militia, no constant oversight, the governors were left to act much as they pleased, and only the direst threat of removal and disgrace could serve to bring them to heel. The crown's only response was much as it had been before: to appoint a single man and give him the unenviable task of imposing its will throughout the colonies.

In 1698, having recently taken the reins of government in New York, Lord Bellomont composed his first letter to the Board of Trade. In some ways it was entirely typical of those that followed: having roundly condemned Benjamin Fletcher for all manner of transgressions, it went on to signal the first of many tolling bells on the evils of pirate patronage. "It may so happen," Bellomont wrote, "that some governors get more by illegal trade, pirates and privateers than their governments are worth." Yet this letter also contained a warning, buried in the many paragraphs of condemnation and righteous sentiment. Perhaps one cannot fault the crown for not heeding it. But it would have great cause to remember Bellomont's words in the coming years:

> I have observed that a great many people in these
> Colonies, especially in those under proprietors and in
> Connecticut and Rhode Island, think that no law of Eng-

land ought to bind them without their own consent; for they foolishly say that they have no representative sent from themselves to the Parliament in England, and they look upon all laws made in England that put any restraint upon them as great hardships.

The colonies were far from open rebellion, however, and the crown still looked to Lord Bellomont to bring the recalcitrant governors back in line. Bellomont understood his role perfectly well, and in the first year of the new century we find him zealously applied to the task. Yet Nemesis was fast approaching, by way of the Red Sea and up the Eastern Seaboard, tacking ever closer to New York.

Captain Kidd's voyage had not gone exactly as planned.

-13-

The Despair of Lord Bellomont

IN APRIL 1698, THE SAME MONTH THAT LORD BELLOMONT arrived in New York, his protégé Captain William Kidd arrived at St. Mary's. Both were chagrined at what they found. Kidd had been anticipating a meeting with Adam Baldridge, whom Kidd's fellow privateers assured him was both sympathetic and discreet. But Baldridge was gone: a native rebellion had risen against him, and Baldridge chose the better part of valor and sailed home to New York. Still, even in his absence, Kidd found many old acquaintances among the pirates there. His welcome was chilly, however; they looked on him with some trepidation, as Kidd's commission to hunt them down was well known. But the fifty-year-old mariner hastened to assure his erstwhile comrades that he was every bit "as bad as they." Greeting the men whom he had sworn to destroy, Kidd promised, "I would have my soul fry in Hell-fire," before he raised a hand against them. Clearly, something was very out of joint.

The Strange Adventures of Captain Kidd, Pirate Hunter

If one's history and connections are any indication of future behavior, Lord Bellomont should have been warned. It was no wonder that many among the St. Mary pirates recognized Kidd: he was drawn from the same society as they. Born in Greenock, Scotland, around 1645 (like most of the Red Sea pirates, his youth and origins are obscure), he surfaced in the Caribbean during King William's War, commissioned by Governor Codrington of Nevis to plunder French ships. As such, Kidd joined the burgeoning ranks of privateers who spent their early careers in service to the crown, working for colonial governors and gaining both their trust and friendship. Commanding an aptly named twenty-gun ship, the *Blessed William*, Kidd proved a skilled mariner but a poor commander: having secured more than £2,000 in captured booty, his crew abandoned him in Nevis and sailed away. Kidd was enraged, but his friend and patron Codrington came to the rescue. Kidd was presented with a brand-new ship, the *Antigua*, and set off to pursue the *Blessed William*. Among the crew who had elected to abandon Kidd were William Mason, Robert Culliford, and Samuel Burgess. They streaked northward, from the Caribbean Sea to the North Atlantic, bound for New York. Kidd left in hot pursuit.

Both ships arrived in New York at a pivotal moment, during the Leislerian Rebellion of 1690. Mason, Burgess, and Culliford sided with the government in power, accepting a commission from Jacob Leisler and sailing for the Red Sea in December with a new, equally well-named vessel, the *Jacob*. Kidd joined the opposite camp, using the *Antigua* to haul guns and ammunition for Colonel Ingolsby in preparation for the final assault on Fort William. It was Kidd, in fact, whom Ingolsby chose to send as a messenger to the arriving Governor Sloughter, informing him of the rebellion.

Yet politics is nothing if not mutable, and by the time the *Jacob* returned, in 1693, things were very different in New York. Leisler was dead, Fletcher was governor, and the Tories were firmly in control. The men of the *Jacob* at once made their overtures to the new regime. Fortunately for them, Governor Fletcher was both accommodating and pragmatic. He received the *Jacob* as a gift, along with £100 from each of the crew. Mason and Culliford quickly received new commissions, and after a brief interval enjoying the delights of New York, the men were off pirating once again. Burgess chose to remain and began his long career in the service of Frederick Phillipse.

Meanwhile Kidd, who by rights should have been enjoying the dividends of backing the winning side, had changed allegiances once again. Now settled in the city and still occasionally making the odd privateering voyage, Kidd struck up a friendship with his neighbor, Robert Livingston. Thus the politically naive captain was drawn, not entirely against his will, into the cadre of Leislerian Whigs whose mission was to topple the Fletcher government. And from there, as related before, Kidd went to London.

William Kidd was thus an exemplar of the professional privateers who haunted the Atlantic colonies in the late seventeenth century—the very men whom Lord Bellomont was charged to destroy. He moved in the same circles as Tew, Want, Wake, and Glover; he had served with Mason and Burgess. Like all of them, he had cut his teeth seizing prizes from the French during the last war; like them, he had forged allegiances with powerful governors and accepted their patronage; like them, he continued to accept commissions from powerful patrons. Yet there was a crucial difference. While Mason, Hoar, Tew, and others purchased their commissions from the colonial governors, Kidd accepted his from Lord Bellomont and the Whig junta. The distinction was in expectations. Men like Fletcher and Codrington granted commissions with the certain knowledge that their terms would never be employed: ordered to the Saint Lawrence or some such place, the pirates sailed at once for the Red Sea, and the governors confidently anticipated a cut of the profits in the end. Bellomont and company, however, fully expected that Kidd would fulfill the obligations of his commission to the letter. He was not only ordered to hunt English pirates (rather than the usual French), he was given a list of names: Thomas Tew, John Ireland, Thomas Wake, William Mays, "and other subjects, natives or inhabitants of New York and elsewhere in our Plantations in America." Furthermore, Kidd was to keep a precise journal of whom he encountered, how the captures were effected, and exactly what cargo he received as prize. "And we do hereby strictly charge and command you, and you will answer the contrary at your peril, that you do not in any manner offend or molest our friends and allies," the commission concluded.

Other terms were harder to bear. Among the papers preserved in the Gilder Lehrman collection in New York are the original Articles of Commission drawn up between Robert Livingston and Captain Kidd, which served as an addendum to the formal commission given by the Whig lords. The very first clause, referring to another investor, Richard Blackham, leaves no doubt as to the expectations of the junta:

> The said Robert Livingston and Captain William Kidd do jointly and severally agree with the said Richard Blackham that in case the said Captain Kidd does not meet with the pirates shipped out from New England, Rhode Island, New York and elsewhere, or does not take from any other pirates or from any of the King's enemies such goods and chattel or anything of value . . . that [Kidd] shall refund and repay the said Richard Blackham in full.

Obligations of this sort were not what a privateer like Captain Kidd was accustomed to. Moreover, they were not what a crew expected or understood. Capturing pirate ships was a messy and dangerous business; the ships were armed, the men desperate, and the rewards often meager. Lord Bellomont might be excused for being unaware of this aspect of seafaring life, but Robert Livingston certainly knew. The terms of the commission reflected back on its unique motive: half pecuniary, half political. The junta had every expectation of profit from the venture, but more important than seized gold was the embarrassment it would cause Governor Fletcher and his Tory backers in the ministry. Given the weight of these expectations and Kidd's own less than savory past, what followed was almost inevitable.

Trouble began even before they left the Thames. As Kidd's ship, the *Adventure Galley*, made its way through the gauntlet of navy brigs at Greenwich, it failed to make proper salute. A navy ship discharged a warning bang of powder to remind him. Kidd's men climbed the shrouds, turned, and slapped their backsides rudely at His Majesty's ship. The navy was not amused and revealed its displeasure by seizing most of the crew during a press-gang raid. Kidd was forced to replace them with men of a lower caliber: "Navy rejects," as one historian has called them.

Things were scarcely better when Kidd reached New York, supposedly to patrol the waters for Tew, Want, and the others. It was 1696, and Governor Fletcher (who was well informed of Kidd's mission, possibly from his great friend William Blaythwayt) looked on Kidd—correctly—as one more threat to his tottering administration. Accordingly he froze the privateer out of New York society and employed his best efforts to make life difficult for him. Still in desperate need of a crew, Kidd found few New Yorkers that wished to take part in a voyage which would brand them pariahs amongst their peers. Once again, Kidd was forced to settle for the dregs—and only then by offering them a disproportionate share of the profits.

Worse still, the pirates he had contracted to capture were not anywhere near New York at all but rather in the Red Sea. Kidd was faced with a difficult choice: his commission required him to remain in the port of New York until the pirates appeared, but it was abundantly clear that neither his supplies nor his crew would hold out that long. Alternatively he could seek them out where they were, though it meant disobeying orders. Kidd's men wanted treasure; the lords wanted prize money. The weight of expectations tipped the balance, as it would again and again. Judging that the lords would prefer action over inaction, Kidd prepared to sail for Madagascar. As the *Adventure Galley* departed the colony for the last time, Governor Fletcher wrote to the Board of Trade, not without some satisfaction, that Kidd had acquired himself a crew of "desperate fortunes and necessities" that expected treasure, not justice. If he "misses in the design named in his commission," wrote Fletcher, "he will not be able to govern such a villainous herd."

Events quickly bore out the governor's words. Reaching Cape Town in late 1696, Kidd fell in with a navy squadron assigned to root out piracy—the very men whom Kidd was charged with aiding. But his manner with them was rude at best and possibly sly. Kidd demanded new sails from the squadron commander, Captain Warren. Warren refused. Something about Kidd's manner stirred his suspicions, and Warren ordered a watch placed on the *Adventure Galley*. Nevertheless, in the dead of night Kidd's ship sprouted oars (not daring to set the sails, as it would reveal his intentions) and slipped away from the navy fleet. Warren relayed his doubts about Kidd to the local agent in Cape Town the next day, and word quickly passed among the pirate hunters that a wolf might be passing amongst the sheep.

Kidd's next encounter with his supposed comrades came at Johanna Island several weeks later. This time it was an East India agent, one of the many private captains that had received commissions from the company to track down pirates in the Red Sea. The East Indiamen proudly flew a navy pennant in recognition of this role. Kidd, insensibly, ordered the ship's captain to strike the pennant, claiming that only he, Kidd, had the right to display such a designation. He waved his commission at the captain, but the captain refused to obey. Such was the heightened suspicion of Kidd that the East Indiamen's guns remained out and trained on the *Adventure Galley* throughout the encounter.

Kidd finally reached the Red Sea in December 1696. The *Adventure Galley* had left London almost a year before, and still Kidd had nothing to show for it. He took up station near Bab's Key, a small island in the Mocha straits. In the meantime, tantalizing visions passed by: Indian ships loaded with specie that must have fired the imaginations of every man on the *Adventure Galley* with dreams of wealth. Kidd let them go. But he could not hold out forever, and the crew was becoming mutinous. The pirates he had been sent to capture were nowhere to be found, tiny specks in an endless tract of empty sea. One can only imagine the pressure Kidd was under at this time. What would happen if the pirates eluded his grasp altogether? If he returned to London empty-handed? Standing on the quarterdeck of the *Adventure Galley*, Kidd must have seen his whole future played out in front of him: frozen out of New York, ridiculed in London, an impoverished, ludicrous failure. But if he returned a wealthy man. . . .

In August 1697 the Mocha fleet sailed by, and Kidd made his choice. He followed the fleet, hoping for a quick strike and an even quicker departure. In this way he could enrich himself, satiate his crew, and appease the lords—but only if he wasn't caught. For the Mocha fleet, while under Indian registry, was managed by the great East India Company—the same company that had, only a few months before, suffered heavily at the hands of the arch pirate Henry Every. When the captain of the *Sceptre*, an English thirty-six gunner, sighted a strange sail in the midst of the convoy, he made chase. Kidd was forced to fall back, his hopes for a surprise raid dashed. He retaliated shortly thereafter by taking a small barque flying English colors and captained by an Englishman, Thomas Parker. Possibly Kidd's intentions were only to take some needed supplies, but his men stormed aboard the barque and set upon its crew. Kidd was forced to put Parker in irons. From his prisoner he learned that the East India Company had already put out the word that he had turned pirate.

This was enough to startle the privateer into spurious redemption. He sailed for the port of Calicut on the southwest coast of India, a well-known stop for East India ships. Arriving with English colors fluttering bravely at the masthead, Kidd sent a message ashore claiming that he could not understand why his reputation had diminished; he was, he said, merely acting out the commission granted him by Lord Bellomont, zealously pursuing the New York pirates in their lairs. Then he boldly demanded supplies, for which he offered payment. The East India Company agent at Calicut gave him the stores, watched his sail depart, and hurriedly wrote to Bombay that the notorious Kidd had just passed through.

Kidd might have been earnest in his letter at Calicut, but his men were not. The privateer-turned-pirate soon discovered the bane of every captain's existence: a mutinous crew. Promised easy work and great riches, the men of the *Adventure Galley* had neither. Suppressed tensions erupted into violence. A gunner named William Moore lashed out at Kidd, calling him a coward for failing to pursue the rich Indian ships. Kidd responded in a rage and struck Moore with a bucket, fracturing his skull. Moore died the next day. By this point, however, the question of Kidd's commission was largely moot. Abandoning the futile search for pirates, he became one himself. His first prize was the *Maiden*, a Moorish ship with a Dutch captain that flew French colors. Seizing upon the last, as well as the "French pass" that the Dutchman produced, Kidd declared, "You are a free prize to England!" and proceeded to divvy up the *Maiden*'s cargo among his crew. Shortly thereafter he took a second ship, a small Moorish ketch, and after that a Portuguese trader laden with East India Company stores. In each of these acts, Kidd genuinely believed he was still within the law. All three captains waved French passes at him, and a state of war still existed between France and England.

The noose was tightening, however, and on January 30, 1698, the trap door finally fell. A 500-ton merchantman appeared on the horizon, flying French colors. Kidd made chase and after four hours overtook her. She was the *Quedah Merchant*, outbound from Bengal with a cargo of cloth, sugar, saltpeter, guns, and gold. At first all seemed well: an aged Frenchman came aboard the *Adventure Galley* and protested the capture of his ship by a fellow countryman—Kidd had run up the French colors, a common ruse to lure the unwary. Kidd scorned both him and the Armenian owners that appeared offering to ransom back the ship. Instead Kidd sold the cargo ashore at Cochin, divided the proceeds among his crew, and sailed for Madagascar with the *Quedah Merchant* in convoy. But just as Kidd had revealed himself an Englishman, the "French" ship finally did the same: a second captain was produced, an Englishman named Wright. The Frenchman had been nothing more than a gunner's mate: a ruse de guerre. Kidd was stunned. "We are lost!" he cried. Then he turned to his crew. "The taking of this ship would make a great noise in England," he told them. They must give her back to Wright at once. Kidd's crew refused, and on they sailed.

Enemy of the East India Company, Friend of the Junta

As the *Adventure Galley* made her way to the safe harbor of St. Mary's, it seemed as though the last brittle cords that connected Kidd to his original purpose finally snapped. Having captured not one but two English captains, Parker and Wright, Kidd had surely damned himself beyond all redemption in the eyes of the East India Company. With nothing to lose, he abandoned his self-imposed restraint toward company vessels and chased an East India ship, the *Sedgewick*, for the better part of a day. Thus the William Kidd who arrived in St. Mary's in the first week of April was a very different man from the one who had departed London several years before: jaded, frustrated, cowed by his crew and bullied by them into murderous revenge, a liar, a cheat, and a thief. In short, a pirate.

Yet Captain Kidd did not seem overly concerned as he sailed into the pirate colony. Having assured his old shipmate and nemesis Captain Culliford that he meant him no harm, he immediately began making plans to return to New York. Such behavior, following upon the complete failure of his commission and his open acts of piracy, would strike most contemporary observers as suicidal. But Kidd felt he had two cards left to play. First were the Whig lords. Tew might have his Governor Fletcher, or Mays his Governor Cranston, or Every his Trott, but Kidd had the greatest trump of all: Lord Bellomont, a peer of the realm and one of the most powerful men in England. Not to mention a cadre of fellow Whigs whose names shone like a constellation of political clout. In the months after his arrival in St. Mary's, Kidd would learn of Bellomont's status as governor of New York and rejoice: his patron had come to power and would surely protect him.

Second, while Kidd knew he was no longer persona grata for the East India Company, he still had reason to feel safe in his homecoming in the colonies. Not only because of the fortuitous events that had resulted in the downfall of Governor Fletcher, but in the longstanding attitude of sanction and accord for pirates such as himself. Kidd had learned the art of patronage under the benign guidance of Governor Codrington and seen for himself how a successful voyage could make up for any number of past sins. Now living amongst the very men he had once been commissioned to destroy, he had every reason to believe that rule still held good. Here was Captain Want, of the *Portsmouth Adventure*, flourishing a commission lately granted from Governor Cranston; there was Captain Glover, who had wangled commissions from no less than three governors for one pirate cruise—a kind of triple insurance policy. Kidd must have looked on these men and taken heart. They were the same rogues that he had been sent to capture, enemies of the crown, yet enjoying their status and in no particular fear of retribution when they returned home. It would have been impressed on Kidd, if he did not know it already, that the situation in the colonies was very different from that in Great Britain: pirates were part of the social fabric, woven in securely with tradesmen, merchants, and governors. And so he made ready to return to New York.

Yet what Kidd failed to realize is that his own position was both distinct and unique: poised exactly halfway in between the complaisance of the colonies and the stern will of the mother country. Even though he had lived among these men both in New York and St. Mary's, and sailed with them, he was not one of them. They belonged to the colonies, had accepted commissions from colonial governors, and thus could expect all the protections that local sympathies and distance from England allowed. Kidd, conversely, had taken his commission in England in furtherance of crown policy and thus was tied securely to the fortunes of the East India Company. Worse yet, the company had recently suffered both disastrous losses to the pirate Henry Every and embarrassment during the botched manhunt and trial for Every's crew. The East India Company was out for blood. When reports filtered back from Bombay to Whitehall that Kidd was menacing its trade, the seeming betrayal of his masters cut deeper than even Every's antics. As Kidd sojourned in St. Mary's, pondering his next move, the Board of Trade took the extraordinary step of offering pardon to any pirate that surrendered himself to the crown. Only two names were specifically excluded: Henry Every and William Kidd.

Across the Atlantic, Lord Bellomont's campaign against piracy, having shown some promise at the outset, sputtered to a virtual halt. He purged the old council, dismissing Bayard, Brooke, and Phillipse; he even arrested old Adam Baldridge, now a chastened resident of New York, and took his deposition. Baldridge's testimony was conclusive and damning, a catalog of every rogue and patron on the Eastern Seaboard. Yet while Bellomont now had in his hands the proofs against them, the pirates had fled to St. Mary's, where Frederick Phillipse continued to supply them. Captain Burgess, on yet another mission to Madagascar, wrote that the pirates "seemed . . . to be very joyful for the said Proclamation of pardon and very ready to embrace it." Whereupon the pirates cheerfully accepted the pardon and returned at once to the Red Sea to await the treasure fleet.

News of Kidd's fall from grace landed on Bellomont with the force of a bombshell. He had received only sporadic reports of the political firestorm heading his way, mostly staunch denials from his friends at court that they had anything but the greatest faith in both Kidd and his master, Bellomont. This was disquieting enough, but worse was to come. Bellomont had sent Benjamin Fletcher back under a cloud of disgrace to face no less than eighteen charges relating to countenancing piracy and illegal trade. After lengthy debate, coinciding with the first outraged reports from the East India Company on Kidd's actions, the Board of Trade exonerated him on nearly every count, confining itself to a gentle censure that the governor might have done more to promote good order in his colony. It was a task, they now acknowledged, that might be beyond the best of men—even beyond Governor Bellomont.

Fletcher, excused if not vindicated, seized upon the revelations of Kidd's actions with intemperate enthusiasm. His old friend William Blaythwayt did likewise, condemning Bellomont for decimating New York trade and spreading anarchy in the colony. Having seized the reins of power just the year before, the Whigs were now steadily losing ground. A single great scandal could topple the whole government. Desperate to shore up support, the Whigs promised an incensed East India Company (which had traditionally allied itself with the Tory party) that they, not the Tories, were the true defenders of the company from the encroachments of pirates. As proof, the Whigs pointed to Bellomont's ongoing efforts to suppress the Red Sea trade from New York. As news of Kidd broke over their heads, the Whigs desperately attempted to contain the damage. Captain Kidd was suddenly very expendable. And so, if need be, was his erstwhile sponsor, Lord Bellomont.

Captain Kidd in New York

In spring of 1699, on the first anniversary of his arrival in New York, it must have seemed to Bellomont as though his tenure in office had lurched from one crisis to another. Gone was the messianic zeal behind the first antipiracy proclamations. All the governors whom he sought to discredit, including the appalling Governor Cranston, were still in office. Having disposed (he thought) of Governor Fletcher and his cabal, he now heard Fletcher braying at him from across the Atlantic, joined with many other voices as well. Bayard was there, stirring up trouble amongst the English merchants that traded with New York. Accusations came that Bellomont had packed every key position with Leislerians (which was true) and that he had undermined the Anglican Church in favor of Dutch Calvinism (which was nonsense). And then, when it seemed as though his fortunes could sink no lower, news came that Captain Kidd's ship was holding position just off the coast of New York.

Bellomont desperately wanted to believe the best of his protégé, even in the face of cold facts. Not for altruistic reasons, but because if any of the charges against Kidd were true, they could only reflect back on his sponsor. "I am in hopes of several reports we have here of Captain Kidd's being forced by his men against his will to plunder two Moorish ships may prove true," Bellomont wrote the Board of Trade in May. "And tis said near 100 of his men revolted from him at Madagascar and were about to kill him because he absolutely refused to turn pirate." But as the evidence piled up, Bellomont quickly came to realize that in the end it would either be Kidd or himself at the dock, or both. His choice was clear.

Bellomont was in Boston, and Kidd was hovering anxiously in Long Island Sound. The governor knew that he had to play a careful role now, luring the pirate in so that the trap could be sprung. For at any moment Kidd, sensing danger, could turn tail and return to St. Mary's, and all would be lost. Bellomont knew that his only chance lay in capturing the wayward Kidd and handing him over to justice in the most public manner possible, all the better to distance himself from Kidd's actions.

Kidd, meanwhile, was equally circumspect. The first guest on board the *Saint Antonio* was a sea lawyer named James Emott, Kidd's old friend, who ushered on Kidd's wife and daughters. After a happy family reunion, the two men moved into Kidd's cabin to talk privately. Kidd must know, Emott told him, of the uproar his arrival had caused on these shores. Outrageous tales of his piracy were exceeded only by even more outrageous estimates of the fortune he carried with him. The colony, said Emott, was gripped by a "gold fever" not seen since Tew's time. Nearly everyone wanted Captain Kidd: either for his gold or for his throat. But Kidd still had friends, the lawyer assured him, and among them was Governor Bellomont. Kidd then dispatched Emott with a letter for his patron, providing a highly glossed account of his adventures— including the spurious claim that all the prizes taken were legitimate and that Kidd had successfully resisted efforts by his crew to chase after East India vessels. Finally there was an offer: Kidd would surrender himself to Bellomont at once and give him his due share of the proceeds (which, as Kidd hinted, were substantial) if Bellomont in turn would grant him pardon.

Emott relayed the message to Bellomont, who received him very civilly. Yet Bellomont's own account of the meeting revealed his true feelings: "He [Kidd] brought Emott from thence to Rhode Island and there landed him, sending him hither to me with an offer of his coming into this port provided I would pardon him. I was a little puzzled how to manage a treaty of that kind with Emott, a cunning Jacobite, a fast friend of Fletcher's and my avowed enemy." Nevertheless, at a second meeting with Emott and another Scot, postmaster Duncan Campbell, Bellomont seemed to acquiesce. Laid up with gout, he appeared to both men as a man intent on finding the best way out of a difficult circumstance. Wincing, either in pain or embarrassment, he showed Emott and Campbell a proclamation denouncing Kidd as a pirate, as ordered by the lord justices. "Now what can I do about that, gentlemen?" he asked them. Emott reiterated Kidd's offer of surrender in return for a full pardon. Bellomont seemed to ponder this and then took pen and paper and began to write.

> I have advised His Majesty's Council and showed them
> this letter, and they are of the opinion that if you can be so
> clear as you (or Mr. Emott for you) have said, then you
> may safely come hither. And I make no manner of doubt
> but to obtain the King's pardon for you, and for those few
> men you have left who I understand have been faithful to
> you, and refused as well as you to dishonor the Commis-
> sion you have from England. I assure you on my word and
> honor, I will perform nicely what I have promised.

Looking over what he had written, Bellomont signed his name with a flourish and scattered sand across the page. Then he carefully folded the paper upon itself, wrote "CAPTAIN WILLIAM KIDD" on the face, and sealed the contents with a blob of red wax and his own signet ring. Take this to Kidd, he told Emott. He will have his pardon.

Emott returned to Long Island, handing Bellomont's letter to an overjoyed Kidd. The pirate made ready to sail for Boston at once. Bellomont, meanwhile, hastened to put his own spin on events. Writing to the Board of Trade shortly thereafter, the governor blandly admitted laying a trap for his former protégé:

> I writ a letter to Captain Kidd inviting him to come in,
> and that I would procure a pardon for him, provided he
> was as innocent as Mr. Emott said he was. I sent my letter
> to him by one Mr. Campbell. . . . Within three or four
> days Campbell returned to me a letter from Kidd full of
> protestations of his innocence, and informing me of his

> design of coming with his sloop into this port. I must not
> forget to tell your Lordships that Campbell brought three
> or four jewels to my wife, which I was to know nothing of.

The implied bribe to Lady Bellomont only deepened Kidd's predicament. When Kidd arrived in Boston, Bellomont summoned him before the council at once. Kidd appeared in his best frock coat and most earnest manner, presenting an account of the prizes taken on the voyage down to the last bale of cloth. It was July 3rd. The council thanked Kidd and dismissed him, politely requesting that he return on the 6th to bring the matter to a close. Kidd readily agreed. In the meantime he made ready a second bribe for Bellomont: a thousand pounds' worth of gold dust and ingots, again to be presented as a "gift" to the governor's wife. This time Bellomont acted swiftly. He summoned an emergency session of the Massachusetts Council, including Deputy Governor (and rival) William Stoughton. "I thought [Kidd] looked very guilty," Bellomont later explained, "and to make me believe so he and his friend Livingston and Campbell aforesaid began to juggle together and embezzle some of the cargo; besides, Kidd did strangely trifle with me and the Council three or four times that we had him under examination."

On the morning of July 6, as Captain Kidd presented himself at Bellomont's door to meet with the council, a gendarme approached and grasped his arm. Kidd recoiled, broke free, and ran into the mansion. His screams echoed through the cavernous rooms as the gendarmes dragged him out the door. He was calling for Lord Bellomont, convinced there had been a mistake.

Downfall of the Governor

If Bellomont fancied that a swift and brutal arrest of Captain Kidd would spare him the censure of the lords, he was much mistaken. As Kidd languished in a Boston jail, a political maelstrom ensued wherein the Whig lords tried desperately to distance themselves from the entire venture, and the Tories dragged them mercilessly back into it. Bellomont and his cronies were branded the "Corporation of Pirates," a label as apt as it was cruel. Even more ironically, the increased attention to the problem of piracy rekindled just the sort of fervent political sentiments that Bellomont would have found invaluable, had he not been caught in the middle of them. As August dragged into September, hearings were held at the Board of Trade in conjunction with the East India Company in order to determine, once and for all, the menace of piracy and its corrosive effects on the colonies. Adam Baldridge was dragged out again, Kidd's shipmates Benjamin Franks and Jonathan Tredway were shipped back from India, and Samuel Burgess was arrested while on yet another voyage for Frederick Phillipse. Having offered a deposition that implicated virtually the entire New York merchant class of pirate brokering, Burgess then waved a commission signed by none other than Governor Bellomont. The Board of Trade, embarrassed, let him go.

Yet the real crux of the matter was still Kidd. With Henry Every lost and gone, probably forever, the East India Company turned the whole of its wrath on Kidd and anyone who had supported him. James Graham, Lord Bellomont's agent in London, wrote to Robert Livingston that "the affair of Kidd has made a great noise in the Parliament, and the malcontents of this place had no small share in the advancing of it." He went on ominously: "It is said that there were private articles between My Lord [Bellomont] and Kidd, which would prove a shame . . . but that matter was managed with great advantage to My Lord, who has said upon occasion that your bond shall never hurt you, so you may put your mind at rest upon that matter." Hints of secret articles, suggestions that Bellomont and others had threatened Kidd to bring back gold to fill their purses, no matter by what means—it was all beginning to look very embarrassing for Lord Bellomont. The governor did himself little credit in his own correspondence, which revealed him to be as greedy and unscrupulous in his own way as Fletcher had ever been. "Try and find if anything be allowed to me for my pains," he wrote his business manager, regarding Kidd's captured booty:

> There is a quantity of gold and the jewels now sent home
> which Kidd had nothing to do with. . . . I am told that as
> Vice Admiral of the Seas I have a right to a 3rd part of
> them, if the rest of the Lords come in for Snacks I shall
> be satisfied, but that Sir Edward Harrison should pretend
> to a greater share of what was not taken by Kidd is very
> unreasonable.

Meanwhile, to preserve appearances, Bellomont redoubled his efforts to root out piracy in the colonies and present himself to the board as an aggrieved innocent. Writing from Boston on November 29, 1699, he crowed of having captured James Gillam, a privateer and friend of Kidd's, who had returned from the Red Sea with a large haul and a commission from Governor Cranston of Rhode Island. "The rest of the evidence about Gillam and some other pirates go numbered from 3 to 23 inclusive," he wrote, "which I recommend to your Lordships' perusal, as what will inform you of the strange countenance given to pirates bye the government and people of Rhode Island."

But the Board of Trade would not be deflected. Kidd was returned to England in the winter of 1699, a grueling passage in the hold of a small, frigid, and ill-kept ship. Bellomont himself was summoned to London shortly thereafter, in considerably more luxury, to testify before Parliament. During five days of heated testimony and debate, Bellomont did all he could to paint himself and his partners as innocent brokers. The success of this campaign was negligible, though Graham wrote a glowing letter back to Livingston claiming that Bellomont "was acquitted with great applause for his conduct." Yet not even Graham could ignore or obfuscate the bitter party politics that underlay the hearings. "His Lordship had many friends in the Parliament and had letters from the King, the Earl of Jersey, and My Lord Chancellor highly commending his conduct and assuring him of their constant friendship," Graham reported, adding in a grim postscript, "notwithstanding the efforts of Colonel Fletcher and Colonel Bayard."

Bellomont returned to Boston, his office still intact but his position desperately insecure. Everything hinged on the trial. Kidd would go before the Old Bailey in the spring, and for the first time the silent prisoner would be given the chance to defend himself. He had only one defense possible: that all his actions were approved and sanctioned by the Whig junta and by His Excellency Lord Bellomont. Kidd, feeling betrayed and desperate to lay the blame for his failures on other shoulders, would not hesitate to implicate him. And the Tories, who awaited the trial with the same fervor that London townspeople did for a public hanging, would be sure to make the most of it. God only knew what Kidd would say on the stand or what papers he would produce. Desperate, Bellomont tried to discredit him by preemptive strike. "There never was a greater liar or thief in the world than this Kidd," he wrote from Boston.

William Kidd's trial, conducted in just two days, May 8 and 9, 1701, represents a watershed in the governors' relationship with the pirates. Just as the trial of Every's crew was intended as an affirmation of crown law and policy, here, too, a successful outcome was pivotal—not, as before, to maintain amicable foreign relations but to maintain the government itself. Consequently, and also akin to the Every trials, the public face of the trial contrasted sharply with the political maneuverings behind the scenes. Kidd signified a threat to the very superstructure of colonial administration, not to mention the English peerage. Historians have made much of the internecine disputes between Whig and Tory that colored the proceedings, and there is no question that both parties had vested interest in the outcome. The Whigs, now holding on to power by the merest thread, desperately needed the trial to reaffirm that Kidd had acted alone, contrary to their instructions and the law of nations. The Tories were equally committed to employing the trial as a means of destabilizing the Whigs still further by attaching them to an unsavory scandal that had equally damaging repercussions for the East India Company. Yet of equal importance (and considerably less historiographical attention) were other divergences that the trial revealed. Not Whig versus Tory but colonies versus the crown.

Just as Sir Charles Hedges had once directed a jury to ignore the presumption of innocence, the men planning Kidd's trial did everything they could to load the dice. Kidd had been held virtually incommunicado for two years, as a series of pitiable petitions from his wife, Sarah, attests. All his papers were taken from him, supposedly held in trust by the Whig lords. With no papers, no ability to contact witnesses to speak in his defense, nor any knowledge of the witnesses that would be produced against him, Kidd could only sit and wait. One piece of intelligence reached him: the so-called "French passes," which proved that most of his prizes were arguably legal, had unaccountably gone missing. William Kidd was under no illusions as to where they had gone. "I would not exceed my authority," he wrote dejectedly to Robert Harley, the speaker of the House of Commons, "and took no other ships than such as had French passes, which I brought with me to New England, and relied upon for my justification. But my Lord Bellomont seized upon them together with my cargo . . . he has kept these passes wholly from me, and stripped me of all defense I have to make, which is barbarous."

Kidd's disillusionment was dangerous. However much the lords might suppress evidence, they could not prevent him from taking the stand. And Kidd had already provided a bullet-point version of his testimony, enough to send shockwaves of terror through Whitehall. For Kidd now claimed that the Whig lords not only forced him to take their commission but drove him by explicit instructions from privateering to piracy:

> I did not seek the Commission I undertook, but was partly cajoled and partly menaced into it by the Lord Bellomont and one Robert Livingston of New York. . . . He [Livingston] was the man admitted into their closets, and received their private instructions, which he kept in his own hands, and who encouraged me in their names to do more than I ever did, and to act without regard to my commission.

This was almost certainly untrue. There is no question that the Whig junta, Lord Bellomont especially, expected to make a profit off of Kidd's venture. But the charge that they had threatened him into open piracy, which Kidd would stoutly maintain until his death, was unfounded. Open piracy that menaced the East India Company would not serve the primary purpose of the commission: embarrassing Governor Fletcher and his Tory patrons.

Following two years of imprisonment, and commencing some six years after Kidd's commission was granted, the trial held at the Old Bailey on May 8, 1701, was anticlimactic. "I cannot be so unjust to myself as to plead an indictment till the French passes are restored to me, unless I would be accessory to my own destruction," Kidd had written, and he was right. Without any documentary evidence to support his claims, he had practically no case at all. Kidd began his defense by lamenting the lost passes and putting the blame securely on the shoulders of Lord Bellomont, who had "frightened and wheedled some of my men to misrepresent me, and by his letters to his friends here advised them to admit me a pirate." After this sensational opening the proceedings quickly settled into a form of majestic drudgery. Six charges were proffered against Kidd, necessitating six separate trials over the course of just two days. Among them were several acts of questionable piracy and one certainty: the *Quedah Merchant*. A separate indictment dealt with the murder of William Moore, gunner.

In the galleries, the luminaries of the age sat tense and expectant. Whigs and Tories alike jostled for seats, leaned over the balustrade, and scowled or smiled alternately. Among them were a few surprising faces. James Graham was on hand, naturally, to provide a running account of the proceedings to Livingston; Benjamin Fletcher and Nicholas Bayard made frequent appearances, no doubt regarding the trial with amused smiles; most surprising of all, Governor Jeremiah Basse of New Jersey was present, staying as a guest of friends in London. Basse was the same man who had denounced the pirate trade several years before, following the Every trials. He watched as several of Kidd's crew produced pardons signed by him, in accordance with the proclamation of pardon in 1699.

When Kidd's turn finally came, he lashed out against the lords who had put him in this terrible position. His demeanor was calm and collected, and his appearance may have made a favorable impression. A portrait done of him at this time shows a ruddy-cheeked burgher with keen brown eyes and a placid expression, a far cry from the slavering monster that Bellomont had described. Yet neither his appearance nor impassioned pleas could make up for the lost papers; in truth, his fate would almost certainly have been sealed even if they had been produced. The Whig lords needed a conviction to pin the blame on Kidd; the Tories wanted as public a spectacle as possible to humiliate the Whigs. Both were satisfied.

Kidd was convicted on all counts and sentenced to hang. The sentence was duly carried out on May 23, 1701. Until that time Kidd had desperately searched for a way out of his predicament, even throwing himself at the mercy of the king. But no mercy was forthcoming. The Whigs were in full retreat from the scandal, and by this time the Tories had found other means of political pressure. The pendulum of English party politics was in motion again, this time in favor of the Tories. Riddled by scandal and charges of mismanagement, the Whigs finally lost their grip on Parliament. A cadre of Tory lords seized the reins of government, and once again men like Benjamin Fletcher emerged triumphant (the lords of the Treasury now reported incredibly that not only was ex-Governor Fletcher innocent of embezzlement, but it appeared the government owed *him* money). None of this was any use to Captain Kidd. On the day of his execution he arrived at the Wapping gallows roaring drunk. He harangued the gathering with yet another diatribe against the Whig lords, cautioned the somber-eyed matrons and bedraggled seamen to beware the enticements of the high and mighty, and said that among all virtues the greatest was prudence. For an eager public clamoring to hear dying confessions and repentance—not to mention the scores of pamphleteers, the seventeenth century's yellow press, on hand to provide accounts of the hanging for an avid public—this was all very unsatisfying. Kidd was hauled off the gallows and given the chance to sober up. Brought up again moments later, he was released into the ether amidst wild cheers, only to have the rope snap almost at once. Brought onto the platform for a third time, dazed and only semiconscious, William Kidd was finally served the Whig lords' vengeance.

Yet even as Kidd dangled from the gallows, another life had already been claimed. Richard Coote, Lord Bellomont, had waited anxiously in Boston for two long years as one accusation after another was leveled at him. Some were overt: William Blaythwayt loudly voiced his opinion that the king would "put a stop to his career." Others were more subtle. A pamphlet published early in 1701, purporting to defend the embittered governor, damns him with the faintest of praise. "It was given out that the Earl of Bellomont was sent Governor to New York on purpose to countenance piracies," it begins, only to quickly deny the charge. "The insinuation that the Earl of Bellomont was sent Governor to New York to countenance Kidd and other piracies was the most unworthy and groundless calumny that was ever invented." Yet in several short paragraphs it laid out the calumny in some detail: how Bellomont certainly never financed illegal privateering voyages, how it was unthinkable that his actions in apprehending Kidd were "pretense," how the charge that he had taken bribes from Kidd was utterly unfounded, despite having been circulated quite extensively. In short, the writer of the pamphlet had come, like Mark Antony, to bury Caesar, not praise him.

The question of Bellomont's complicity would not go away. It was openly questioned in Parliament whether "the letters patents granted to the Earl of Bellomont and others of pirates goods were dishonourable to the King, against the law of nations, contrary to the laws and statutes of this realm, invasive of property, and destructive to trade and commerce." There was only so much of this a man could withstand. Now riddled with gout and almost unable to walk, Bellomont watched his noble dreams fall apart. It was a humiliating end, even worse than the rebellion that had consumed Governor Andros, the last man that tried to "purge" the colonies. At the end of his life, Bellomont was forced to admit that—despite his own efforts, despite the downfall of Fletcher and Markham and others—piracy in the Atlantic colonies was just as rampant as ever. The seventeenth century closed with a final, cruel irony: just as the pirate hunter Kidd had turned pirate, so, too, had the pirate-hunting Governor Bellomont become derided as a pirate broker himself. Broken, "so jaded with writing" that he could barely summon the courage to do so, Lord Bellomont died in March 1701.

Events followed quickly thereafter. Joseph Dudley, the staunch Tory whose candidacy the Whigs in Massachusetts had been desperate to forestall, finally became governor. New York was given to Edward Hyde, Lord Cornbury, a genial aristocrat who immediately purged the council of Bellomont's Leislerian friends, brought back the old merchant cabal (what was left of it; Bayard remained in London and Frederick Phillipse died shortly thereafter), and sanctified the defunct Fletcher government as a model of good administration. The changeover was no less dramatic in Whitehall than in the colonies. In November 1701 a friend of Governor Fletcher's wrote exultantly that "most or all of the knot of Lords whereof the Earl of Bellomont was one are Removed and Dead."

The trial of Captain Kidd is often cited as a microcosm of Whig and Tory factionalism, in which the pirate is depicted as an unfortunate pawn in the great chess game of English politics. Yet to understand Kidd and Bellomont we must look not only to the political and social climate of England but to that of the Atlantic world as well. The case of William Kidd reveals stark disparities between the two. Kidd's background, his life in New York, his relations with the pirates, and ultimately his fateful decisions both to turn pirate himself and to return to New York all spring directly from the pirate culture of the Atlantic colonies. It was, as we have seen, a culture composed largely of relationships: between merchant and captain, consumer and seller, customs agent and governor, and governor and privateer, as well as among privateers. All of these relationships in one way or another came under scrutiny and attack during the disastrous career of Captain Kidd, and all testify to a very different understanding of the "crime" of piracy in the colonies—not only among the colonists, but among their governors as well.

It was an understanding of which the Whig junta was sadly unaware. In their zeal to send a pirate to catch a pirate, they failed to reckon with the powerful lure of the colonial antimodel: piracy not as a crime but as a legitimate occupation; pirates not as "enemies of the human race" but as respected members of the community acting with the cognizance and collaboration of powerful gubernatorial patrons. The tragedy of William Kidd was that he became pinioned between these two conflicting paradigms, unable to move as they slowly crushed him to death.

-14-

"That Race of Wicked Men"

IT WAS A NEW CENTURY. THE LAST WAS BARELY LAMENTED. IT HAD begun with the death of the Virgin Queen, seen decades of misman- agement and religious fervor erupt into civil war, and settled finally into four decades of increasing corruption and decadence. Yet it had also seen England's rise as a maritime empire, fostering colonies and a navy that would transform the Isles from a small, windblown, and soggy rock into one of the dominating mercantile forces of the next two hundred years. Already, by 1700, there were precursors of a new and very different age. Isaac Newton had provided the mechanics of the world in his *Philosophia Naturalis Principia Mathematica* in 1687, suggesting for the first time that there was a natural order in the universe that could be not only understood but applied. Perfectibility became the ubiquitous aspiration: perfect machines, perfect governments, perfect souls. The eighteenth century would be an age of reform, of legalism, of bureaucracy. It would also witness the severing of ties between two of the most cohesive and closely bound societies in human history: England and America.

Piracy balanced on the cusp. The relationship of governors and pirates was a legacy of the preceding era, when every man had his patron and, depending on his station, his protégé as well. Piracy itself was something of an anachronism: an unwanted side effect from decades of intermittent war coinciding with the draconian Navigation Acts. Yet for as much as it seemed backward-looking, tied to the flawed policies of the previous century, it contained within itself elements that would come to define the next: notions of freedom, equality, and iconoclasm that clashed against the rigid social castes and the emergence of a distinct legal and social identity in the American colonies. In 1700 piracy appeared to be among the most formidable challenges to the new English bureaucracy. In a short time, it would prove to be very fragile indeed.

A Brief Resurgence

Chroniclers might mark it as a milestone, but for the ever-pressed Board of Trade the new century began mired in the problems of the old. The same names still haunted their correspondence: Every, Kidd, even Tew. In May 1700 a packet of letters arrived in Whitehall, containing depositions from such men as "Nicholas Churchill, of Lower Lichet . . . who sailed with Captain Kidd," "James Brown, who sailed from Rhode Island on the *Susanna* with Commander Wake," "John Eldrich, of Lynn in Norfolk, who joined Captain Hoar's privateer in Jamaica," and others. Some even overlapped, as in the curious story of Turlagh Sullivan, of Pennsylvania, "who sailed in 1694 on the *Dolphin*, Richard Want, Commander, who declared he had a Commission from Governor Jones of Providence against the French. The ship sprang a leak and Captain Every took them on board and landed them at New Providence."

Nor were the reports confined to past evils. Edward Randolph— now in his sixties, crippled by gout, and rapidly losing his sight—was still in the colonies and still writing. His communications with the board became more and more querulous with age. He complained of ill health, of fevers and joint pains, of the sacrifices made in service to the crown. But most of all he complained about the governors, who still seemed bent on flouting the royal will. Having left New York in late 1699, he commenced his tour of the Caribbean and the Carolinas. What he found could be summed up by the French expression *plus ca change, plus c'est pareil.* New governors had replaced old, but there was little change in policy. Randolph wrote from Charleston: "The Lords have appointed another governor to succeed Governor Webb. [He is] Mr. Blake, the present Governor, [who] drives a fine trade of seizing and condemning vessels. Right or wrong, he is sure to be the gainer."

Peace had been declared some five years hence, but still the governors pleaded that they must grant privateering commissions only to forestall and counter pirate raids from neighboring islands. This had a kernel of truth, as Randolph discovered. The governor of Havana "entertains and protects pirates," he wrote the board, and those colonies that fell near the Gulf of Florida routinely saw their trade plundered by Spanish or French privateers. But it was impossible, as Randolph found to his chagrin, to distinguish between legitimate commissions granted to pirate hunters and those merely concealing outright piracy. The legal template was the same. As late as 1703, when another war had arrived, the Board of Trade was still writing in dismay to Governor Bennett of Bermuda:

> We at present observe to you that though in the commission you sent us the day and the month be left blank, yet the year 1701 is expressed, and the reign is that of King William; so that such commissions must have been given in time of peace, which we take to be contrary to your instructions and without example, unless in the time of your predecessor Mr. Day, whose irregularities we well hoped you would not have imitated.

Even as the same names and the same problems echoed, a new strain of militancy also appeared. As the preceding quotation alludes, Governor Day had recently been removed from office on charges of countenancing pirates and imprisoning the industrious and long-suffering customs inspector, George Larkin. Having accused Larkin of pirate brokering, thievery, treason, profanity, ridiculing the council, and "lewd

suggestions" made to one of the council members' wives, the Bermudians finally went for the jugular. Responding to a direct order from the
board to release Larkin (who had languished in the same prison that
Edward Randolph briefly occupied, also for attempting to do his duty),
the council made its most outrageous charge yet. George Larkin, it
declared, "amongst his other horrid evil practices," had ravished "a slave
belonging to His Majesty's Service." The board, unamused, promptly
removed Day and appointed Bennett in his place. But the situation was
scarcely any better for Larkin: he remained in prison, writing piteously
to Whitehall, "if I had not my own innocency and God's protection, it
would be hard for me to stand out against their stratagems and conflicts
of malice. . . . I verily believe that some of them don't care if the islands
were under the dominion of the Turk, provided that piracy and that
which they call a Free Trade were encouraged."

Strains on the Relationship: Pirate Patronage in the Early Eighteenth Century

The disgrace and sudden death of Governor Bellomont removed from
the scene the one man that appeared most likely—and most committed—to combating the pirate menace. Yet even as industrious men like
Larkin suffered, there were signs elsewhere that a new generation of colonial administrators was taking up the cudgels, renouncing the piratical
patronage of their forebears. Among these was Francis Nicholson of Virginia, a vigorous administrator with a patrician's disdain for the slovenly,
ill-mannered lot that he perceived as local pirates. "All the news of America is the swarming of pirates," his lieutenant, Robert Quarry, wrote,
"not only on these coasts but all the West Indies over, which doth ruin
trade ten times worse than a war. Nothing but extraordinary means can
remedy this great evil." Governor Nicholson's means were extraordinary
indeed. While others, including Bellomont, wrote long and moaning
letters to the Board of Trade and wrung their hands in despair, Nicholson commissioned his own pirate hunter out of his own pocket, the
Shoreham, and assumed command himself. He cornered a pirate ship,
a formidable vessel with some 140 men, just off the Virginia coast. The
battle commenced at eight in the morning and was still raging at five
that afternoon. Nicholson showed great courage, remaining on the quar-

terdeck throughout the engagement and exhorting his men. Finally, with both ships crippled, the pirates surrendered. Both the governor and his men were rewarded handsomely for their pains: the pirate ship proved to be full of captured gold. "A few more such expeditious, brave and generous actions from other governments," Quarry concluded, "would quickly clear these coasts of pirates."

Other governors also showed a willingness to recognize the problem, though few went as far as Nicholson in combating it. Gone was the traditional stone-walled denial (with the exception of Governor William Beeston of Jamaica, who in August 1700 still maintained stoutly, "We have no pirates about this island," though he admitted there were "many in the West Indies"). Governor Blake of the Carolinas begged the board to dispatch a warship to the Bahamas to sweep out the pirates there, "for as it is now there doth hardly a ship come from the gulf or on our coast but is plundered."

The demand for a naval presence became a common refrain, both from governors eager to suppress the pirate trade and from governors attempting to justify their own granting of "pirate hunter" commissions. As early as the 1680s colonies that had been plagued by foreign pirates began requesting naval force to patrol the coasts and protect local shipping. These requests were largely ignored. It was in this naval vacuum, in fact, that some governors began commissioning their own pirate protégés, on the principle that two (or three, or four) could play that game.

Other circumstances also forced a radical shift in pirate cruising grounds. Thanks largely to the antics of Every and Kidd, the English navy began convoying East India vessels through the Red Sea. Within a year, pirate trade off the African coast diminished to almost nil, and the pirate colonies in St. Mary's and Madagascar simply melted away. Yet with the navy occupied in the Red Sea, the pirates returned to their old haunts: the Caribbean and the Atlantic. Ironically, English policy had exacerbated the pirate menace by transferring it from a distant coast halfway round the world to the very shores of America. This also meant that piracy, which had hitherto been an English problem, as it depleted ships bound for London and belonging to the East India Company, now became largely an American problem, as the pirates preyed on any vessel departing colonial ports. While some governors still granted commissions to those who sought them, others despaired over the growth of piracy just off their shores. Those men, like Nicholson, Quarry, Blake, and a good many others, began pleading with the crown to send the fleet.

Yet there seemed to be a vacuous lack of understanding in Whitehall. The governors demanded warships; the Board of Trade responded with proclamations. In answer to Lieutenant Governor Quarry's almost weekly demands for action, it said blandly:

> We are very hopeful all difficulties of this or any other
> kind relating to pirates will for the future be in great mea-
> sure removed by an Act of Parliament . . . so that everyone
> in authority will thereby plainly understand their duty,
> and we hope the suppression of that race of wicked men
> will in the end be effectually obtained. So we bid you
> heartily farewell.

The solution to this conundrum would be neither ships nor proclamations but war. As it had so often in the past century, the conflagration of hostilities in Europe brought enormous changes to the colonies. In 1701 King Charles II of Spain died, and Louis XIV finally exercised his long-cherished claim on the Spanish throne, installing his grandson, the Duc d'Anjou. Emperor Joseph I of the Holy Roman Empire, who had an equally strong claim, promptly declared war on France. What followed was almost a carbon-copy of the last great conflict: France and Spain mounted a brilliant campaign, while England, Holland, Portugal, and the Holy Roman Empire combined to check French aggressions. The war, which would come to be known as the War of the Spanish Succession, would rage on for longer than a decade. In the colonies it had a different name: Queen Anne's War, after the young queen who had succeeded William III on his death in 1701. It would be among the bloodiest and most brutal conflicts ever fought in North America. In 1702 the English sacked the city of St. Augustine in Spanish Florida; in 1704 Indian tribes sponsored by the French commenced raids on towns throughout New York and New England, razing Deerfield, Massachusetts, to the ground. The English retaliated in Florida, combining with the Creek tribe to massacre the Spanish-allied Apalachee. For the colonists it seemed as though the enemy was all around them: in the forests beyond, in the hills above.

And on the sea. If the Atlantic and Caribbean had seemed hostile before, they were now chaotic. English, French, Spanish, Dutch, and

Portuguese pirates roamed freely, taking whatever ship crossed their path. Just as King William's War had trained an early generation of pirates, so, too, would Queen Anne's. The resurgence of war turned the Board of Trade's careful plan for quashing piracy on its head. Just as the relationship between governor and pirate seemed about to wane, as Governors Fletcher, Markham, and Day and others paid the price for such sponsorship, the outbreak of war rescued all those that remained.

Perhaps no one in America was more relieved than Samuel Cranston of Rhode Island. In the first year of the eighteenth century, Lord Bellomont still pursued the errant colony of Rhode Island; his last letter to the Board of Trade before his death stated grimly, "The Government of Rhode Island continue their irregularities with more boldness than ever." It seemed for the moment as though the constant stream of reports was finally building to a head. Responding to Bellomont's charges, Cranston in late 1700 offered his most cloying answer yet:

> We have examined the late Governors and the late Deputy
> Gov. Major Green concerning what commissions have
> been granted by them to any captains of ships, etc., and
> cannot understand of any more than one besides you have
> received. . . . We most humbly beg your Lordships' pardon
> for what of negligence doth appear in us. If there hath
> been any misinformation by us, it was through misunder-
> standing. It was never in our hearts to shuffle with you.
> We have many enemies who endeavor to render us con-
> temptible and obnoxious. . . .

Less than six months later the most determined of those enemies, Lord Bellomont, was dead. What had appeared for the moment to be a crisis now simmered down into a state of mutual antipathy between the board and the colony. The coming of war later that year seemed an additional reprieve, as both Cranston and Green hurriedly changed the dates of their privateering commissions ex post facto. The success of this ploy was negligible. As late as 1706 the Board of Trade would still bemoan Rhode Island and nearby Connecticut as a "refuge and retreat of pirates and illegal traders, and the receptacle of goods imported thither from foreign parts contrary to Law."

Nor was the board insensible to the germination of independence therein, which seemed to spread like a contagion to nearby Massachusetts and New York. "They have assumed to themselves a power of making laws contrary and repugnant to the Laws of England," the board reported, "and directly prejudicial to Legal Trade." This was a grave charge, and it followed with another:

> These mischiefs chiefly arise from the ill use they make of the powers intrusted to them by their Charters, and the independency which they pretend to, presuming that each Government is obliged only to defend itself, without any consideration of its neighbors, or the general preservation of the whole.

In the midst of the charges leveled against him, it might have afforded the governor a grim satisfaction to witness the disgrace of one of his most virulent accusers, Massachusetts governor Joseph Dudley. In 1703 Dudley submitted to the Board of Trade a list of charges against Rhode Island, naming it as the foremost pirate broker of the colonies. He maintained both public and private reasons for singling out Rhode Island and Cranston. Pirates sailing out of Newport regularly plundered ships bound to and from Boston. But there was also a more personal element: Dudley, as will be recalled, lost his own share of privateering gains to Cranston when the Massachusetts-commissioned pirates Lawrence and Blew condemned their prizes in Newport.

Yet much of Dudley's antipathy for Cranston might have been an attempt to deflect similar charges against himself. Buried in the records of the Public Record Office at Kew is a commission granted by Dudley to Captain John Quelch of the brigantine *Charles*. Dated July 3, 1703, it is almost a carbon copy of those given out by Cranston and others the decade before:

> Foreasmuch as you have application unto me for license to arm, furnish and equip the brigantine in warlike manner against Her Majesty's enemies I do accordingly permit and allow the same, and reposing special trust and confidence in your loyalty, courage and good conduct . . . commission you to take, kill, suppress and destroy any pirates, privateers, or other subjects and vessels of France and Spain, in whatsoever place you shall meet them . . . and make prize of the same.

Perhaps, as the wording suggests, Governor Dudley truly did intend for Quelch to restrict his attacks to the French and Spanish. On the other hand such language was standard for commissions granted during this time; Governor Cranston's commissions were almost identical. Moreover, there was that interesting phrase "in whatsoever place you shall meet them." Most pirate-hunting commissions restrained the captain to a particular coastline, usually that of the governor's own colony. The fact that Dudley gave Quelch license to roam the seas at will appears, on the face of it, rather suspicious. Either way, Quelch and his confreres soon proved themselves to be anything but pirate hunters. Leaving from Boston in August, the *Charles* hurriedly made for Brazil, where it captured and plundered nine Portuguese vessels in a single month—a spectacular coup. The only snag was that Portugal and England were then allies. Quelch returned to Boston in triumph, the *Charles*'s hold filled with captured gold and silver. Dudley, who had been apprised of the ship's arrival, made no immediate move. But his ambitious lieutenant governor, Thomas Povey, was less circumspect. Povey had been among the many Whigs displaced by Dudley's appointment. Now he seemed determined on embarrassing his superior, perhaps in the hopes of replacing him. When Dudley left for New York on business in May 1704, a proclamation appeared almost at once, signed by the Honorable Thomas Povey, Esq. Whereas Quelch and his men had brought ill-gotten gold into the colony and knowingly plundered ships belonging to Her Majesty's allies, "I have therefore thought fit, by and with the advice of Her Majesty's Council, strictly to command and require all officers civil and military . . . to apprehend and seize the said persons, and bring them before the Council." The proclamation concluded with a warning: "And all Her Majesty's subjects, and others, are hereby strictly forbidden to entertain, harbour or conceal any of the said persons, or their treasure . . . on pain of being proceeded against with utmost severity of law." This, presumably, included the governor himself.

Within days, Quelch and nearly all his crew were in irons. Dudley, returning to his colony and presented with a fait accompli, made the best of it. He quickly penned a note to the Board of Trade placing all the blame on Quelch and his fellow captain, John Plowman. Then he began to turn the great machinery of law against them. A special Court of Vice-Admiralty was summoned, presided over by none other than Governor Dudley himself. Quelch, who, looking from the dock to the judge's dais, must surely have known what was in store for him, presented before the court his commission, signed by Joseph Dudley. It was entered into the record without comment. Then the prosecution laid before the court all the evidence of Quelch's piracy, to which Quelch could only reply that he had enriched the colony considerably through his efforts. He and twenty others were condemned. Quelch, brought to the scaffold, demanded to know why this unjust sentence had been passed on him, claiming that he had been "convicted on circumstances."

Strangely enough, Quelch's sentiments were echoed by Governor Dudley himself. Having disposed of Quelch and thus redeemed himself in the eyes of his superiors, Dudley was moved to be merciful. Writing shortly thereafter to the Board of Trade, he pleaded clemency for the remaining sixteen of Quelch's crewmates, most of whom were no more than boys. It seems, he wrote, "very harsh to hang people that bring in gold to these Provinces."

The swift justice brought against Quelch and his men seemed to presage a hardening of attitudes against piracy in the colonies. Not long after their execution, Cotton Mather ascended the podium of Boston's North Church and delivered an impassioned (and lengthy) tirade against the "tragic spectacle" of piracy, depicting it as a mortal sin almost without equal. "Behold," he thundered, "how Evil does pursue the sinners! They that have refused and reviled the Savior of the world, must be exemplarily given into the hands of the Destroyer!" Yet as the war dragged on, fewer and fewer "sinners" were thus destroyed; incidents of outright piracy like Quelch's diminished. There was little reason to attack English-allied ships when so much French or, more particularly, Spanish trade was available. Two years after the Quelch trials, Governor Dudley wrote to thank the board for its kind words regarding his prosecution of pirates, noting that it was both the first and the last time such a trial had taken place on American shores. "It was an affair of difficulty," he admitted, "to persuade people of the justice of pursuing those men that brought in gold."

Lord Hamilton and the Last Pirate Golden Age

The war ended in 1713 with the Treaty of Utrecht, and the pirates that had enriched themselves off Spanish trade now were unemployed once again. The year 1713 thus marked the dawn of the last pirate golden age, the era that generated most of the romantic legends of piracy that persist today. The pirate colonies that sprung up in the Caribbean would inspire novelists like Robert Louis Stevenson to dream of Treasure Islands, and historians like Marcus Rediker to write of "pirate Libertalia," the mythical land where equality and classlessness among buccaneers contrasted sharply with the rigid caste structures they left behind. Yet, for all its colorful aspects, this last flourishing era for piracy was also its shortest. By the third decade of the eighteenth century Atlantic piracy was all but finished, and the trade had shifted to the Muslim warlords of the Mediterranean.

Yet there were still those willing to make a profit off illegal trade, even in a new climate of increased censure. By far the most flagrant display of pirate brokering in the early eighteenth century was that of Governor Archibald Hamilton of Jamaica. His case, which falls at the end of the golden age of piracy, is perhaps the most revealing of the curious relationship between pirate and governor. In 1716 a pamphlet appeared in Port Royal titled "Articles exhibited against Lord Archibald Hamilton," presenting an excerpted series of documents which claimed that Lord Hamilton had commissioned and financed a pirating voyage just off the coast of his own colony. The emergence and circulation of this pamphlet is itself a testament to how the times had changed. Never before had an accusation of pirate brokering come from within the colony itself; what was once quietly countenanced now became public scandal. Lord Hamilton, it alleged, heard through agents at the port of three Spanish treasure ships, departing Havana, which had inadvertently grounded themselves on the shoals of an island. Hamilton thereupon sought out three well-known pirates and commissioned them—ironically as pirate hunters—"to go out to the said wrecks, and if stronger than the Spaniards to beat them off, and take what money they could get." The governor himself took a partial share in the enterprise. "Consider me what [percentage] you please," he instructed the captain of one such sloop, the *Eagle*.

The expedition was markedly successful, and Lord Hamilton took delivery of some two thousand pieces of eight. The matter might thus have been closed, were it not for the persistence of Don Juan de Valle, deputy governor of Cuba. News of the incident having reached him by way of an outraged Spanish captain, he sent a courteous letter to Hamilton that described it, pointedly ignored the governor's own involvement, and concluded:

> Therefore the said deputy [de Valle] should think himself wanting to the respect he owes to the said Governor and Council of Commerce [of Cuba] to humbly represent to you the mischiefs that may ensue such proceedings [as the attack on the Spanish treasure ships], and likewise pray Your Excellency to inhibit and discountenance the like practices in the future. . . . Nothing more now remains unto me but to wait Your Excellency's favorable answer that I may have the honor of laying the same before the said Governor and Commerce, with what speed the necessity of the affair requires.

Governor Hamilton reacted to the letter as though he had never received it. Months wore on, and he continued to finance such voyages, seldom bothering to conceal his involvement. De Valle's second letter was more blunt:

> Very guilty persons are since permitted, with Your Excellency's commission, again in the same vessels to proceed to sea and repeat the same crimes. This my lord with your good favour looks so very strange from friends and allies, I am at a loss what to say. . . . Instead of that mutual friendship, good neighborhood and correspondence stipulated and agreed upon, nothing on the one hand but depredations, plunderings, robberies and piracies daily committed. What have other sloops and vessels, commissioned by Your Excellency, since done? Attack and seize, upon the high seas, and bring into your ports, sloops richly laden belonging to subjects of His Catholic Majesty without reason, or other crime than that they were valuable.

De Valle's third and final letter was sent directly to London and thus, at last, received a response. The Board of Trade authorized an investigation, relieved Lord Hamilton of his governorship pending its outcome, and sent Lord Heywood as interim governor and chief inquisitor. His instructions must have been singular, for no sooner had he arrived than he at once declared the matter officially closed. Hamilton did not regain his office, however. His reputation shattered, he returned to London in disgrace. Shortly thereafter he penned his own justification, entitled "An Answer to an Anonymous Libel." He referred, of course, to the earlier "Articles" pamphlet. Interestingly, Hamilton's purported denial admitted nearly everything his opponents had alleged. He began by offering a meticulous accounting of each gold piece, demonstrating that the proper share had been paid into crown coffers, exactly as it would be for a legitimate privateering voyage. The crown, he argued, had been enriched by some £3,500. An affidavit from the customs office in Port Royal was reproduced to that effect. The fact that England and Spain were currently at peace was tactfully avoided. Hamilton's later justifications provide so lucid and neatly stated a summary of the colonial governors' collective position that they merit quotation in full:

> At the time I was pressed most for these commissions, we had only one man of war, and one sloop left on the Jamaica station, both foul, and in that light unfit to go after such nimble vessels which infested us, and even such as they were the commanders had given me notice that they had received orders to return to Britain. . . . I thought it my duty in the mean time to provide the best I could for the safety and trade and commerce in those parts, precedents were brought me of the like commissions having been granted by Sir William Beeston, and others, my predecessors. This application was *general*, and made even *by some of the very same persons who have since been my judges and prosecutors*. . . . As to the general insinuations that there was nothing on the one hand but depredations, plunderings, robberies, and piracies daily committed, I suppose he [Valle] means on our side; I can only say he was not so ignorant as he pretended, for I had taken care to inform him of many more depredations, plunderings and robberies committed by the Spaniards upon us than even he complained of.

It was a masterful response, arguing that (1) inadequate naval protection forced governors to resort to privateering commissions; (2) such commissions were of longstanding practice, committed not only by predecessors but by some of the same men who were now his accusers; and (3) the Spaniards themselves engaged in such acts and thus could be paid back with the same coin. All these reasons were true. They were also the thin reeds upon which every governor rested when explaining his behavior vis-à-vis the pirates.

Woodes Rogers on the Attack

Even as Hamilton was busily defending himself, a new force had appeared in the Caribbean. As it had many times before, the Board of Trade again chose one man to serve as governor (though of the Bahamas, not New York) and gave him the unenviable task of suppressing piracy in the Atlantic. This time, however, they chose wisely. Woodes Rogers was a privateer himself. In an earlier era he would have been reckoned alongside Drake or Morgan, for he was cut from the same cloth. A gentleman buccaneer, he amassed a vast fortune for himself during the late war by sacking the Spanish city of Guayaquil in South America, a raid that Drake himself would have envied and that netted Rogers some £800,000 in captured gold. He had also undertaken a circumnavigation of the globe between 1708 and 1711—again, following on the model of Drake. Such a man had not appeared in maritime circles for some time: still in his mid-thirties, handsome, charming, and daring, Rogers was the sort of mariner that had made England great. The only thing he lacked—and yearned for—was imperial glory. Rogers was a visionary: he saw the Caribbean as a vast untapped commodity, teeming with fertile fields and undeveloped colonies of great potential. The apex of this rich new land was a chain of islands that had until recently been almost abandoned: the Bahamas.

In a new era of imperial strategy, the Bahamas were ideal. From their ports nearly every ship passing from Central America or the Caribbean to Europe could be intercepted, and their myriad shoals and inlets offered innumerable safe harbors. It was this strategic advantage, indeed, that had made the Bahamas so attractive to their longtime inhabitants, the pirates. Almost from their inception, the Bahamas and their capital, New Providence, were a pirate haven. It was here that Henry Every had made first landfall in the *Fancy*, receiving the protection of Governor Trott. It was here, too, that Edward Randolph had decried the corruption of both of Trott's successors, Governor Nicholas Webb and Governor Read Elding. In one of his last letters to the Board of Trade, Randolph had written, "I intend to go to [New] Providence, where Mr. Read Elding, a known and late pirate, is by the death of Capt. Webb the present governor." By 1717, the date of Rogers's commission, all pretence at governing the isles was lost. The last governor had fled, and what administrative structure remained was left in the hands of the pirates: Benjamin Hornigold, Thomas Barrow, Edward Teach. Thus New Providence became to the Caribbean what St. Mary's had been for the Red Sea, except worse. For all his faults, Adam Baldridge had been both an astute businessman and a loyal (within his bounds) subject. If he had an Achilles' heel it was an aggrandizement of power; his self-proclaimed status as "King" Baldridge might well have explained the native inhabitants' discontent. Hornigold, Teach, and the others had no such imperial visions. They saw the Bahamas as a safe port, a place to careen their ships, amuse their crew, and lie in wait for the next passing cargo ship.

Woodes Rogers knew many of the Caribbean pirates and had even served with some of them. When he recommended himself as governor for the Bahamas, along with the pledge to end the scourge of piracy therein, one can imagine the trepidation with which the Board of Trade regarded his offer: it was not much different than Captain Kidd offering himself as a pirate hunter. Nevertheless his record, during the war and after, did him credit, and he seemed sincere. The board not only granted him a commission as governor, but it also authorized him to displace the pirates by any means at his disposal and replace them with some 250 planters: the nucleus of a new plantation colony. The most likely explanation for the board's largesse was that, after thirty years of combating the pirate menace without success, it had no other options.

Rogers left the Thames estuary with a convoy of navy warships: the frigates *Rose* and *Milford* supported by sloops *Buck* and *Shark*. The voyage across the Atlantic, begun in the spring of 1718, took three months. At some point during that time word reached Hornigold and the others of a navy flotilla on its way. Had the pirates mounted serious resistance to Rogers, they would certainly have emerged victorious. But such was the dread of an oncoming naval fleet, its size unknown, that most of them simply fled. Teach headed for the Carolinas, where he would pass the remainder of his life under the protection of Governor Eden. His erstwhile companion Stede Bonnet did the same. Others fled to Cuba or Hispaniola, while some remained hidden in the cays, hoping to be overlooked.

Of those who remained on the island when Rogers made landfall in July, only a handful proved combative. Charles Vane, who would shortly be captured and hanged for his piracies, set flaming torches to a French prize and sent her as a fire ship to decimate Rogers's fleet. The vessel passed through without doing any damage, however, and it was Vane who was forced to retreat. He fired a salute to Rogers as he went by.

It was a strange but telling precursor to the welcome Rogers received as he arrived in Nassau. As his longboat approached the shore, Rogers could see several hundred pirates gathered at the water's edge, awaiting him with muskets drawn. Benjamin Hornigold was there, and so was Thomas Burgess (no relation to Samuel), Edward England, Henry Jennings, John Martel, and some three hundred others whose names had regularly appeared in the Board of Trade's correspondence. It was a tricky moment. Rogers, who rightly believed he would be regarded as a turncoat, looked into the faces of the men he had come to subdue and, if necessary, destroy. Suddenly, as his foot first trod upon Bahamian soil, the muskets turned upward. The pirates fired a volley into the air and began shouting, "Hurrah for King George! Hurrah for Governor Rogers!"

What followed was scarcely less extraordinary. Of the nearly one thousand pirates still inhabiting the Bahamas, almost all presented themselves for pardon. Benjamin Hornigold, who had once been Blackbeard's mentor, offered his services to Rogers as a pirate hunter, and Rogers dispatched him at once. It would have been a difficult decision—many pirates had accepted such commissions and promptly abandoned them—but Hornigold was as honest as he was ferocious, and Rogers's trust paid off. Captain Hornigold became the fiercest of the pirate hunters and convinced many of his former protégés either to surrender or join him.

For those pirates who did not surrender themselves, Rogers had no specific instructions, so he improvised. Some were given tracts published by the Society for Promoting Christian Knowledge; others were hanged. The combination of carrot and stick seemed to work, for within a few months of his arrival Rogers congratulated himself that he had subdued the pirate menace and established a safe colony for future settlement. This assessment was precipitous, however. After just three months, more than half the initial settlers were dead from disease; Rogers himself was in chronic ill health. Stores were running low, and without the influx of captured booty (which had maintained the Bahamas almost exclusively for thirty years), fresh supplies were hard to come by. The crops failed, recouped briefly, and failed again. The Spanish, who occupied far better defended and stocked colonies nearby, constantly menaced Rogers with threats of invasion. Worst of all, Governor Rogers was forced to create a working, harmonious society from a bizarre collection of English, French, and Spanish pirates and Swiss, Dutch, and German farmers from the Palatinate. The results, as Rogers himself admitted to the Board of Trade, were mixed. The farmers kept to themselves, and the pirates kept to the grog shops. Rogers kept them all as occupied as possible by constructing large and elaborate defensive barriers for the expected Spanish invasion; what Rogers did not say, and would not admit except to his superiors at Whitehall, was that the fortress walls were of equal importance should the pirates still roaming the Caribbean suddenly decide to take back New Providence for themselves.

Decline and Fall

The Bahamian enterprise never turned a profit, and by 1721 Rogers was back in London, exhausted and almost penniless. But in one sense the experiment was a resounding success: the pirate colony had been displaced and would never return. The last great safe harbor had been removed. For as many pirates as had fled on Rogers's approach, many more had either remained and converted to more honest employment or taken commissions to hunt down their brethren. The example of the Bahamas was indicative of a trend that permeated throughout the colonial world. The colonies were turning on the pirates, and the pirates were turning on themselves. The unique combination of patronage and good business that had maintained piracy in the Atlantic world was unraveling fast, and a new generation of administrators was ruthlessly driving the pirates from port to port.

No single circumstance can account for the rapid disintegration of pirate patronage in the second decade of the eighteenth century. What we find instead is a combination of factors coalescing at a pivotal moment, some from as far away as the Red Sea, others from Whitehall, and still others close to home.

First and perhaps most important was the loss of the Red Sea pirate trade, due to improved East India convoys and an increasingly aggres-

sive naval presence in the area. The pirate "lords," men like Adam
Baldridge, had long since gone, and the former safe haven of Madagascar was becoming increasingly unsafe. Faced with stronger opposition,
the Red Sea pirates simply melted away. Some cut their losses and sailed
home, while others settled as planters on the island and tried to disappear. In most cases they were successful. The remainder of the pirates,
as mentioned earlier, shifted hunting grounds to the Caribbean and
began harassing colonial trade.

In a classic case of cause and effect, the shifting of piracy from the
far-flung Red Sea to the colonies' own backyard was the catalyst that
accelerated its ultimate demise. The proximity of prey drew a different
sort of character to the profession: pirate captains no longer needed the
skills nor the vessels for years-long transatlantic voyages. Now they could
remain in shoals and inlets not far from their homes, sailing out in tiny
sloops to harass and plunder any ship unlucky enough to cross their
path. The attributes best suited for this sort of work were not seamanship and enterprise but ruthlessness and cunning. Accordingly, "gentlemen" pirates of the likes of Thomas Tew virtually disappeared, and a
new breed appeared. Rough, brutal, and often cruel, they were the man-
ifestation of Justice Hedges's earlier definition—"sea robbers"—and
exemplified by that consummate scoundrel Edward Teach.

Not surprisingly, these men were less concerned with gaining legal
imprimatur for their voyages. The reasons for obtaining commissions—
preservation of reputation, insurance against capture and trial—no
longer applied. Teach and his confreres had no illusions about their status: they were criminals and frequently reveled in that status. They
accepted the hangman's noose as a necessary risk, sometimes articulat-
ing it with grim humor through elaborate mock piracy trials in which
one of their number would stand as the accused, another (usually the
captain) as judge, and the remainder as prosecution, defense, and jury.
Pirates in the last golden age typically viewed themselves as standing
apart from, not within, colonial society. "I am a free prince," Captain
Edward Low declares in Daniel Defoe's account, "and have as much
authority to make war on the whole world as he who has a hundred sail
of ships and an army of a hundred thousand men in the field." Pirates
formed extraterritorial enclaves in the thousands of cays and uncharted
islands of the Caribbean, transient and volatile colonies that could

appear and disappear in a week. Some drew up "pirate articles," quasi-constitutions that delineated each man's role, responsibilities, and rights within the pirate band. One such document, drafted by Captain John Phillips in 1723, astonishes with its scope and breadth, its articles including:

> 1. Every man shall obey civil command; the captain shall have one full share and a half of all prizes; the master, carpenter, boatswain and gunner shall have one share and a quarter.
> 2. If any man shall offer to run away, or keep any secret from the company, he shall be marooned with one bottle of powder, one bottle of water, one small arm, and shot. . . .
> 8. If any man shall lose a joint in time of engagement, he shall have 400 pieces of eight; if a limb 800.
> 9. If at any time you meet with a prudent woman, that man that offers to meddle with her, without her consent, shall suffer present death.

The change of self-perception also presaged a marked change in choice of prey. While the Spanish trade still provided adequate income, the new generation of pirates in the eighteenth century was less cautious about restricting itself to plundering "enemy" vessels. Often they simply took whatever they could find: given that they were already branded as criminals (both by themselves and by the colonies), it little mattered whether they attacked Spanish vessels or English ones. Fewer and fewer bothered to seek commissions, and fewer governors—faced with this new and uncouth band of ruffians—felt inclined to grant them. Patriotic declarations like Henry Every's were noticeably absent. Governor Elding of the Bahamas, who would himself be accused by Edward Randolph of sponsoring pirate voyages, went so far as to claim that many Bahamian pirates had taken commissions from Spanish ports to attack *English* vessels.

There were still pockets of support: port towns where pirates and their ill-gotten goods were still welcomed, governors who still offered the hand of friendship. Increasingly, however, the motivations for pirate patronage were less concerned with colonial society and more with simple greed. Among the most notorious of the eighteenth-century pirate patrons was North Carolina's Governor Eden, whose close friendship with the pirate Blackbeard is related in the Prologue. Yet what is most significant about that relationship is not that it occurred but when. By 1718 the indulgence North Carolina offered pirates was already something of an exception. Even as Eden was protecting Teach, governors of nearly every surrounding colony were expurgating pirates from their midst and issuing stern proclamations against harboring or trading with them. Francis Nicholson of Virginia had changed posts and now served as acting governor of Nova Scotia, but his successor, Alexander Spotswood, was a man of much the same stamp. It was Spotswood, as will be recalled, who commissioned Lieutenant Maynard to track down Blackbeard and destroy him. His animus against the pirate was indicative of the state of piracy in this period: Blackbeard had been cruising the waters off Virginia, attacking Virginian ships, and selling their wares at auction in North Carolina.

Whereas governors were once at odds with the crown in their regard for the pirates, the immediacy of pirate activity off their coasts led to a rapid change of heart. Governor Pulleine of Bermuda, who had recently replaced the notorious pirate broker Benjamin Bennett and would become an ardent supporter of the crown's antipirate policy, would write in 1717 that "North and South America are infested with these rogues," the pirates. One by one, the old pirate brokers disappeared, replaced by new administrators who harbored nothing but loathing for the "sea peoples" who used their ports as refuge. It was less a matter of personal morality than outside circumstance: the cruising grounds had changed. Pirates no longer departed for three-year voyages around the Cape of Good Hope, returning laden with riches. They were there, in the colonies, all the time: drinking, whoring, carousing, spending lavishly but leaving a trail of chaos in their wake. They plundered the ships of one colony and sold their wares to another. The pecuniary advantages they offered now had to be set against the burden of having these loutish brutes constantly in evidence.

The decline of the pirates' character, if one may term it thus, coincided with a renewed effort by the English government to stamp them out of existence. The Board of Trade emerged from the Treaty of Utrecht more formidable than ever and no longer had to rely solely on toothless proclamations or acts of Parliament to enforce its will on the colonies. Having successfully secured the East India trade through increased naval presence in the Red Sea, it embarked on a similar policy in the Atlantic. Naval vessels were dispatched to the Caribbean, forming patrols in the key areas of pirate infestation, especially around Jamaica, the Bahamas, and the Carolinas. Naval captains were now posted in nearly all the major port cities, visibly present and working in close conjunction with the local governments. This static Admiralty presence had a dual purpose: for honest governors, it provided the necessary force they had long demanded to eradicate the pirate scourge; for dishonest ones, the post captains were a means of constant oversight and a stern check on any "aberrant" behavior regarding the pirates.

Yet it is undeniable that the success of the English navy during this time hinged in no small part on the receptivity of colonial administrations and colonial society as a whole. Policing the Red Sea was a comparatively simple matter, as there were no sympathetic governments therein to offer safe harbor to the pirates or subvert their capture. Had the navy appeared in New York in 1695, for example, the situation would have been markedly different. There the post captains would have encountered a governor and colony actively engaged in protecting the pirate trade, which they regarded collectively as an essential branch of commerce. By the second decade of the eighteenth century, however, the colonies had wearied of this new generation of pirates and their feckless ways. Ships were bottled up in port, unable to move for fear of attack. Piracy was no longer a supplement to local economies but rather was a drain.

One can gauge the hardening of sentiments against the pirates by the sudden surge of trials in the colonies. Previously, as late as 1710, successful pirate trials were virtually unknown outside Great Britain. It was for that reason that the Admiralty had long maintained the prerogative to extradite all pirates back to London for trial; they believed, correctly, that no pirate would ever be convicted by the people who had profited from him. But by the time of Rogers's arrival in New Providence, attitudes had changed dramatically. In 1718 the colony of Massachusetts tried eight men for piracy and convicted all but two. The accused maintained, rather ingeniously, that the antipiracy proclamations of Queen Anne were no longer in force, as their author—the queen—was dead. It was an argument that might well have swayed an earlier Massachusetts court. Now, however, the court firmly rejected it, maintaining in its conclusion that the pirate "can claim the protection of no prince, the privilege of no country, the benefit of no law; he is denied common humanity, and the very rights of nature . . . and is to be dealt with [as a] wild and savage beast, which every man may lawfully destroy."

Soon court dockets throughout the colonies were clogged with piracy trials. In July 1726 another sixteen pirates were tried in Massachusetts, of whom four were convicted. The rest proved to be nothing more than unwitting accomplices, but of the four that went to the scaffold, the presiding judge declared with fury that they "had not the fear of God before their eyes, but [were] Instigated by the Devil." It was a speech that could have been written by Cotton Mather himself—who, now in his sixty-third year, still preached the evils of piracy before an increasingly receptive audience. The July trials were followed by another set in October, as another five pirates were condemned, to the general delight of the populace.

Several interesting facts emerge from the trial transcripts. First, the men who appear in them do not flourish commissions but rather plead almost unanimously that they were pressed into piracy by another, usually a comrade at the dock. This finger-pointing was a significant departure, for it indicates that pirates now acted on their own accord, without any local sponsor. Second were the amounts of plunder involved. Gone were the days when Thomas Tew could seize a king's ransom from the Great Mogul: Samuel Van Vorst, John Brown, Thomas South, and Hendrick Quinter all went to their deaths for "piratically and feloniously embezzling" a cargo of wine, sundry goods, and wearing apparel. Piracy had retracted: it now looked less like a business and more like petty thievery. Thus, having once exceeded and confounded the laws of England, it now fit squarely within the realm of criminal law. The dichotomy between English and American attitudes toward the practice diminished, and the crime itself faded into obscurity.

If piracy trials in Massachusetts were remarkable, their counterparts in Rhode Island were nothing short of astounding. In 1723 the colony tried no fewer than thirty-six pirates and convicted twenty-eight of them. What makes this even more extraordinary is that the trials occurred during the tenure of Governor Cranston, who would remain governor of the colony for another four years, until his death in 1727. In 1769, long after the age of piracy had passed, a pamphlet appeared in circulation that purported to relate the dying speeches of many of these Rhode Island pirates executed at Newport. The passage of time from execution to pamphlet renders these accounts suspect at least, but even in their idealized form they tell us much about how the perception of piracy had altered in even so notorious a place as Rhode Island. "Live soberly, and let not yourselves be overcome with strong drink," one pirate counsels from the scaffold. "Alas! It is a sad thing, a too reigning vice among men, the inlet of numberless sins and evils, the ruin of a great many families." Another allegedly writes to his mother, "I beg that this may be a warning to all young people, to keep themselves from all bad courses, especially Sabbath-breaking, drinking to excess, and blaspheming the name of God. And I beseech all that are servants to keep with and be faithful to their masters, for if I had been dutiful to mine, 'tis likely I had not been brought to this untimely end."

Like beggars and whores, pirates were now cautionary figures whose piteous example reinforced the mores of the status quo. The age of pirates and the patronage was truly ended.

A New World

What can we conclude about these strange bedfellows, the governors and their pirate protégés? From a legal standpoint, this relationship is crucial. English law was not monolithic but rather was conducted through a series of communications from sovereign to administrator to subject. Thus the law is only as strong as the willingness of administrators to communicate and enforce it. Much of English state building during this period was centered on enforcing compliance through an increasingly intricate legal bureaucracy: sheriffs, judges, local administrators. The law, in short, was brought to the localities. But the establishment of overseas colonies added a new and untenable dimension. How could crown law be enforced across a distance of several thousand miles, when even its edicts took months to be heard? Throughout the seventeenth and eighteenth centuries, the English government never fully solved this problem.

The willingness to countenance pirates was one aspect—indeed, the most crucial aspect—of an overall dichotomy between crown and colonial law. Just as the bureaucratic structures of England developed, its colonies developed as well. They became not legal and social extensions of the mother county but independent social entities, each composed of myriad ethnicities. English, French, Dutch, Germans, Native Americans, and Africans all lived in close proximity, moving from one colony to another. Similarly, the problems that confronted the Atlantic colonies were radically different from those of their European masters. Frontiers were insecure, subject to constant raids either by other colonists or by Indian tribes. Crops failed. Trade was a constant problem, all the more so after the Navigation Acts. And so it went on. Governors arriving, as Benjamin Fletcher did in 1691, soon found themselves thrust into the midst of conflicts for which they were entirely unprepared. Little wonder that, while confronting problems unknown to their masters at Whitehall, they quietly condoned other practices that likewise had not entered into the imperial imagination.

This is not to suggest, however, that the legal and social bonds between crown and colony were nonexistent. For as many examples as we find of governors flouting crown policy, there are an equal number of how that policy had direct consequences in the colonies. The most obvious, of course, is war. The outbreak and cessation of hostilities invariably produced a sea change in piratical sponsorship—not necessarily in the number of commissions granted but in how they were perceived. Similarly, the constant shift of political fortunes in London also had ramifications on the pirate trade. Consider, for example, how closely tied were the fates of men like Benjamin Fletcher, Lord Bellomont, Frederick Phillipse, or William Kidd to the prevailing parties in power at Whitehall. The century-long tussle between Whig and Tory created an almost comical state of affairs wherein the pirate patrons of one party could be excoriated by those of the other, and vice versa. Thus the career of Tory gentleman Benjamin Fletcher would be shattered by his relation with Thomas Tew; then, just a few years later, he would see his Whig nemesis Lord Bellomont disgraced through his own dealings with Captain Kidd. Piracy and the pirates themselves were constantly caught in the crosshairs of party faction, an unavoidable consequence of the patron-protégé relationship.

There were also the personal relationships between these men, pirate and governor, which cannot be overestimated. Thomas Tew and Benjamin Fletcher were not just business associates but friends; William

Markham felt sufficiently akin to Every's crew that he took one into his family. None of these gestures could be written off as entirely commercially motivated. As the business of piracy became increasingly common and regulated, financed by local merchants and controlled (albeit at arm's length) by local governments, the social dichotomy between pirates and governors disappeared. These were men often drawn from the same or similar classes, whose daily life in the colonies brought them frequently into contact with one another. The assumption that their relationship could only be monetary rests on the equally erroneous premise that their status in society differed substantially and that therefore no other social relationship could exist.

A similar misconception centers on the nature of the commissions. Historians have by and large referred to payments for commissions as bribes, concluding therefore that governors who accepted money from pirates were irredeemably corrupt. *Res ipsa loquitur*; the thing speaks for itself. Yet to condemn the governors as venal for accepting such payments is to apply a twenty-first-century perspective to a seventeenth-century practice. Throughout the era we have considered, such "bribery" was not only an accepted form of contract but the oil that greased the machinery of English politics. Members of Parliament regularly charged fees to submit a particular bill or accepted gifts from hopeful or grateful constituents. The seventeenth and eighteenth centuries were an era of patronage, when the entire English class system operated through a series of master-servant relationships: one had one's patron and one's protégés. For governors to have protégés among the pirates was as natural as an English aristocrat having favored tenants; it was equally natural that the governors, having bestowed on the pirates the measure of their trust and sanction, would expect to be compensated in turn.

Piracy—forever maligned, obscured, or misinterpreted as the pirates' rebellion against the status quo—was indeed a radical challenge to the English state. Yet that challenge came not from the pirates themselves. It was their patrons, the earnest colonial governors, who through quiet accord and longstanding practice signaled the limits of crown law and the germination of a distinct Atlantic community.

A community that would one day be known as the United States of America.

Sources

AS IT WAS MY INTENTION TO BRING THE RELATIONSHIP BETWEEN governors and pirates to the light, I have tried wherever possible to let them tell the story in their own words. Two primary sources furnish the bulk of this documentation: the *Calendar of State Papers, Colonial Series,* which is a compilation of nearly all colonial correspondence to the English crown, and the archives of the Public Record Office at Kew, England. In addition, three archives in the United States have proved enormously helpful: the John Carter Brown Library of Providence, Rhode Island, which has the largest collection of colonial maritime documents in North America and was pivotal in reconstructing the career of Governor Cranston; the Gilder Lehrman Collection in the Museum of the City of New York, which contains nearly all the correspondence between Livingston, Governor Fletcher, and Captain Kidd; and the archives of Colonial Williamsburg, Virginia, which contain one of two surviving copies of the Blaythwayt Papers. I am greatly indebted to all these archives for allowing me access to their collections. In addition, the preserved colonial records of Virginia, Pennsylvania, North Carolina, New York, New Jersey, Massachusetts, and Bermuda have all been of great assistance, as have the trial records preserved in many of these former colonies. Three collections of private papers have also been extensively quoted and thus deserve special note: the aforementioned Blaythwayt Papers, the correspondence of William Penn, and the letters of Edward Randolph. The first exists only in its original form, but the latter two are readily available in bound reproductions. Secondary sources were obtained through the enormous collection available at Brown University, in conjunction with numerous other university libraries throughout the United States, as well as the stunning array of sources available at the British Library in London.

Preface

xi **needed by the colonial economies.** Alan Taylor, *American Colonies: The Settling of North America* (New York: Viking, 2001), 294.

Prologue

2 **the old pirate told him.** Lloyd Haynes Williams, *Pirates of Colonial Virginia* (Richmond, Va.: The Dietz Press, 1937), 105.

2 **to answer the *Adventure Command*'s eight.** Ibid., 108.

3 **pirate hunter for the crown,** Governor Woodes Rogers to the Council of Trade and Plantations, October 31, 1718, *Calendar of State Papers*, 372.

3 **his fourteenth wife.** Williams, 101.

3 **might send Intelligence to Teach."** Alexander Spotswood to Lord Cartwright, February 14, 1718, *Colonial Records of North Carolina*, 324.

4 **Blackbeard taunted him.** Cyrus Karraker, *Piracy Was a Business* (Rindge, N.H.: Richard Smith, 1953), 155–156.

5 **as Daniel Defoe termed them—** Daniel Defoe, *A General History of the Robberies and Murders of the Most Notorious Pirates* (New York: Carroll & Graf, 1985), 66. There is some dispute over whether Defoe is indeed the author of this seminal text, which is the principal source for many current works on the history of piracy. The author is listed as Captain Charles Johnson, almost certainly a pseudonym. Until the authorship question is resolved, I will continue to refer to it as Defoe's.

6 **cut the rest to pieces!"** Ibid., 66.

6 **clattering uselessly to the ground.** Ibid., 66.

7 **prolonging their Lives a few Days,"** Ibid., 67.

8 **agent of Governor Charles Eden.** Karraker, 157.

8 **another sixty with Eden.** Ibid., 151.

8 **be on his guard."** Williams, 108.

8 **your real friend and servant, T. Knight."** Tobias Knight to Edward Teach, November 17, 1718, *Colonial Records of North Carolina*, 345.

8 **Maynard's men interrupted him.** Williams, 112.

9 **Blackbeard had presented them.** Defoe, 68.

9 **died of fright several days later,** Ibid.

9 **in April of the following year.** *Council Journal for the Colony of Virginia*, May 27, 1719.

10 **a few discontented Men."** Alexander Spotswood to Lord Cartwright, February 14, 1719, from *The Spotswood Letters*, vol. II, 272.

Chapter 1

14 **the history of individual cases.** Edward Jenks, *Sources of Judicial Organization of English Law* (London: Sack & Montanuz, 1931), reviewed by Thorsten Sellin in *Journal of Criminal Law and Criminology*, vol. 131 (1933), 474.

14 **acts of Parliament and Orders in Council.** Ibid., 474. In addition, there are also statutory rules and procedures and bylaws of corporation, but neither concerns us here.

14 **in the early modern period.** Ibid., 475.

15 **great displeasure of God and men."** Ibid., 146.

15 **"enemies of the human race."** Unfortunately, no copy of *Articuli Admiralitis* survives, but it is referred to by contemporary Richard Zouch and referenced by William Blackstone in his *Commentaries on the Laws of England* (Boston: Beacon Press, 1962), 66.

15 *sed communis hostis omnium."* "Piracy is not a crime directed against a definite number of persons but rather aggression against the community as a whole." Cited in John W. Sundberg, "Piracy: Air and Sea," *De Pauw Law Review*, 20 (winter 1970), n. 17, p. 338.

16 **"waged war against the world entire."** Daniel Defoe, 300.

16 **otherwise entitled to do.** Blackstone, 66.

16 **amounted to felony there,"** Ibid., 67.

17 **a revolt on board."** Ibid.

17 **under criminal law in the assizes.** For a comprehensive overview of the assize courts and their function in criminal law, see J. H. Baker, "Criminal Courts and procedure at Common Law 1550–1800," in *Crime in England 1550–1800*, ed. J. S. Cockburn (Princeton: Princeton University Press, 1977), 25–28.

18 **the trade of the crown.** John William Bund, *A Selection of Cases from the State Trials* (London: Cambridge Warehouse, 1879), 8–9.

18 **deemed inadmissible evidence.** Hugh Rankin, *The Golden Age of Piracy* (New York: Henry Holt, 1969), 5.

19 **according to the common law."** Blackstone, 67.

19 **per course of common law"** Sir Matthew Hale, *Pleas of the Crown* (London: Richard Tonson, 1678).

19 **cases properly belonging to that court."** Richard Zouch, "The jurisdiction of the Admiralty in England asserted against Sir Edward Coke's *Articuli Admiralitis"* (London: Francis Tyton, 1663).

20 **or hostile to the state.** K. R. Andrews, "The expansion of English privateering and piracy in the Atlantic, c. 1540–1625," in Michel Mollat, *Cours et Piraterie* (Paris: Imprimerie Nationale, 1975), 200.

20 **vessels one could legally plunder.** Grover Clark, "The English Practice Regarding Reprisals by Private Persons," *American Journal of International Law*, vol. XIV (1933), 694. The text of reprisals may be found in R. G. Marsden, *Documents Relating to Law and Custom of the Sea*, vol. I (London: Naval Records Society, 1915), 38.

20 **Their efforts had limited results.** N. A. M. Roger, "The Naval Service of the Cinque Ports," *English Historical Review*, vol. 111, no. 442 (1996), 638.

21 **led a boarding party.** Peter Earle, *The Pirate Wars* (New York: St. Martins, 2006), 20.

21 **to the local authorities.** Karraker, 25–30.

22 **refer to it as "confused."** Ibid., 21.

22 **commingled and coalesced.** A recent work does a credible job of examining the growth of privateering and its impact on English foreign policy. See Susan Ronald, *The Pirate Queen: Queen Elizabeth, Her Pirate Adventurers, and the Dawn of Empire* (New York: Harper Collins, 2007).

Chapter 2

24 **the marriage was almost a certainty.** John Hampden, ed., *Francis Drake, Privateer: Contemporary Narratives and Documents* (Tuscaloosa: University of Alabama Press, 1972), 245.

25 **the Spanish imperial crest.** George Thompson, *Sir Francis Drake* (New York: William Morrow, 1972), 162–163.

25 **fluttered in the breeze.** For a complete account of Drake's knighthood and its attending circumstances, see Sir Julian Corbett, *Drake and the Tudor Navy* (London: Longmans Green, 1892).

25 **both at home and abroad.** See, for example, G. E. Aylmer, "Britain Transformed," in *The Age of Expansion: Europe and the World, 1559–1660*, ed. H. R. Trevor-Roper (New York: McGraw-Hill, 1968).

26 **of the next three hundred years.** For a complete history of this transformation, see John Brewer, *Sinews of Power* (New York: Alfred Knopf, 1989).

26 **naval captains became privateers.** Ronald, 54–60.

26 **to man the fleet once it was ready.** Rankin, 3–5.

26 **the pretense of curtailing them.** Karraker, 40–41.

27 **raids on Spanish ports.** Ronald, 165–169.

27 **sometimes even aristocratic antecedents.** Ibid., 17.

28 **fell to him.** Ibid., 215–230. For Drake's own account of his voyages, see "The World Encompassed: Sir Francis Drake, His Voyage Around the World," in *Francis Drake, Privateer: Contemporary Narratives and Documents*, ed. John Hampden (Tuscaloosa: University of Alabama Press, 1972), 124.

28 **the inspiration.** Kenneth Andrews, *Drake's Voyages: A Re-assessment of Their Place in Elizabethan Maritime Expansion* (London: Weidenfeld & Nicholson, 1967), 180–184.

29 **turned pirates."** John Smith, *The True Travels and Adventures of Captaine John Smith*. First published 1629 (Birmingham: Arber, 1884), 69.

30 **"Proclamation against Pirats."** J. F. Larkin and P. L. Hughes, eds. *Stuart Royal Proclamations* (1973–1983), vol. 1, nos. 15, 28, 46, 50, 53, 67, 93. Note: this is only a partial list of such proclamations against piracy from that period.

30 **shall terrify all others. . . ."** Ibid., n. 28, 53.

30 **take order in that behalf."** Ibid., n. 46, 99.

30 **allowed to the defendant."** Ibid., n. 93, 204.

30 **complices and associates."** Ibid., n. 67, 146.

31 **loathing and detestation.** Ibid., n. 93, 203.

31 **ports and maritime counties."** Ibid., n. 93, 203.

31 **an effete, homosexual king.** See, for example, C. H. Haring, *The Buccaneers in the West Indies in the XVII Century* (Hamden, Conn.: Archon, 1966); Robert Carse, *The Age of Piracy* (New York: Rinehart, 1957).

31 **steering, and the like.** A point made most forcefully in David Cordingly's *Under the Black Flag: The Romance and the Reality of Life Among the Pirates* (New York: Random House, 1995).

32 **sundries while aboard ship.** George Francis Dow, *The Pirates of the New England Coast, 1630–1730* (Salem, Mass.: Marine Research Society, 1923), 2.

32 **discipline was stringently enforced.** It would not be until the late eighteenth century that the Royal Navy saw fit to introduce guidelines for the limits to which a captain could punish his crew. Until that time such matters were left entirely at the master's discretion. Abuses were common and sometimes horrific.

32 **they are hardly reclaimed."** Smith, 84.

32 **pirates of the usual type."** Dow, 6.

32 **fugitive thieves and murderers,"** John Andrew Doyle, *The English Colonies in America* (New York: Henry Holt, 1907), 383.

33 **many volunteers, many compelled.** *Calendar of State Papers, Colonial Series, 1614*, 432.

33 **"ligne de l'enclose des Amities,"** Haring, 48.

33 **makes people here cry out,"** *Calendar of State Papers, Venetian, 1603–1607*, 199.

34 **the space of two years more."** Sir Ralph Winwood, document collection titled *Memorials of Affairs of State*, ed. Edmund Sawyer (London: 1725), 75.

34 **in harbors throughout England.** A circumstance that, as already indicated, led in turn to a surplus of unemployed mariners and thus augmented the pirate problem as well.

35 **logwood, sugar, and spices.** For a complete account of Spanish trade routes, see Charles Weiss, *L'Espagne depuis Philippe II.*

35 **Sir Henry Mainwaring.** Despite his extraordinary success, very few accounts of piracy mention Henry Mainwaring beyond a cursory reference. The most complete account of his life appears in Mainwaring, *Life and Works of Sir Henry Mainwaring.*

38 **"had committed no great wrong."** Philip Gosse, *The History of Piracy* (New York: Benjamin Franklin, 1968), 120.

39 **"a very just man of his word."** Sir Henry Mainwaring, *The Beginnings, Practices and Suppression of Pirates.* First published 1624. (London: 1717), courtesy of the British Museum.

41 **"is no great matter."** Secretary Windebank to Sir Arthur Hopton, *Clarendon State Papers* II, 87.

42 **Spanish traders in the Caribbean.** William Bradford, *Of Plymouth Plantation 1620–1647* (New York: Knopf, 1952), 441.

42 **"poor thatched house."** John Winthrop, *Journal of John Winthrop* (New York: Scribners, 1908), vol. II, 273.

42 **had enjoyed in years.** Gosse, 140.

43 **from Dutch competition.** Douglas Botting, *The Pirates* (Alexandria, Va.: Time-Life Books, 1978), 27.

Chapter 3

45 **over and over."** Kris Lane, *Pillaging the Empire* (Armonk, N.Y.: M. E. Sharp, 1998), 169.

45 **an otherwise bare peninsula."** Michael Pawson and David Buisseret, *Port Royal, Jamaica* (Oxford: Clarendon Press, 1975), 37.

47 **to such raids themselves.** Pawson, 20.

48 **lacked the approval of the Admiralty;** See Helen Crump, *Colonial Admiralty Jurisdiction in the Seventeenth Century* (London: Longmans, Green & Co., 1931).

48 **upon spoil and depredations."** *C.S.P. Colonial Series, 1661–8*, 61, March 1661.

49 **at Puerto Caballo one year later.** Angus Konstam, *Pirates: Predators of the Seas* (New York: Skyhorse Publishing, 2007), 99–101.

50 **Castillo del Morro.** Not to be confused with the Castillo del Morro of Puerto Rico, which still stands.

50 **150,000 pieces of eight.** Konstam, 101.

50 **the crown received £200.** *C.S.P. Colonial Series, 1661–8*, 379, October 20, 1662.

52 **suppress these raids at once.** *C.S.P. Colonial Series, 1661–8*, 443, April 23, 1663.

52 **whether the crown received a share.** This may be the first recorded example of an excuse that would be repeated throughout the history of piracy in the British Atlantic: that governors had no power to curb the pirates even if they wanted to. In some cases (and almost certainly Lyttelton's) this was the truth. Later, however, as the relationship between the governors and pirates deepened, the excuse would be a frequent and convenient obfuscation.

52 **his duty to call them in."** *C.S.P. Colonial Series, 1661–8*, 566, October 15, 1663.

54 **the strictness of his instructions."** *C.S.P. Colonial Series, 1661–8*, 767, June 30, 1664.

54 **slender account in the Admiralty."** Ibid., 942, February 20, 1665.

54 **His Majesty's service."** Ibid., 946, April 12, 1665.

55 **brought in and fitted out again."** Ibid., 1264, August 21, 1666.

56 **havoc on Spanish trade.** Botting, 13.

56 **ferocious and inspired.** Rosita Forbes, *Admiral Sir Henry Morgan, King of the Buccaneers* (Gretna, La.: Pelican, 2005). For other accounts of Morgan's life and career, see E. A. Cruikshank, *Life of Sir Henry Morgan* (Toronto: Macmillan, 1935), which contains an excellent narrative of Morgan's political struggles as lieutenant governor of Jamaica; W. Adolphe Roberts, *Sir Henry Morgan, Buccaneer and Governor* (New York: Friede, 1933).

56 **to invade Jamaica."** *C.S.P. Colonial Series, 1661–8,* 1838, September 7, 1668.

57 **an all-out assault on Jamaica.** Ibid.

58 **"three thousand men,"** Ibid.

58 **Sir James noted sadly.** A. P. Thornton, "The Modyfords and Morgan," in *Jamaican Historical Review,* ii.2 (1952), 48.

59 **depredations against English trade.** *C.S.P Colonial Series, 1669–74,* 162, 172, 206.

59 **forbear all hostilities on land."** Ibid., 194.

60 **the defense of this island."** Ibid., 211.

60 *or any other place."* Ibid., 211.

60 **on Cuba in 1668.** Haring, 143–157.

61 **and call him off.** Ibid., 359.

62 **broad, blue smile of the Pacific.** Ibid., 169–178.

62 **huge alacrity of their minds."** Alexander Esquemeling, *The Buccaneers of America.* Orig. published Netherlands, 1684. (London: George Allen, 1951), 217.

Chapter 4

63 **"Dogs! We will meet you!"** Esquemeling, 217.

63 **could not conveniently reach."** Ibid., 217.

64 **with great repose and satisfaction."** Ibid., 217–218.

64 **outnumbered by more than two to one.** Roberts, 149–150.

64 **kindled very hot."** Esquemeling, 219.

65 **which was accordingly done."** Ibid., 220.

65 **poisoned by the Spaniards."** Ibid., 221.

66 **the whole year long.** Ibid., 223–224.

66 **40 of his soldiers in it."** Morgan's full account of the battle, dated April 20, 1671, appears in *C.S.P. Colonial Series, 1669–74,* 504.

66 **no good example in this point."** Esquemeling, 229.

66 **behind the procession, as slaves.** Cruikshank, 197.

67 **a considerable sum of money.** *C.S.P. Colonial Series, 1671,* n. 484, 534.

67 **uncharacteristically bleak mourning.** *State Papers of Spain,* vol. 58, 156–157.

67 **His Majesty's good brother the Catholic King."** *C.S.P. Colonial Series, 1669–74,* 405.

68 **would live to regret.** For a detailed account of Modyford's removal, see Cruikshank, 200–225.

68 **security for his father's good conduct.** Thornton, 57.

68 **taken his son's place in the tower.** *C.S.P. Colonial Series, 1669–74*, 653, 654.

68 **strength or commerce."** Ibid., 608.

69 **silver and gold in the entire world."** Ibid., 547.

69 **to the vanquished enemy."** Ibid., 608.

70 **followed after his carriage wherever he went.** A very different account of Morgan's stay in London can be found in Sir Thomas Dalby's account, *An Historical Account of the Rise and Growth of the West India Colonies* (London, 1690). Dalby claims that "under the perpetual malice of the court faction" Morgan lost both his income and his health, returning to Jamaica plagued by "a lingering consumption" brought on by stress and the prevailing English damp.

71 **The interrogation was adjourned.** Roberts, 193–202.

71 **in the entire Caribbean Sea.** *C.S.P. Colonial Series, 1669–74*, 863.

72 **endeavored to restrain and prevent,"** *C.S.P. Colonial Series, 1675–6*, 863, April 4, 1676.

72 **set the course for Jamaica.** See Cruikshank, 226–258.

72 **that curse of life."** *C.S.P. Colonial Series, 1675–6*, 912, May 2, 1676.

73 **punishing criminals with death."** *BA, C.O.* I:48, no. 37.

73 **the French government on Tortuga.** *C.S.P. Colonial Series, 1675*, 998.

74 **via the Lords of Trade.** *C.S.P. Colonial Series, 1675–6*, 566.

74 **damns and curses most extravagantly."** *C.S.P. Colonial Series, 1681–85*, 501, 522.

75 **the cause of his present indisposition.** Sir Hans Sloane, *Voyage to Jamaica* (London, 1707), vol. I, pp. xcviii–xcix.

75 **his friend Sir Leoline Jenkins.** *Cal. St. Pap., Col., 1677–1680*, p. li, reprinted in John Franklin Jameson, *Privateering and Piracy in the Colonial Period: Illustrative Documents* (New York: MacMillan, 1923), 134.

76 **"French falls," and so on.** Pawson, 187.

77 **"but more for New England."** Ibid., 48.

Chapter 5

79 **depending thereon, in America."** Commission for Benjamin Fletcher, *Minutes of the provincial Council of Pennsylvania* (Philadelphia: Jo. Severns, 1852), 357.

79 **commissions to execute the Law martiall."** Ibid., 361.

80 **execute with relative impunity.** Among the most comprehensive studies of the extent of gubernatorial administrative power in the colonies is Lauren Benton, *Law and Colonial Cultures* (London: Cambridge University Press, 1997).

81 **waged war against the entire world.** Alfred Rubin, *The Law of Piracy*, 2nd ed. (New York: Transnational, 1998); Philip Buhler, "New Struggle with an Old Menace: Towards a Revised Definition of Maritime Piracy," *Currents International Trade Law Journal* 61 (1999).

81 **under international law.** M. J. Peterson, "An Historical Perspective on the Incidence of Piracy," in *Piracy at Sea*, ed. Eric Ellen (1989), 41.

81 **British colonial governors.** Karraker, 69–71; Robert Ritchie, *Captain Kidd and the War Against the Pirates* (Cambridge: Harvard University Press, 1986), 38. Ritchie writes, "Money in any form warmed Fletcher's heart; he never refused a present or a bribe, no matter how small."

82 **may be hostile to His Majesty,"** Edward Rowe Snow, *Pirates and Buccaneers of the Atlantic Coast* (Boston: Yankee Publishing, 1944), 98.

82 **a cadre of Whig noblemen,** Whig and Tory were titles denoting the two primary political factions of the age. Very generally, Whigs were ardent Protestants and the linear political descendants of the Puritans of Charles I's time. They sought to preserve the Protestant Church of England at all cost and viewed the Catholic states of both France and Spain as hereditary enemies. The Tories were those who supported James II in his battle against Parliament, a loose collection of ardent Royalists, Anglicans, and Catholics. In the Glorious Revolution, a Whig junta invited William of Orange to invade, but it was the tacit acceptance by a number of key Tories that allowed the invasion to succeed as quickly and bloodlessly as it did.

83 **to plague the enemy's ships.** *C.S.P. Colonial Series, 1689–92,* 293.

83 **without crown approval.** *C.S.P. Colonial Series, 1689–92,* 2034, 2044, 2047.

83 **the papist king, James II.** Mary Lou Lustig provides a comprehensive account of Andros's dictatorial regime in *The Imperial Executive in America: Sir Edmund Andros 1627–1714* (Madison, N.J.: Fairleigh Dickinson University Press, 2002).

84 **Royal Colony of Virginia.** See, generally, Joseph Moran, *An Historical Survey of Three Colonial Rebellions, Including Bacon's Rebellion, Leisler's Rebellion, and the Andros Overthrow in Boston* (master's thesis, Brown University, 1963).

84 **by his Majesty for the same.** Case of William Coward, *Records of the Court of Assistants of Massachusetts Bay,* v. 8, 1685–1700, 319–322.

85 **for the ruin of it.** "An account of the late revolutions in New England, in a letter." [Boston: printed by Samuel Green, 1689] Early American Imprints, 1st series, no. 462 (filmed).

85 **ignorant of the news."** Ibid., 2.

86 **where the Moslem Muslim treasure ships awaited.** Deposition of Samuel Burgess, May 3, 1698, *BA, Colonial Office Papers* 5/1040.

86 **the American colonies were governing themselves.** See, generally, Jerome Reich, *Leisler's Rebellion: A Study of Democracy in New York, 1664–1720* (Chicago: University of Chicago Press, 1953).

86 **two days after the attack,** In one of the greatest ironies of colonial history, the man dispatched to inform Sloughter of Ingolsby's raid was none other than Captain William Kidd, who accrued a handsome fee of £150 for aiding the new government in engineering Leisler's ultimate capture. Ritchie, 35.

87 **tradesmen, sailors, and farmers.** Reich, 126.

86 **their own Whig revolution in the colonies.** Michael Kammen, *Colonial New York: A History* (New York: Scribner's, 1975), 118–119.

87 **"Great White Arrow."** James S. Leamon, "Governor Fletcher's Recall," *William and Mary Quarterly* (1985), 527.

88 **were ardent Whigs.** Ibid., 531.

88 **"tread softly."** William Penn to Benjamin Fletcher, December 5, 1692, in *The Papers of William Penn*, vol. III, ed. Marianne Wokeck et al. (Philadelphia: University of Pennsylvania Press, 1986), 358.

89 **most effectual for the present service.** "An account of several passages and letters between His Excellency Benjamin Fletcher, captain general and governour in chief of the province of New-York . . ." Printed and sold by William Bradford, printer to Their Majesties, King William and Queen Mary, in New-York, 1693. In *Early American Imprints*, 1st series, no. 674 (filmed).

89 **in this commission to me.** Ibid., 674.

90 **trade and customs.** Karraker, 71.

90 **prosecution of witches in Salem.** For a devastating account of Phipps's activities, see Mary Beth Norton, *In the Devil's Snare: The Salem Witchcraft Crisis of 1692* (New York: A. A. Knopf, 2002).

90 **to the great impoverishing and hurt of the same"),** "At a General Court for Their Majesties' Colony of the Massachusetts Bay . . . ," December 22, 1691, *Early American Imprints*, 1st series, no. 554; 39285.

90 **loses his integrity in the process.** James Lydon, *Pirates, Privateers and Profits* (Upper Saddle River, N.J.: Gregg Press, 1970), 37–41.

90 **blackened greed, and vice versa.** Ritchie, 37–38.

91 **Calvinists and Anglicans, and so on.** See, generally, Reich, *Leisler's Rebellion;* Henry H. Kessler, *Peter Stuyvesant and His New York* (New York: Random House, 1959).

91 **will never be able to pay them."** *Journal of Jaspar Dankaerts*, ed. Bartlett James and J. Franklin Jameson (New York, 1913), 244.

92 **crushing tyranny of the merchant cabal.** Reich, 134.

92 **prominent offices to local merchants** *Second Annual Report of the State Historian of the State of New York* (Albany: 1897), vol. II, 312.

92 **on account of dishonesty.** *Documents Relative to the Colonial History of the State of New York* (Albany: 1855–83), vol. III, 314.

92 **disposal of confiscated goods.** *Select Cases of the Mayor's Court of New York City, 1674–1784* (Washington, D.C.: 1935), 63.

92 **the most notorious of the cabal, Frederick Phillipse.** Danckaerts, 244.

93 **shipowner and man of substance.** Jacob Judd, "Frederick Phillipse and the Madagascar Trade," *William and Mary Quarterly* (1993), 354–359.

94 **pirate-turned-entrepreneur named Adam Baldridge.** Deposition of Adam Baldridge, May 5, 1699. *BA, Colonial Office 5/1042, no. 30 II.*

Chapter 6

97 **things of no great moment.** James Ovington, *A Voyage to Suratt in the Year 1689* (London: Bradcliff, 1929), 461.

97 **made goods, tea, and coffee.** Lydon, 39.

98 **the shops of Boston.** *C.S.P. Colonial Series, 1681–85*, no. 1845.

98 **never had a spot upon our Garment.** William Penn to the Lords of Trade, *BA Colonial Series, 5/1260/43.*

99 **seventy bars of iron,"** Deposition of Adam Baldridge, May 5, 1699, noted supra.

99 **a long and profitable relationship.** Judd, 357.

100 **and three dozen hoes.** Deposition of Adam Baldridge, May 5, 1699, noted supra.

100 **children 3 yrs suckling."** Frederick Phillipse to Adam Baldridge, February 25, 1695, *High Court of Admiralty Papers, BA 1/98.*

100 **though I had the advantage so to be."** Ibid.

100 **the white men upon Madagascar."** Deposition of Adam Baldridge, May 5, 1699, noted supra.

100 **Samuel Burgess.** No known relation to the author, alas.

101 **married to one of his cousins.equal profit and danger on both sides."** For a full account of Burgess's relations with Phillipse (some of which will be covered later in this text), see Deposition of Samuel Burgess, May 3, 1698, *Colonial Office Papers BA*, 5/1040.

101 **equal profit and danger on both sides."** Frederick Phillipse to Adam Baldridge, December 24, 1695, *High Court of Admiralty Records BA*, 1/95.

101 **a separate class of proto-revolutionaries,** Marcus Rediker, *Between the Devil and the Deep Blue Sea: Merchant Seamen, Pirates and the Anglo-American World 1700–1750* (Cambridge: Cambridge University Press, 1993).

101 **might join a different firm.** See, generally, Karraker; Lydon.

101 **without Speciall lycence for soe doing."** "An Act for Restraining and Punishing Privateers and Pyrates" (New York: William Bradford, 1692). Courtesy of the Huntington Library.

102 **those sort of men in the West Indies.** Colonel Quarry to the Lords of Trade, June 6, 1699, *New Jersey Colonial Documents, 1687–1703*, ed. William Whitehead (Newark: Daily Advertiser, 1881), 281.

102 **made to do so with Burgess.** Judd, 360–361.

103 **some sixteen known privateering commissions,** *Documents Relative to the Colonial History of the State of New York, IV*, 221–224, 304, 320–326.

103 **recorded as having granted ten,** Case of Isaac Richier, August 31, 1694, *Colonial Office Records, BA*, 37/10.

104 **none yet that have done so."** Governor Fletcher to the Board of Trade, *C.S.P. Colonial Series, 1697–98*, 587.

104 **a typical fee of £300),** Lord Bellomont to the Board of Trade, *C.S.P. Colonial Series, 1696–97*, 259–260.

104 **was guilty of treason.** One might also make the claim that the members of his council, as officers of the government, were likewise guilty of treason. Yet as the crown's appointed representative it was Fletcher who bore the responsibility for implementing crown law; the council's function was merely advisory.

105 **tall, florid, and pompous."** Lydon, 37–38.

Chapter 7

106 **information to me to hear him talk.** Fletcher to the Board of Trade, *C.S.P. Colonial Series, 1697–98*, 587.

107 **though in value not much.** Ibid.

107 **time must show that.** Peter Delanoy to the Lords of Trade, June 13, 1695, *Documents Relative to the Colonial History of the State of New York IV*, 221–224.

108 **The "ramblings"** Dow, 84.

108 **"Tew, Esq."** Ibid.

108 **he had before then been a pirate."** George Weaver, Case of Benjamin Fletcher, *C.S.P. Colonial Series, 1699*, 44.

109 **received, entertained, and befriended him.** Dow, 84.

109 **the French fortress at Goree.** Defoe, 399.

109 **sixty men apiece);** Deposition of Adam Baldridge, May 5, 1699, *BA Colonial Office Series*, 5:1042, no. 30 II.

109 **without the least prospect of booty."** Defoe, 400.

109 **we'll stand by you!"** Ibid.

110 **money that he hath demanded."** Case of Isaac Richier, August 31, 1694, *Colonial Office Series, BA* 37/10; the full account of the charges on both sides is available at the Bermuda Archives at the Government Administration Building, 30 Parliament Street, Hamilton, Bermuda.

110 **charged poor Larkin with piracy.** George Larkin to the Board of Trade, *C.S.P. Colonial Series, 1702–1703*, 1014.

111 **skill and courage."** Defoe, 401.

111 **blow up the ship.** Ibid.

111 **bound for America.** Deposition of Adam Baldridge, *BA, C.O. 5:1042, no. 30 II*.

112 **an equally ironic name: *Liberty*.** Defoe, 405.

112 **carry the goods himself.** Dow, 87.

112 **any agent of William Outerbridge).** Testimony of Captain Stone, *C.S.P. Colonial Series, 1702–1703*, 1014.

113 **"harass the French."** Dow, 89.

113 **going against their wills,"** Report of Thomas Dyer, June 5, 1693, *Colonial Office Series, BA*, 5/1259, no. 40.

113 **number of passengers they carried,"** Defoe, 405.

113 **the dates do not add up.** Ibid., 407–413.

114 **soliciting him to make another trip."** Ibid., 416.

114 **join Tew in the same account."** Personal letter of John Graves, *C.S.P. Colonial Series, 1696–97,* 744.

114 **make New York his port of return."** *C.S.P. Colonial Series, 1697–8,* 860.

114 **the merchants of New York,"** Karraker, 69.

114 **for his next cruise,** Dow, 89.

115 **just three years before),** Don Seitz, *Under the Black Flag* (London: Stanley Paul, 1937), 34–35.

115 **along the Gulf of Saint Lawrence.** Lydon, 41.

115 **valued at £2,000, as a present.** Ibid., 42.

115 **redundant scraps of paper.** Ibid., 69.

115 **a ruby-encrusted saddle for the Great Mogul.** *C.S.P. Colonial Series, 1696–97.*

116 **taken without making resistance."** Defoe, 422.

116 **preparing for their reception there.** Jeremiah Basse to the Board of Trade, *C.S.P. Colonial Series, 1696–1697,* 1203.

117 **the second time in New York.** Lord Bellomont to the Board of Trade, *C.S.P. Colonial Series, 1696–97,* 259–260.

118 **been kindly received.** Ibid.

118 **Governor Samuel Gorton.** Lydon, 42.

118 **more than one hundred men.** Ibid., 43.

119 **"agents" in piratical deals;** *N.Y. Col. Docs IV,* 307–308.

119 **deals with notorious pirates were thrashed out.** Ibid., 398, 535.

119 **for the other councilors as well.** Ibid., 457–461.

119 **as they squandered their booty."** Lydon, 45.

119 **between £1,000 and £1,500 per voyage.** Ibid., 45.

119 **somewhere in the region of £100,000.** *Documents Relative to the Colonial History of the State of New York* (Albany: 1855–83), vol. IV, 327.

120 **I hope it will meet with no opposition."** Governor Fletcher to the Pennsylvania Assembly, May 17, 1693, *Minutes of the Provincial Council of Pennsylvania,* 406. Clearly Fletcher was not too committed to the passage of the act; shortly thereafter he wrote the assembly: "The Bill which I sent you was originally drawn at Whitehall. I cannot pass it as you have altered it. There are other laws to punish privateers & I am Vice Admiral as well as Governor here. Since you did not pass it in form I shall not insist. I remember some of you said it was too sanguinary; it can do you but little good or harm."

120 **none yet that have done so.** *C.S.P. Colonial Series, 1697–98,* 587.

121 **had been committed on the land.** "An Act for Restraining and Punishing Privateers and Pirates," *Early American Imprints,* 1st series, no. 664.

121 **ought to be wholly suppressed."** Lydon, 48.

121 **under the severest penalties."** Lords of Trade to Benjamin Fletcher, February 6, 1696, *C.S.P. Colonial Series, 1695–96.*

Chapter 8

124 **"much addicted to his Punch,"** Daniel Defoe, 24.

124 **fat and of a jolly complexion."** Botting, 80.

124 **I'll let you into the secret."** Defoe, 25.

124 **the cheerful first mate, Henry Every.** Examination of John Dann, August 3, 1696, *BA, Colonial Office 323:2, no. 25 IV.*

125 **the *James* men swarmed on deck.** Seitz, 39.

125 **all the brave fellows joined with me."** Defoe, 25.

126 **guide them back to shore.** Examination of John Dann, noted supra.

126 **many of his closest friends admitted,** See, for example, the depositions of John Dann and Philip Middleton, who sailed with Every, cited elsewhere in this chapter.

126 **a captain in Cromwell's navy.** Seitz, 39.

127 **seized them and carried them away."** Quoted in Botting, 80.

127 **many subjects of the King have experienced.** Deposition of Philip Middleton, *BA, Colonial Office 5:1257, no. 47 I.*

127 **shackled them in the hold.** Examination of John Dann, noted supra.

127 **Tew, Glover, Hoar, and Wake),** Deposition of Adam Baldridge, May 5, 1699, *BA, Colonial Office 5:1042, no. 30 II.*

128 **As yet an Englishman's friend, HENRY AVERY** Petition of the East India Company, July 1696, Privy Council Unbound Papers, 1:46.

129 **from thence to England.** Robert Blackborne to the King's Council, contained in ibid.

129 **our above expected goods."** East India Company letter from Bombay, author unknown, May 28, 1695, Privy Council Unbound Papers, 1:46.

129 **if contemporary accounts can be trusted, as Meat.** Examination of John Dann, noted supra.

130 **fitted out at New York.** Examination of John Dann, noted supra.

130 **not the hero they took him for."** Defoe, 27.

131 **defray the charges of their journey by land."** Ibid.

131 **produce a severe storm."** East India Company letter from Bombay, author unknown, October 12, 1695, Privy Council Unbound Papers, 1:46.

132 **some even in murder.** *The Trials of Joseph Dawson, Edward Forsyth, etc. . . . . for Several Piracies and Robberies* (London: John Everingham, 1696), 13–17.

132 **almost certainly an exaggeration.** Botting, 83. Other estimates are as high as £4,000,000.

132 **no idea of this incredible windfall.** Examination of John Dann, noted supra.

132 **some misfortune in the voyage."** Defoe, 28.

133 **were all gone.** A somewhat more prosaic account is given by John Dann, Every's crewmate: "The *Portsmouth* did not come into the fight and therefore had no div-

idend, but the brigantine had, which was taken away from them again by reason that the *Charles*' men changing them with silver for gold found the brigantine men had clipped the gold, so they left them only 2000 pieces of eight to buy provisions. They gave a share to the captain of the *Portsmouth* and brought him away with them." Dann's account may be factually correct and still not entirely inconsistent with Defoe's: in both cases chicanery of some kind was definitely being practiced. Given Every's past actions, it is likely the "clipped gold" story was fabricated to justify making off with the spoils. Examination of John Dann, August 3, 1696, *BA, Colonial Office, 323:2, no. 25 IV.*

133 **was known to be persuadable.** Defoe, 29.

133 **disappeared from history.** But not, apparently, from genealogical folklore. Many longtime residents on the island of Reunion—where Every's men settled—claim to trace their antecedents back to his crew. Though there is scant record of this, there is no particular reason to doubt the possibility.

134 **Timothy Tugmutton and Simon Whifflepin.** Botting, 85.

134 **Cayenne, in French Guiana.** Examination of John Dann, noted supra.

134 **make war upon [English] subjects."** Petition of Thomas Bulkley, February 4, 1697, *C.S.P. Colonial Series 1697–8,* n. 681, 349.

134 **a ship infected with pestilence."** Ibid.

135 **"to high places of trust."** Ibid.

135 **their agents Jones and Trott."** Ibid.

135 **and all that was in her.** Affidavit of Philip Middleton, November 11, 1696, *BA, Colonial Office 5:1257, no. 47 I.*

135 **which he promised them."** Examination of John Dann, noted supra.

136 **as effectually as they could desire."** Affidavit of Philip Middleton, noted supra.

136 **sent to Governor Trott."** Ibid.

136 **a collection of African elephant tusks.** Ibid.

136 **outnumbered the settlers two to one).** The Case of Nicholas Trott, October 25, 1698, *C.S.P. Colonial Series, 1698,* 928, p. 506.

136 **had been improperly ballasted** Affidavit of Philip Middleton, noted supra.

137 **Surat, Broach, Agra, and Ahmedabad.** Petition of the East India Company, noted supra.

137 **one was even stoned to death.** Botting, 91.

137 **that no letters might pass to us.** East India Company Letters from Bombay, October 12, 1695, Privy Council Unbound Papers, BA 1:46.

137 **any trade could be securely maintained?** Seitz, 42.

138 **apprehend the said Henry Every.** "By the Lords Justices, A PROCLAMATION . . ." August 10, 1696. Printed in London by Charles Bill. Copy from British Library microform 1632:12.

138 **discovery and seizure of the said Henry Every.** Ibid.

139 **could not tempt me from my duty."** Botting, 87.

139 **most notorious band of criminals in the Atlantic.** The case of Nicholas Trott, *C.S.P. Colonial Series, 1698,* 928, p. 506.

139 **allowed all but a handful to escape.** Ibid.

140 **scarce sufficient to pay his debts.** Defoe, 30–31.

140 **as much as would buy him a coffin."** Ibid., 31.

141 **are now in Dublin."** Examination of John Dann, noted supra.

141 **£1,045 of gold sewn into the lining.** Ibid.

141 **the supposed charge of piracy."** Certificate for John Devin, Suffolk Court Files, Boston, no. 3765, paper 2.

Chapter 9

144 **for several *other* piracies.** *The Trials of Joseph Dawson, etc.*, 4.

145 **Destruction of our Navigation and Trade.** Ibid., 5.

146 **the party accused upon his trial."** Ibid., 7.

146 **all Laws forbid such methods."** Ibid., 8.

147 **a good witness for all that."** Ibid., 14–15.

147 **they did not run so far as that."** Ibid., 18.

148 **Middleton answered grimly.** Ibid., 21.

148 **and at Providence.** A.k.a. New Providence, the Bahamas.

148 **and could not go abroad.** *Trials*, 22–23.

149 **dishonour to the justice of the nation."** Ibid., 11.

149 **for the Execution of Pirates. FINIS."** Ibid., 28.

149 **nor countenanced any such things,"** Ibid., 110.

150 **concealed all manner of illegal activities.** See, generally, Michael Garibaldi Hall, *Edward Randolph and the American Colonies* (Chapel Hill: University of North Carolina Press, 1960).

150 **who took no notice of it."** Robert Snead to Sir John Houblon, September 20, 1697, *C.S.P. Colonial Series, 1697*, 1331, p. 613.

150 **but seemed very angry, so I left him."** Ibid.

151 **and had the proclamation read."** Ibid., 614.

152 **who was frightened by the Governor."** Ibid.

153 **the proclamation was published.** Ibid., 614. Further charges are contained in a second letter from Snead to Houblon, dated April 25 of the following year. *C.S.P. Colonial Series, 1698*, 403, p. 181.

154 **rather than adventure themselves here."** Governor Codrington to the Privy Council, July 5, 1697, *C.S.P. Colonial Series, 1697*, 1148–1149, p. 538.

154 **cast upon Massachusetts in that regard."** William Stoughton to the Board of Trade, August 15, 1697, *C.S.P. Colonial Series, 1697*, 1359, p. 625.

154 **governed by so great a King.** Governor Nicholson to the Privy Council, July 30, 1697, *C.S.P. Colonial Series, 1697*, 1363, p. 629.

155 **such a herd of men under no pay."** Governor Fletcher to the Board of Trade, April 5, 1697, *C.S.P. Colonial Series, 1697*, 892, p. 518.

155 **gave us our liberty."** Jeremiah Basse to William Popple, July 26, 1697, *C.S.P. Colonial Series, 1697*, 1203, p. 564.

156 **a power that they dare not disobey.** Jeremiah Basse to Secretary Popple, July 18, 1697, *BA Colonial Papers*, vol. 1, A 48.

157 **what law have they there to do it?** William Popple to Jeremiah Basse, July 22, 1697, *C.S.P. Colonial Series, 1697*, 1198, p. 561.

157 **some no doubt from the prospect of gain."** Jeremiah Basse to William Popple, July 26, noted supra.

158 **and now by Thomas Day."** The same Captain Thomas Day whom Markham had earlier granted a commission.

158 **a rich prize from the French,** This was Basse's error. In fact, the two Glovers were one and the same, the pirate to whom Fletcher had granted a commission the year before.

158 **on the coast of Arabia."** Ibid.

159 **Vice Admirals in every province."** Ibid.

160 **carried on as much as ever."** Edward Randolph to the Board of Trade, received August 17, 1696, *C.S.P. Colonial Series, 1696*, 149, pp. 213–214.

160 **approved by the King as Governors."** Ibid., 213.

Chapter 10

163 **now took for granted.** Karraker, 104.

164 **eventually to be termed *mercantilism*.** See Lars Magnussen, *Mercantilism, the Shaping of an Economic Language* (London: Routledge, 1994).

166 **replaced by William Markham.** Hall, 136.

167 **as both vied for control.** Peter Laslett, "John Locke, the Great Recoinage, and the Origins of the Board of Trade: 1695–1698," *William and Mary Quarterly*, 3rd Series 14 (July 1957), 370–402.

167 **the Board of Trade would not be.** Committee Minutes of the Board of Trade, February 17, 1696, *C.S.P. Colonial Series, 1696*, 2275.

167 **first among them.** *Journals of the House of Lords XV*, 7.

167 **chief detriments to their livelihood.** *Proceedings and Debates of Parliaments*, vol. II, 1696, p. 104.

168 **iciness bordering on contempt.** Edward Randolph, *Edward Randolph; Including His Letters and Official Papers from the New England, Middle and Southern Colonies in America, with Other Documents Relating Chiefly to the Vacating of the Royal Charter of the Colony of Massachusetts Bay, 1676–1703*. Robert Toppan, ed. (Boston: Prince Society, 1898–1909), vol. II, 206–207. Herein referred to as *Randolph Letters*.

168 **"subjection and slavery."** *Randolph Letters*, vol. II, 253–254.

168 **by James II several years later.** Hall, 98–128.

169 **this kingdom much more."** *Randolph Letters*, vol. II, 225–259.

169 **Henry Morgan's nemesis.** *C.S.P. Colonial Series, 1675–76*, 787.

169 **owned by local merchants.** Hall, 57.

169 **they charged him court costs.** Ibid., 57–58.

169 **charges of sedition and treason.** Randolph had actually been captured in Boston in the company of Edmund Andros; a pistol was put to the head of each man and they were escorted swiftly from their holdout on Castle Island to the nearest jail. Hall, 122.

170 **bring the recalcitrant colonies firmly into line.** *Randolph Letters*, vol. V, 70.

170 **"silly animals";** Ibid., vol. VII, 353.

170 **"scurrilous and haughty."** Ibid., vol. V, 77.

171 **cruel slavery and oppression rampant."** Ibid., vol. VII, 433–434.

171 **by color of his office."** *Randolph Letters*, vol. V, 88.

171 **which will end all disputes,"** Ibid., 93.

171 **for a man in his sixties.** Ibid., vol. VII, 606.

172 **for preventing frauds."** *Randolph Letters*, vol. V, 135–136.

172 **Abuses in the Plantation Trade."** Leo Stock, ed. *Proceedings and Debates of the British Parliament Representing North America* (Washington, 1924–41), vol. II, 155.

173 **whatsoever he shall judge proper."** *Randolph Letters*, vol. VII, 523.

173 **further marks of our displeasure."** *House of Lords Journal*, XVI, 125–126.

174 **Every's men came to Maryland."** Randolph to William Popple, May 12, 1698, *C.S.P. Colonial Series, 1698*, n. 451, 211.

174 **is both foul and false."** *Papers of William Penn*, 486.

174 **embrace pirates, ships and men."** Ibid., 518.

174 **forbidden trade and piracy."** Ibid.

174 **I never saw nor heard."** Ibid., 512–513.

175 **and say no more."** Peter Alricks to Governor Markham, October 18, 1696, *C.S.P. Colonial Series, 1697*, n. 76, 44.

175 **the abuse of government."** Governor Markham to Captain Daniell, October 20, 1696, *C.S.P. Colonial Series, 1697*, n. 76 vi, 44.

176 **as well as I am capable."** Captain Daniell to Governor Markham, March 9, 1697, ibid., n. 76 vii, 45.

176 **a good voyage and a better temper.** Governor Markham to Captain Daniell, March 30, 1697, ibid., n. 76 viii, 45–46.

176 **this I never believed."** Governor Markham to the Board of Trade, November 29, 1697, ibid., n. 76 x, 48.

177 **for three weeks [during] my stay."** Randolph to William Popple, May 12, 1698, ibid., n. 451, 211.

177 **sent directly to the Board of Trade.** Ibid.

177 **by piracy or illegal trade."** Governor Markham to the Board of Trade, October 20, 1698, ibid., 381.

177 **as his enclosed letters show."** Ibid.

178 **what wood my cudgel was made of.** *Papers of William Penn*, 513.

178 **there are such diligent informers?"** William Markham to William Penn, November 29, 1698, *C.S.P. Colonial Series, 1698*, n. 76 xvi, 51.

178 **continues their steady friend."** Randolph to the Board of Trade, April 25, 1698, *C.S.P. Colonial Series, 1698*, n. 401, 181.

179 **they were quite unwilling to do.** Hall, 182.

179 **an external and objective review.** Aside, it must be noted, from Governor Nicholson's personal campaign to oust Markham, which had more than a contributory effect on Randolph's reports.

Chapter 11

181 **both New York and New England.** Leamon, 538.

181 **composed almost exclusively of Whigs.** Ibid., 534.

182 **festering corruption in both colonies.** The melding of New York and Massachusetts would also have the additional benefit of forestalling the return of Joseph Dudley, former governor and committed Tory. Dudley would have to wait for his commission until 1701.

182 **his fellow Whigs.** Ritchie, 49–53.

182 **if I still continued obstinate."** Ibid., 58.

183 **execution of their respective offices."** Letter from the Board of Trade to Lord Bellomont, March 9, 1699, reprinted in ibid., 113.

183 **letters of revocation."** Shrewsbury to Blaythwayt, July 13, 1697, *Manuscripts of the Duke of Buccleuch and Queensbury* (London: Historical Manuscripts Commission, Fifteenth Report, 1903), 492.

184 **neglecting the Sabbath.** Ritchie, 169.

184 **and tweaked hard.** Ibid.

184 **regress without control."** *C.S.P. Colonial Series, 1698*, n. 235, 114.

185 **the bargain between them."** Two accounts exist of this extraordinary council meeting. The first are the Minutes of the Council of New York, *C.S.P. Colonial Series, 1698*, n. 433, 203, from which these quotations are drawn. A similar account can be found among the Early American Imprints, Series I, erroneously dated May 18.

186 **as the laws in such cases do direct."** "By His Excellency . . . A proclamation," Early American Imprints, Series I, n. 842.

186 **encouraged privateers."** *C.S.P. Colonial Series, 1698*, n. 451, 211.

186 **large sums of money."** Ibid., n. 472, 222.

187 **censured by the King."** Ibid., 223.

187 **Government out of frame."** *C.S.P. Colonial Series, 1698*, n. 475, 231.

188 **the worst form of robbery."** Ibid., 231.

188 **publicly in his coach."** *C.S.P. Colonial Series, 1698*, n. 473, 225.

189 **caused Governor Fletcher great loss.** Ibid., 226.

189 **to be sold to pirates.** Judd, 360–361.

189 **Governor Fletcher's protection."** *C.S.P. Colonial Series, 1698*, n. 473, 227.

190 **a present of the ship."** Ibid., 228.

190 **try what he could do.** Ibid.

190 **driving New York into the ground.** Lydon, 51.

190 **from the late Governor."** "Proclamation," noted supra.

190 **without the King's orders."** *C.S.P. Colonial Series, 1698*, 226.

191 **Three hundred fifty weight of gun powder** List of freight on board the *Margaret*, June 7, 1698, CO 5/1042.

191 **we entreat you to continue them."** *C.S.P. Colonial Series, 1698*, n. 929, 507.

191 **have been himself a pirate."** Ibid., 507.

Chapter 12

193 **desperate for passage home.** Judd, 369.

194 **on the charge of piracy.** "Examination of John Powell of New York," HCA 1/53 BA.

194 **with all sorts of stores."** *C.S.P. Colonial Series, 1698*, n. 224, 108.

194 **Frederick Phillipse.** *BA Colonial Office*, 5:1042, no. 30 II.

195 **also the Governor of Rhode Island."** *C.S.P. Colonial Series, 1698*, n. 224, 108.

195 **But he never did so."** *C.S.P. Colonial Series, 1698*, n. 84, 193.

195 **delivered part of her goods."** Ibid., n. 404, 183.

195 **or any other place.** Ibid., n. 194, 95.

196 **agreeable to his deserts."** John Goddard to the Board of Trade, June 29, 1697. Courtesy of the Bermuda Archives.

196 **than Richier and Trott.** *C.S.P. Colonial Series, 1698*, n. 647, 326.

196 **removing Goddard from office.** Ibid., n. 183, 91.

196 **depart the island.** Ibid., n. 1035, 571.

196 **successively imprisoned him."** Randolph to the Board of Trade, July 4, 1699. Courtesy of the Bermuda Archives.

197 **more fit for a pasha than a governor."** Ibid.

197 **Thomas Tew master."** Ibid.

197 **writing for a pardon."** *C.S.P. Colonial Series, 1698*, n. 444, 208.

198 **Suspicion is not proof."** *C.S.P. Colonial Series, 1698*, n. 928, 506.

198 **and submit his findings.** Within a year it seemed that Nicholas Webb had fallen into his predecessor's transgressions. Edward Randolph reports in October 1698 that "Mr. Webb at Providence has forgotten his oath (I am informed), seizing and discharging vessels as he pleases, the masters paying well for it." *C.S.P. Colonial Series, 1698*, n. 402, 181.

199 **illegal traders of all places."** *Calendar of State Papers, Colonial Series, America and West Indies, 1696–7*, ed. J. W. Fortescue, London, 1898–1905, November 16, 1696, 396.

199 **virtually impossible to do so.** David Starkey, "A Restless Spirit: British Privateering Enterprise," in *Pirates and Privateers* (Exeter: University of Exeter, 1997), 128.

199 **owed their livelihoods to the sea.** William Owen, "Privateering and Piracy in Rhode Island 1653–1712" (master's thesis, Brown University, June 1959), 79.

200 **Christopher Almy, merchant.** Howard Chapin, *Privateer Ships and Sailors: The First Century of American Colonial Profiteering* (Toulon: Imprimerie G. Mouton, 1926), 39.

200 **several hundred pounds richer.** Ibid., 44.

200 **through trading voyages.** Owen, 19–24.

200 **fair and true commission.**" *Records of the Colony of Rhode Island and Providence Plantations in New England,* ed. John R. Bartlett, vol. III (New York, 1858), 176.

200 **by virtue of the same.**" Ibid., 176.

201 **from Rhode Island's shores.** Chapin, 63.

201 **incredible riches which Tew displayed.** *C.S.P. Colonial Series, 1698,* February 19, 1697, 396.

201 **£1,200 apiece.** Lydon, 41.

201 **enlist for Tew's next voyage.** Botting, 67.

202 **when the complaint arose.** *RCRI,* vol. III, 337.

202 **for nearby pirate vessels.** *C.S.P. Colonial Series, 1696–7,* April 5, 1697, 894.

202 **the Governor of Rhode Island.**" *C.S.P. Colonial Series, 1698,* February 14, 1698, 108.

202 **to the Red Sea.** Ibid., 108.

202 **for unlawful purpose.**" Ibid., December 21, 1698, 1071.

202 **by the privateers on receiving them.** *C.S.P. Colonial Series, 1698,* n. 896, 477.

203 **releases the goods for public sale.** Lydon, 55–58.

203 **but also each other.**" Owen, 93.

204 **who have visited Rhode Island.** Bartlett, 124.

204 **the hands of Governor Cranston.** Ibid.

204 **turned out to be successful.**" Edmund Berkeley, *Three Philanthropic Pirates* (Virginia: 1890), 15.

204 **for restoring them their money.**" Ibid., 20.

204 **restored to the petitioners.** Ibid.

204 **increasing crown revenue.** Owen, 38.

205 **the rest turned pirate as well.** Ibid., 31–32, 47–50.

205 **the said inhabitants or Plantations.**" Quoted in ibid., 39, from the Henry Stevens Collection (unpublished), vol. VIII, 498.

205 **You know better.**"). Bartlett, 115.

205 **make them tender prosecutors.**" *C.S.P. Colonial Series, 1698,* n. 642, 323.

206 **to fight the French.** Ibid., n. 434, 204.

206 **out of any hearty zeal.** Letter from Lord Bellomont to the Board of Trade, April 5, 1699, reprinted in Bartlett, 116.

206 **we were otherwise informed.**" Letter from the Board of Trade to King William III, February 9, 1699, reprinted in Bartlett, 113.

207 **as ridiculous as they can.**" Letter from Governor Cranston to the Board of Trade, March 1699, reprinted in ibid., 113.

207 **how you could write them.**" Letter from the Board of Trade to Governor Cranston, June 1699, reprinted in ibid., 115.

207 **laden with plunder.** The term *condemn* in maritime parlance has a different meaning than that commonly assigned to it; to condemn a ship and her cargo means to declare them legal prizes and thus the property of their captor.

208 **a private man of war.** Letter from Colonel Byfield to the Board of Trade, November 28, 1702, reprinted in Bartlett, 118.

208 **according to law."** Ibid.

208 **The *Charles* was thus condemned."** Ibid.

209 **the rights of the lord high admiral.** Bartlett, 131.

209 **as the law directs."** Quoted in Owen, 88.

209 **to secure themselves.** Bartlett, 120.

210 **five times that amount.** Lydon, 42–46.

210 **good business all around.** Ibid., 45.

210 **has been greatly enriched."** Bartlett, 115.

212 **as great hardships.** *C.S.P. Colonial Series, 1698*, n. 846, 383.

Chapter 13

213 **sailed home to New York.** Karraker, 63.

214 **"as bad as they."** Deposition of Robert Bradinham, *BA fol. 7, 1/15*.

214 **raised a hand against them.** Ritchie, 117.

214 **and Samuel Burgess.** Ritchie, 32–33.

215 **his neighbor, Robert Livingston.** Correspondence to, from, and concerning Kidd and Livingston can be found at the Museum of New York, in the Gilder Lehrman Collection.

215 **our Plantations in America."** Original commission reprinted in Defoe, 387.

216 **our friends and allies,"** Ibid., 387–388.

216 **Richard Blackham in full.** Courtesy of the Gilder Lehrman Collection, Museum of New York.

217 **as one historian has called them.** Botting, 107.

217 **a disproportionate share of the profits.** Ibid., 108.

217 **such a villainous herd."** See Fletcher to the Board of Trade, noted supra.

218 **passing amongst the sheep.** Botting, 108.

218 **throughout the encounter.** Ibid.

219 **he had turned pirate.** Ritchie, 96–99.

219 **Kidd had just passed through.** Botting, 111.

219 **Moore died the next day.** *A Complete Collection of State Trials and Proceedings for High Treason and Other Crimes and Misdemeanors, from the Reign of King Richard II to the End of King George I* (London, 1730), vol. 5, 287–296.

219 **between France and England.** Ibid., 291.

220 **with the *Quedah Merchant* in convoy.** Defoe, 392.

220 **a great noise in England,"** Botting, 116.

222 **surrendered himself to the crown.** "Pardon for persons on Madagascar, engaged in piracy . . ." BA, High Court of Admiralty 1/98.

222 **Henry Every and William Kidd.** For a detailed account of the East India Company's manhunt for Captain Kidd, see Ritchie, 127–159.

222 **patron on the Eastern Seaboard.** Deposition of Adam Baldridge, BA, Colonial Office 5/1042, no. 30 II.

222 **very ready to embrace it."** Examination of Samuel Burgess, BA, High Court of Admiralty 1/53.

223 **good order in his colony.** "Representation of the Lords of Trade on the Charges Against Colonel Fletcher," *Documents Relating to the Colonial History of New York,* IV, 304.

223 **(which was nonsense).** "Heads of Accusation Against the Earl of Bellomont," *Doc. Rel. Col. His. N.Y.,* IV, 620–623.

224 **refused to turn pirate."** Bellomont to the Board of Trade, BA Colonial Office 5/1042, 203–208.

224 **grant him pardon.** Ritchie, 176–177.

225 **my avowed enemy."** Bellomont to the Board of Trade, BA Colonial Office 5/860, n. 62.

225 **what I have promised.** Memorial of Duncan Campbell, BA Colonial Office 5/860, n. 64.

226 **to know nothing of.** Bellomont to the Board of Trade, noted supra.

226 **we had him under examination."** Bellomont to the Board of Trade, noted supra.

226 **there had been a mistake.** Ritchie, 182.

226 **as apt as it was cruel.** Ibid., 197.

227 **none other than Governor Bellomont.** Judd, 371.

227 **at rest upon that matter."** James Graham to Robert Livingston. Courtesy of the Gilder Lehrman Collection.

227 **is very unreasonable.** Lord Bellomont to Sir John Stanley, British Library 29/207, 65–66.

228 **and Colonel Bayard."** Graham to Livingston, noted supra.

228 **he wrote from Boston.** Bellomont to the Board of Trade, BA Colonial Office 5/680, n. 64.

229 **his wife, Sarah, attests.** *Massachusetts Colonial Archives,* vol. 62, n. 317.

229 **which is barbarous."** William Kidd to Robert Harley, reprinted in Jameson, 250.

230 **without regard to my commission.** Kidd to Harley, noted supra.

230 **accessory to my own destruction,"** Ibid., 251.

230 **to admit me a pirate."** Kidd to unknown, BA 1/29, 285–286.

231 **proclamation of pardon in 1699.** Ritchie, 216.

231 **owed *him* money).** Leamon, 541.

232 **the Whig lords' vengeance.** Many accounts exist of the execution of Captain Kidd. The most commonly cited, though not necessarily the most reliable, is that of Paul Lorraine, pastor of Newgate Prison. Like many prison pastors, Lorraine did a brisk business in transforming dying confessions to pamphlet literature. His

depiction of Kidd can be found at the British Library: *A True Account of the Behavior, Concession and Last Dying Speeches of Captain William Kidd* (London: 1701).

232 **that was ever invented."** "A full account of the proceedings in relation to Captain Kidd in two letters written by a person of quality to a kinsman of the Earl of Bellomont," 1701. Courtesy of the John Carter Brown Library.

232 **destructive to trade and commerce."** Ibid., 19.

233 **"so jaded with writing"** Bellomont to the Board of Trade, BA Colonial Office 5/861, n. 4.

233 **Removed and Dead."** William Sharpass to Robert Livingston, reprinted in Leamon, 540.

Chapter 14

236 **landed them at New Providence."** *C.S.P. Colonial Series, 1700,* n. 466, 277.

237 **sure to be the gainer."** Ibid., n. 476, 286.

237 **"entertains and protects pirates,"** Ibid., 286.

237 **would not have imitated.** *C.S.P. Colonial Series, 1703,* n. 1313, 832.

238 **belonging to His Majesty's Service."** Ibid., n. 1014, 623.

238 **a Free Trade were encouraged."** Ibid., n. 503, 292.

238 **remedy this great evil."** *C.S.P. Colonial Series, 1700,* n. 500, 301.

239 **clear these coasts of pirates."** Ibid., 301.

239 **"many in the West Indies").** Ibid., n. 685, 458.

239 **but is plundered."** Ibid., n. 521, 307.

239 **Madagascar simply melted away.** Botting, 177.

240 **bid you heartily farewell.** *C.S.P. Colonial Series, 1700,* n. 721, 487.

240 **in the hills above.** Henry Kamen, *The War of Succession in Spain 1700–15* (London: Weidenfeld & Nicholson, 1969); Samuel Drake, *The Border Wars of New England* (New York: Scribner & Sons, 1897).

241 **more boldness than ever."** *C.S.P. Colonial Series, 1700,* n. 543, 363.

241 **render us contemptible and obnoxious. . . .** Ibid., n. 433, 251.

241 **contrary to Law."** *C.S.P. Colonial Series, 1706,* n. 18, 4.

242 **general preservation of the whole.** Ibid., 4.

242 **condemned their prizes in Newport.** *C.S.P. Colonial Series, 1706,* n. 673, 408.42

242 **make prize of the same.** Piracy Trial of the *Charles,* Court of Vice Admiralty 1704, 43BA, HCA 30/861.

243 **captured gold and silver.** *C.S.P. Colonial Series, 1704,* n. 437, 216.

243 **utmost severity of law."** Proclamation, May 24, 1704, Early American Imprints, 1st Series, n. 39411.

244 **bring in gold to these provinces."** *C.S.P. Colonial Series, 1704,* 216.

244 **the hands of the Destroyer!"** Cotton Mather, "Faithful Warnings to Prevent Fear Judgments" (Boston: Timothy Green, 1704).

244 **those men that brought in gold."** *C.S.P. Colonial Series, 1706,* n. 432, 233.

245 **what money they could get.**" "Articles exhibited against Lord Archibald Hamilton," 1716, 5. Courtesy of the John Carter Brown Library.

245 **one such sloop, the *Eagle.*** Deposition of Captain John Beswick, in ibid., 15.

246 **necessity of the affair requires.** Letter from Don Juan de Valle to Lord Archibald Hamilton, June 5, 1715, in ibid., 10.

246 **they were valuable.** Letter from Don Juan de Valle to Lord Archibald Hamilton, September 18, 1715, in ibid., 14.

247 **than even he complained of.** Lord Archibald Hamilton, "An Answer to an Anonymous Libel," 1716, 48–49. Courtesy of the John Carter Brown Library.

248 **following on the model of Drake.** See Colin Woodard, *The Republic of Pirates* (New York: Harcourt, 2007).

248 **the Bahamas.** For a fascinating account of Rogers's life, see Bryan Little, *Crusoe's Captain: The Life of Woodes Rogers, Seaman, Trader and Colonial Governor* (London: Oldham's Press, 1960).

248 **Capt. Webb the present governor.**" *C.S.P. Colonial Series, 1700*, n. 61, 40.

249 **of a new plantation colony.** Botting, 140.

249 **hoping to be overlooked.** A recent book provides a superb account of Rogers's reception amongst the pirates. See Colin Woodard, *The Republic of Pirates* (New York: Harcourt, 2007).

250 **to Rogers as he went by.** Karraker, 182.

250 **the Board of Trade's correspondence.** Ibid.

250 **Hurrah for Governor Rogers!**" Little, 153.

251 **take back New Providence for themselves.** See Rogers's reports to the Board of Trade, BA Colonial Office 23/1, 21–24, 63.

252 **prosecution, defense, and jury.** Botting, 46.

252 **a hundred thousand men in the field.**" Rankin, 22.

253 **shall suffer present death.** Ibid., 31.

253 **to attack *English* vessels.** Karraker, 174.

254 **infested with these rogues,**" Botting, 138.

254 **enforce its will on the colonies.** Lydon, 260–263.

256 **which every man may lawfully destroy.**" "The trials of eight persons indicted for piracy . . . held in Boston," Early American Imprints, Series 1, n. 2003.

256 **Instigated by the Devil.**" "The trials of sixteen persons for piracy . . ." (Boston: Joseph Edwards, 1726).

256 **to the general delight of the populace.** "The trials of five persons for piracy . . ." Early American Imprints, 1st Series, n. 2818.

256 **sundry goods, and wearing apparel.** "The trials of eight persons," noted supra, 3.

257 **brought to this untimely end.**" "An account of the pirates," Early American Imprints, 1st Series, n. 11129.

Index